LLEWELLYN'S 2023
DAILY PLANETARY GUIDE

Copyright 2022 Llewellyn Worldwide Ltd. All rights reserved.
Typography property of Llewellyn Worldwide Ltd.
Llewellyn is a registered trademark of Llewellyn Worldwide Ltd.

ISBN: 978-0-7387-6391-0. Astrological calculations compiled and programmed by Rique Pottenger, based on the earlier work of Neil F. Michelsen.

Astrological proofreading by Beth Rosato
Cover design by Shannon McKuhen

GettyImages/182759596©da-kuk
GettyImages/857877866©kevron2001

Llewellyn Publications
A Division of Llewellyn Worldwide Ltd.
2143 Wooddale Drive
Woodbury, MN 55125-2989
www.llewellyn.co

Printed in China

2022

SEPTEMBER
S	M	T	W	T	F	S
				1	2	3
4	5	6	7	8	9	10
11	12	13	14	15	16	17
18	19	20	21	22	23	24
25	26	27	28	29	30	

OCTOBER
S	M	T	W	T	F	S
						1
2	3	4	5	6	7	8
9	10	11	12	13	14	15
16	17	18	19	20	21	22
23	24	25	26	27	28	29
30	31					

NOVEMBER
S	M	T	W	T	F	S
		1	2	3	4	5
6	7	8	9	10	11	12
13	14	15	16	17	18	19
20	21	22	23	24	25	26
27	28	29	30			

DECEMBER
S	M	T	W	T	F	S
				1	2	3
4	5	6	7	8	9	10
11	12	13	14	15	16	17
18	19	20	21	22	23	24
25	26	27	28	29	30	31

2023

JANUARY
S	M	T	W	T	F	S
1	2	3	4	5	6	7
8	9	10	11	12	13	14
15	16	17	18	19	20	21
22	23	24	25	26	27	28
29	30	31				

FEBRUARY
S	M	T	W	T	F	S
			1	2	3	4
5	6	7	8	9	10	11
12	13	14	15	16	17	18
19	20	21	22	23	24	25
26	27	28				

MARCH
S	M	T	W	T	F	S
			1	2	3	4
5	6	7	8	9	10	11
12	13	14	15	16	17	18
19	20	21	22	23	24	25
26	27	28	29	30	31	

APRIL
S	M	T	W	T	F	S
						1
2	3	4	5	6	7	8
9	10	11	12	13	14	15
16	17	18	19	20	21	22
23	24	25	26	27	28	29
30						

MAY
S	M	T	W	T	F	S
	1	2	3	4	5	6
7	8	9	10	11	12	13
14	15	16	17	18	19	20
21	22	23	24	25	26	27
28	29	30	31			

JUNE
S	M	T	W	T	F	S
				1	2	3
4	5	6	7	8	9	10
11	12	13	14	15	16	17
18	19	20	21	22	23	24
25	26	27	28	29	30	

JULY
S	M	T	W	T	F	S
						1
2	3	4	5	6	7	8
9	10	11	12	13	14	15
16	17	18	19	20	21	22
23	24	25	26	27	28	29
30	31					

AUGUST
S	M	T	W	T	F	S
		1	2	3	4	5
6	7	8	9	10	11	12
13	14	15	16	17	18	19
20	21	22	23	24	25	26
27	28	29	30	31		

SEPTEMBER
S	M	T	W	T	F	S
					1	2
3	4	5	6	7	8	9
10	11	12	13	14	15	16
17	18	19	20	21	22	23
24	25	26	27	28	29	30

OCTOBER
S	M	T	W	T	F	S
1	2	3	4	5	6	7
8	9	10	11	12	13	14
15	16	17	18	19	20	21
22	23	24	25	26	27	28
29	30	31				

NOVEMBER
S	M	T	W	T	F	S
			1	2	3	4
5	6	7	8	9	10	11
12	13	14	15	16	17	18
19	20	21	22	23	24	25
26	27	28	29	30		

DECEMBER
S	M	T	W	T	F	S
					1	2
3	4	5	6	7	8	9
10	11	12	13	14	15	16
17	18	19	20	21	22	23
24	25	26	27	28	29	30
31						

2024

JANUARY
S	M	T	W	T	F	S
	1	2	3	4	5	6
7	8	9	10	11	12	13
14	15	16	17	18	19	20
21	22	23	24	25	26	27
28	29	30	31			

FEBRUARY
S	M	T	W	T	F	S
				1	2	3
4	5	6	7	8	9	10
11	12	13	14	15	16	17
18	19	20	21	22	23	24
25	26	27	28	29		

MARCH
S	M	T	W	T	F	S
					1	2
3	4	5	6	7	8	9
10	11	12	13	14	15	16
17	18	19	20	21	22	23
24	25	26	27	28	29	30
31						

APRIL
S	M	T	W	T	F	S
	1	2	3	4	5	6
7	8	9	10	11	12	13
14	15	16	17	18	19	20
21	22	23	24	25	26	27
28	29	30				

MAY
S	M	T	W	T	F	S
			1	2	3	4
5	6	7	8	9	10	11
12	13	14	15	16	17	18
19	20	21	22	23	24	25
26	27	28	29	30	31	

JUNE
S	M	T	W	T	F	S
						1
2	3	4	5	6	7	8
9	10	11	12	13	14	15
16	17	18	19	20	21	22
23	24	25	26	27	28	29
30						

JULY
S	M	T	W	T	F	S
	1	2	3	4	5	6
7	8	9	10	11	12	13
14	15	16	17	18	19	20
21	22	23	24	25	26	27
28	29	30	31			

AUGUST
S	M	T	W	T	F	S
				1	2	3
4	5	6	7	8	9	10
11	12	13	14	15	16	17
18	19	20	21	22	23	24
25	26	27	28	29	30	31

Contents

Introduction to Astrology *by Kim Rogers-Gallagher* 4
    Planets: The First Building Block 4
    Signs: The Second Building Block 10
    Houses: The Third Building Block 15
    Aspects and Transits: The Fourth Building Block 18
    Retrograde Planets 23
    Moon Void-of-Course 24
    The Moon's Influence 25
    The Moon Through the Signs 26
2023 Eclipse Dates 30
2023 Retrograde Planets 31
2023 New and Full Moons 32
2023 Planetary Phenomena 33
2023 Weekly Forecasts
    by Michelle Perrin, aka Astrology Detective 35
Finding Opportunity Periods *by Jim Shawvan* 77
Business Guide 83
Calendar Pages 85
    How to Use Your *Daily Planetary Guide* 85
2023 Calendar with Aspects and Opportunity Periods
    by Paula Belluomini 86
World Time Zones 192
World Map of Time Zones 193
2023 Ephemeris Tables 194
The Planetary Hours 206
Table of Rising and Setting Signs 207
Blank Horoscope Chart 208

Introduction to Astrology

by Kim Rogers-Gallagher

Your horoscope is calculated using the date and time you were born from the perspective of your birth location. From this information, a clock-like diagram emerges that shows where every planet was located at the moment you made your debut. Each chart is composed of the same elements, rearranged, so everyone has one of everything, but none are exactly alike. I think of planets, signs, houses, and aspects as the four astrological building blocks. Each block represents a different level of human existence.

The eight planets along with the Sun and Moon are actual physical bodies. They represent urges or needs we all have. Chiron also falls into this category. The twelve signs of the zodiac are sections of the sky, and each is 30 degrees. The signs describe the behavior a planet or house will use to express itself. The twelve houses in a chart tell us where our planets come to life. Each house represents different life concerns—values, communication, creativity, and so on—that we must live through as life and time progress.

Basically, aspects are angles. Some of the planets will be positioned an exact number of degrees apart, forming angles to one another. For example, 180 degrees is a circle divided by two and is called an opposition. A square is 90 degrees and divides the circle by four. A trine is 120 degrees and divides the circle by three, and so forth. Aspects show which planets will engage in constant dialogue with one another. The particular aspect that joins them describes the nature of their "conversation." Not all planets will aspect all other planets in the houses.

Planets: The First Building Block

Each planet acts like the director of a department in a corporation, and the corporation is, of course, you. For example, Mercury directs your Communications Department and Jupiter oversees your Abundance and Growth Department. When you have the need to communicate, you call on your Mercury; when it's time to take a risk or grow, you use your Jupiter. Let's meet each of the planets individually and take a look at which job duties fall under each planet's jurisdiction.

The Sun

Every corporation needs an executive director who makes the final decisions. The Sun is your Executive Director. The Sun in your chart is your core, your true self. Although each of the planets in your chart is important in its own right, they all "take their orders," figuratively speaking, from the Sun.

Everyone's Sun has the same inner goal: to shine. The house your Sun is in shows where you really want to do good, where you want to be appreciated and loved. Your Sun is your inner supply of pride and confidence, your identity. The Sun is you at your creative best, enjoying life to the fullest.

The Sun shows the focus of the moment, where the world's attention will be directed on that particular day. In fact, in horary and electional astrology, the two branches that pertain most to timing and prediction, the Sun represents the day, the Moon the hour, and the Midheaven the moment. In the physical body, the Sun rules the heart, upper back, and circulatory system.

The Moon

Speaking of the Moon, a good place to meet her and begin to understand her qualities is by the water on a clear night when she's full. Whether you're looking up at her or at that silvery patch she creates that shivers and dances on the water, take a deep breath and allow yourself to be still. She represents the soft interior of each of us that recalls memories, fears, and dreams.

She's a lovely lady who oversees the Department of Feelings; she's the bringer of "moods" (a great Moon word). Her house and placement in your chart reveal how your intuition works, what your emotional needs are, and how you want your needs met. She is the ultimate feminine energy, the part of you that points both to how you were nurtured and to how you will nurture others. In the body, the Moon has jurisdiction over the breasts, ovaries, and womb. She also rules our body fluids, the internal ocean that keeps us alive.

Mercury

☿ Back when gods and goddesses were thought to be in charge of the affairs of humanity, Mercury shuttled messages between the gods and mortals. In today's world, Mercury is the computer, the telephone, and the internet. He's the internal computer that constantly feeds you data about the world. His position and house in your chart show how you think and reason, and how you express yourself to others. You'll recognize him in your speech patterns, in your handwriting, and in the way you walk, because moving through your environment means communicating with it. He operates through your five senses and your brain, and makes you conscious of opposites—light and dark, hot and cold, up and down. He's what you use when you have a conversation, exchange a glance, gesture, or interpret a symbol. Mercury represents the side of you living totally in the present.

If you've ever tried to collect mercury after it escaped from a broken thermometer, you've learned something about Mercury. Just as your Mercury never stops collecting data, those tiny beads you tried so hard to collect brought back a bit of everything they contacted—dog hair, crumbs, and grains of dirt. In the body, Mercury also acts as a messenger. He transmits messages through his function as the central nervous system that lets your eyes and hands collaborate, your eyes blink, and breathing continue.

Venus

♀ Venus spends her energy supplying you with your favorite people, places, and things. If you want chocolate, music, flannel sheets, or the coworker you've got a mad crush on, it's your Venus that tells you how to get it. Venus enjoys beauty and comfort. She shows how to attract what you love, especially people. When you're being charming, whether by using your manners or by adorning yourself, she's in charge of all behavior that is pleasing to others—social chitchat, smiles, hugs, and kisses. Whenever you're pleased, satisfied, or content enough to purr, it's your Venus who made you feel that way. Since money is one of the ways we draw the objects we love to us, she's also in charge of finances. Venus relates to your senses—sight, smell, taste, touch, and sound—the body's receptors. After all, it's the senses that tell us what feels good and what doesn't. Venus responds to your desire for beautiful surroundings, comfortable clothing, and fine art.

Mars

♂ Mars is in charge of your Self-Defense and Action Department. He's the warrior who fights back when you're attacked—your own personal SWAT team. Your Mars energy makes you brave, courageous, and daring. His placement in your chart describes how you act on your own behalf. He's concerned only with you, and he doesn't consider the size, strength, or abilities of whomever or whatever you're up against. He's the side of you that initiates all activity. He's also in charge of how you assert yourself and how you express anger.

"Hot under the collar," "seeing red," and "all fired up" are Mars phrases. Mars is what you use to be passionate, adventurous, and bold. But he can be violent, accident-prone, and cruel, too. Wherever he is in your chart, you find constant action. Mars pursues. He shows how you "do" things. He charges through situations. This "headstrong" planet corresponds to the head, the blood, and the muscles.

Jupiter

♃ Jupiter is called "the Greater Benefic," and he heads the Department of Abundance and Growth. He's the side of you that's positive, optimistic, and generous. He's where you keep your supply of laughter, enthusiasm, and high spirits. It's Jupiter's expansive, high-spirited energy that motivates you to travel, take classes, and meet new people. Wherever he is in your chart is a place where you'll have an extensive network of friends and associates—folks you can visit, count on, and learn from. Jupiter is the side of you that will probably cause you to experience the "grass is greener" syndrome. Your Jupiter is also what you're using when you find yourself being excessive and wasteful, overdoing, or blowing something out of proportion. Words like "too" and "always" are the property of Jupiter, as are "more" and "better." In general, this planet just loves to make things bigger. In the body, Jupiter corresponds with the liver, the organ that filters what you take in and rids your body of excess. Jupiter also handles physical growth.

Saturn

♄ Saturn represents withholding and resistance to change. He heads the Boundaries and Rules Department. Locate Saturn in your chart to find out where you'll build walls to keep change out, where you may segregate yourself at times, where you'll be most likely to say no. Your Saturn is the authority inside you, the spot where you may inhibit or stall yourself throughout life—most often because you fear failure and would rather not act at all than act inappropriately. This planet teaches you to respect your elders, follow the rules, and do things right the first time. Wherever Saturn is in your chart is a place where you'll feel respectful, serious, and conservative. Your Saturn placement is where you'll know that you should never embellish the facts and never act until you're absolutely sure you're ready. Here is where you won't expect something for nothing. Saturn is also where you're at your most disciplined, where you'll teach yourself the virtues of patience, endurance, and responsibility. Because this planet is so fond of boundaries, it's also the planet in charge of organization, structures, and guidelines. In the physical body, Saturn correlates with the bones and the skin, those structures that hold your body together.

Uranus

♅ There's a spot in everyone's chart where independence is the order of the day, where rules are made specifically to be broken, and where personal freedom is the only way to go, regardless of the consequences. Here's where you'll surprise even yourself at the things you say and do. Meet Uranus, head of the Department of One Never Knows, the place in your chart where shocks, surprises, and sudden reversals are regular fare.

Your Uranus energy is what wakes you up to how confined you feel, breaks you out of the rut you're in, and sets you free. He's a computer wizard and involved in mass communications. Where he's strong in your chart, you will be strong, too. Here is where you'll have genius potential, where you'll be bold enough to ignore the old way to solve a problem and instead find a whole new way. Major scientific and technological breakthroughs like the space program and the internet were inspired by Uranus. In the body, Uranus rules the lower part of the legs, including the calves and ankles, and he co-rules with Mercury the central nervous system.

Neptune

♆ Next time you hear yourself sigh or feel yourself slip into a daydream, think of Neptune. This is the planet in charge of romance, nostalgia, and magic. Although her official title is head of the Department of Avoidance and Fantasy, she's also one of the most creative energies you own. Wherever she is in your chart is where you're psychic. It's also where you're capable of amazing compassion and sensitivity for beings and creatures less fortunate than yourself. It's where you'll be drawn into charity or volunteer work because you realize that we're all part of a bigger plan, that there are no boundaries between you and what's out there.

This combination of sensitivity and harsh reality doesn't always mix well. This may also be a place where you'll try to escape. Sleep, meditation, and prayer are the highest uses of her energies, but alcohol and drugs are also under her jurisdiction. Neptune's place in your chart is where you're equally capable of fooling all of the people all of the time, and of being fooled yourself. In the body, Neptune and the Moon co-rule fluids. Neptune also has a connection with poisons and viruses that invisibly infiltrate our bodies and with the body's immune system, which is how we keep our barriers intact.

Pluto

♇ Pluto is head of the Department of Death, Destruction, and Decay. He's in charge of things that have to happen, and he disposes of situations that have gone past the point of no return, where the only solution is to "let go." He also oversees sex, reincarnation, recycling, regeneration, and rejuvenation. Pluto's spot in your chart is a place where intense, inevitable circumstances will arrive to teach you about agony and ecstasy. Pluto's place in your chart is where you'll be in a state of turmoil or evolution, where there will be ongoing change. This is the side of you that realizes that, like it or not, life goes on after tremendous loss. It is the side of you that will reflect on your losses down the road and try to make sense of them. Most importantly, since

Pluto rules life, death, and rebirth, here's where you'll understand the importance of process. You'll be amazingly strong where your Pluto is—he's a well of concentrated, transforming energy. In the body, Pluto is associated with the reproductive organs since here is where the invisible process of life and death begins. He is also in charge of puberty and sexual maturity. He corresponds with plutonium.

Signs: The Second Building Block

Every sign is built of three things: an element, a quality, and a polarity. Understanding each of these primary building blocks gives a head start toward understanding the signs themselves, so let's take a look at them.

The Polarities: Masculine and Feminine

The words "masculine" and "feminine" are often misunderstood or confused in the context of astrology. In astrology, masculine means that an energy is assertive, aggressive, and linear. Feminine means that an energy is receptive, magnetic, and circular. These terms should not be confused with male and female.

The Qualities: Cardinal, Fixed, and Mutable

Qualities show the way a sign's energy flows. The cardinal signs are energies that initiate change. Cardinal signs operate in sudden bursts of energy. The fixed signs are thorough and unstoppable. They're the energies that endure. They take projects to completion, tend to block change at all costs, and will keep at something regardless of whether or not it should be terminated. The mutable signs are versatile, flexible, and changeable. They can be scattered, fickle, and inconstant.

The Elements: Fire, Earth, Air, and Water

The fire signs correspond with the spirit and the spiritual aspects of life. They inspire action, attract attention, and love spontaneity. The earth signs are solid, practical, supportive, and as reliable as the earth under our feet. The earth signs are our physical envoys and are concerned with our tangible needs, such as food, shelter, work, and responsibilities. Air signs are all about the intellectual or mental sides of life. Like air itself, they are light and elusive. They love conversation, communication, and mingling. The water signs correspond to the emotional side of our natures. As changeable, subtle, and able to infiltrate as water itself, water signs gauge the mood in a room when they enter, and operate on what they sense from their environment.

Aries: Masculine, Cardinal, Fire

♈ Aries is ruled by Mars and is cardinal fire—red-hot, impulsive, and ready to go. Aries planets are not known for their patience, and they ignore obstacles, choosing instead to focus on the shortest distance between where they are and where they want to be. Planets in Aries are brave, impetuous, and direct. Aries planets are often very good at initiating projects. They are not, however, as eager to finish, so they will leave projects undone. Aries planets need physical outlets for their considerable Mars-powered energy; otherwise their need for action can turn to stress. Exercise, hard work, and competition are food for Aries energy.

Taurus: Feminine, Fixed, Earth

♉ Taurus, the fixed earth sign, has endless patience that turns your Taurus planet into a solid force to be reckoned with. Taurus folks never, ever quit. Their reputation for stubbornness is earned. They're responsible, reliable, honest as they come, practical, and endowed with a stick-to-it attitude other planets envy. They're not afraid to work hard. Since Taurus is ruled by Venus, it's not surprising to find that these people are sensual and luxury-loving, too. They love to be spoiled with the best—good food, fine wine, or even a Renoir painting. They need peace and quiet like no other, and don't like their schedules to be disrupted. However, they may need a reminder that comfortable habits can become ruts.

Gemini: Masculine, Mutable, Air

♊ This sign is famous for its duality and love of new experiences, as well as for its role as communicator. Gemini is mutable air, which translates into changing your mind, so expect your Gemini planet to be entertaining and versatile. This sign knows a little bit about everything. Gemini planets usually display at least two distinct sides to their personalities, are changeable and even fickle at times, and are wonderfully curious. This sign is ruled by Mercury, so if what you're doing involves talking, writing, gesturing, or working with hand-eye coordination, your Gemini planet will love it. Mercury also rules short trips, so any planet in Gemini is an expert at how to make its way around the neighborhood in record time.

Cancer: Feminine, Cardinal, Water

♋ Cancer is cardinal water, so it's good at beginning things. It's also the most privacy-oriented sign. Cancer types are emotionally vulnerable, sensitive, and easily hurt. They need safe "nests" to return to when the world gets to be too much. Cancer types say "I love you" by tending to your need for food, warmth, or a place to sleep. The problem is that they can become needy, dependent, or unable to function unless they feel someone or something needs them. Cancer rules the home and family. It's also in charge of emotions, so expect a Cancer to operate from his or her gut most of the time.

Leo: Masculine, Fixed, Fire

♌ Leo is fixed fire, and above all else represents pride and ego. Sun-ruled Leo wants to shine and be noticed. Natural performers, people in this sign are into drama and attract attention even when they don't necessarily want it. Occasionally your Leo friends may be touchy and high maintenance. Still, they are generous to a fault. Leo appreciates attention and praise with lavish compliments, lovely gifts, and creative outings designed to amaze and delight. Leo's specialties are having fun, entertaining, and making big entrances and exits.

Virgo: Feminine, Mutable, Earth

♍ Virgo may seem picky and critical, but that may be too simplistic. As a mutable earth sign, your Virgo planet delights in helping, and it's willing to adapt to any task. Having a keen eye for details may be another way to interpret a Virgo planet's automatic fault-finding ability. When Virgo's eye for detail combines with the ability to fix almost anything, you have a troubleshooter extraordinaire. This sign practices discrimination—analyzing, critiquing, and suggesting remedies to potential problems. This sign is also wonderful at making lists, agendas, and schedules. Keep your Virgo planet happy by keeping it busy.

Libra: Masculine, Cardinal, Air

Libra adores balance, harmony, and equal give and take—no easy task. A more charming sign would be difficult to find, though. Libra's cardinal airy nature wants to begin things, and entertaining and socializing are high priorities. These expert people-pleasing Venus-ruled planets specialize in manners, courtesy, and small talk. Alone time may be shunned, and because they're gifted with the ability to pacify, they may sell out their own needs, or the truth, to buy peace and companionship. Seeing both sides of a situation, weighing the options, and keeping their inner balance by remaining honest may be Libra's hardest tasks.

Scorpio: Feminine, Fixed, Water

Planets in this sign are detectives, excelling at the art of strategy. Your Scorpio planets sift through every situation for subtle clues, which they analyze to determine what's really going on. They're also gifted at sending subtle signals back to the environment, and at imperceptibly altering a situation by manipulating it with the right word or movement. Scorpio planets are constantly searching for intimacy. They seek intensity and may be crisis-oriented. They can be relentless, obsessive, and jealous. Remember, this is fixed water. Scorpios feel things deeply and forever. Give your Scorpio planets the opportunity to fire-walk, to experience life-and-death situations.

Sagittarius: Masculine, Mutable, Fire

The enthusiasm of this mutable fire sign, ruled by Jupiter, spreads like a brushfire. These planets tend to never feel satisfied or content, and to always wonder if there's something even more wonderful over the next mountain. Your Sagittarius planets are bored by routine; they're freedom-oriented, generous, and optimistic to a fault. They can be excessive and overindulgent. They adore outdoor activities and foreign places and foreign people. They learn by first having the big picture explained. They're only too happy to preach, advertise, and philosophize. Sagittarius planets can be quite prophetic, and they absolutely believe in the power of laughter, embarrassing themselves at times to make someone laugh.

Capricorn: Feminine, Cardinal, Earth

♑ Your Capricorn planets, ruled by Saturn, have a tendency to build things, such as erecting structures and creating a career for you. Saturn will start up an organization and turn it into the family business. These planets automatically know how to run it no matter what it is. They're authority figures. They exercise caution and discipline, set down rules, and live by them. Capricorn is the sign with the driest wit. Here's where your sense of propriety and tradition will be strong, where doing things the old-fashioned way and paying respect to elders will be the only way to go. They want a return for the time they invest, and don't mind proving how valuable they are.

Aquarius: Masculine, Fixed, Air

♒ Aquarian planets present some unexpected contradictions because they are fixed air and unpredictable. This sign's ruler, Uranus, gets the credit for Aquarius's tumultuous ways. Aquarian energy facilitates invention and humanitarian conquests, to the amazement of the masses, and planets in this sign are into personal freedom like no other. They create their own rules, fight city hall whenever possible, and deliberately break tradition. They adore change. Abrupt reversals are their specialty, so others often perceive them as erratic, unstable, or unreliable. But when Aquarius energy activates, commitment to a cause or an intellectual ideal has a steadfastness like no other sign possesses.

Pisces: Feminine, Mutable, Water

♓ Mutable Pisces can't separate itself emotionally from whatever it's exposed to. While this is the source of Pisces' well-deserved reputation for compassion, it's also the source of a desire to escape reality. Planets in this sign feel everything—for better or worse—so they need time alone to unload and reassemble themselves. Exposure to others, especially in crowds, is exhausting to your Pisces planets. Here is where you may have a tendency to take in stray people and animals and where you'll need to watch for the possibility of being victimized or taken advantage of in some way. Pisces planets see the best in people or situations, and they can be disappointed when reality sets in. These planets are the romantics of the zodiac. Let them dream in healthy ways.

Houses: The Third Building Block

Houses are represented by twelve pie-shaped wedges in a horoscope chart. (See blank chart on page 208.) They're like rooms in a house, and each reflects the circumstances we create and encounter in a specific area of life. One room, the Sixth House, relates to our daily routine and work, while the Eleventh House relates to groups we may be affiliated with, for example. The sign (Aries, Taurus, etc.) on the cusp of each house tells us something about the nature of the room behind the door. Someone with Leo on the Sixth House cusp will create different routines and work habits than a person with Capricorn on that cusp. The sign influences the type of behavior you'll exhibit when those life circumstances turn up. Since the time of day you were born determines the sign on each of the houses, an accurate birth time will result in more accurate information from your chart.

The Twelve Houses

The First House

The First House shows the sign that was ascending over the horizon at the moment you were born. Let's think again of your chart as one big house and of the houses as "rooms." The First House symbolizes your front door. The sign on this house cusp (also known as the Rising Sign or Ascendant) describes the way you dress, move, and adorn yourself, and the overall condition of your body. It relates to the first impression you make on people.

The Second House

This house shows how you handle the possessions you hold dear. That goes for money, objects, and the qualities you value in yourself and in others. This house also holds the side of you that takes care of what you have and what you buy for yourself, and the amount of money you earn. The Second House shows what you're willing to do for money, too, so it's also a description of your self-esteem.

The Third House

This house corresponds to your neighborhood, including the bank, the post office, and the gym where you work out. This is the side of you that performs routine tasks without much conscious thought. The Third House also refers to childhood and grammar school, and it shows your relationships with siblings, your communication style, and your attitude toward short trips.

The Fourth House

This house is the symbolic foundation brought from your childhood home, your family, and the parent who nurtured you. Here is where you'll find the part of you that decorates and maintains your nest. It decides what home in the adult world will be like and how much privacy you'll need. The Fourth House deals with matters of real estate. Most importantly, this house contains the emotional warehouse of memories you operate from subconsciously.

The Fifth House

Here's the side of you that's reserved for play, that only comes out when work is done and it's time to party and be entertained. This is the charming, creative, delightful side of you, where your hobbies, interests, and playmates are found. If it gives you joy, it's described here. Your Fifth House shines when you are creative, and it allows you to see a bit of yourself in those creations—anything from your child's smile to a piece of art. Traditionally this house also refers to speculation and gambling.

The Sixth House

This house is where you keep the side of you that decides how you like things to go along over the course of a day, the side of you that plans a schedule. Since it describes the duties you perform on a daily basis, it also refers to the nature of your work, your work environment, and how you take care of your health. It's how you function. Pets are also traditionally a Sixth House issue, since we tend to them daily and incorporate them into our routine.

The Seventh House
Although it's traditionally known as the house of marriage, partnerships, and open enemies, the Seventh House really holds the side of you that only comes out when you're in the company of just one other person. This is the side of you that handles relating on a one-to-one basis. Whenever you use the word "my" to describe your relationship with another, it's this side of you talking.

The Eighth House
Here's the crisis expert side of you that emerges when it's time to handle extreme circumstances. This is the side of you that deals with agony and ecstasy, with sex, death, and all manner of mergers, financial and otherwise. The Eighth House also holds information on surgeries, psychotherapy, and the way we regenerate and rejuvenate after a loss.

The Ninth House
This house holds the side of you that handles new experiences, foreign places, long-distance travel, and legal matters. Higher education, publishing, advertising, and forming opinions are handled here, as are issues involving the big picture, including politics, religion, and philosophy.

The Tenth House
This spot in your chart describes what the public knows about you. Your career, reputation, and social status are found here. This is the side of you that takes time to learn and become accomplished. It describes the behavior you'll exhibit when you're in charge, and also the way you'll act in the presence of an authority figure. Most importantly, the Tenth House describes your vocation or life's work—whatever you consider your "calling."

The Eleventh House
Here's the team player in you, the side of you that helps you find your peer groups. The Eleventh House shows the types of organizations you're drawn to join, the kind of folks you consider kindred spirits, and how you'll act in group situations. It also shows the causes and social activities you hold near and dear.

The Twelfth House
This is the side of you that only comes out when you're alone, or in the mood to retreat and regroup. Here's where the secret side of you lives, where secret affairs and dealings take place. Here, too, is where matters like hospital stays are handled. Most importantly, the Twelfth House is the room where you keep all the traits and behaviors that you were taught early on to stifle, avoid, or deny—especially in public. This side of you is very fond of fantasy, illusion, and pretend play.

Aspects and Transits: The Fourth Building Block

Planets form angles to one another as they move through the heavens. If two planets are 90 degrees apart, they form a square. If they're 180 degrees apart, they're in opposition. Planets in aspect have twenty-four-hour communication going on. The particular angle that separates any two planets describes the nature of their conversation. Astrologers use six angles most often, each of which produces a different type of relationship or "conversation" between the planets they join. Let's go over the meaning of each of the aspects.

Ptolemic Aspects

The Conjunction (0–8 degrees)

♂ When you hear that two things are operating "in conjunction," it means they're operating together. This holds true with planets as well. Two (or more) planets conjoined are a team, but some planets pair up more easily than others. Venus and the Moon work well together because both are feminine and receptive, but the Sun and Mars are both pretty feisty by nature, and may cause conflict. Planets in conjunction are usually sharing a house in your chart.

The Sextile (60 degrees)

✳ The sextile links planets in compatible elements. That is, planets in sextile are either in fire and air signs or earth and water signs. Since these pairs of elements get along well, the sextile encourages an active exchange between the two planets involved, so these two parts of you will be eager to work together.

The Square (90 degrees)

☐ A square aspect puts planets at cross-purposes. Friction develops between them and one will constantly challenge the other. You can see squares operating in someone who's fidgety or constantly restless. Although they're uncomfortable and even aggravating at times, your squares point to places where tremendous growth is possible.

The Trine (120 degrees)

△ Trines are usually formed between planets of the same element, so they understand each other. They show an ease of communication not found in any of the other aspects, and they're traditionally thought of as "favorable." Of course, there is a downside to trines. Planets in this relationship are so comfortable that they can often get lazy and spoiled. (Sometimes they get so comfy they're boring.) Planets in trine show urges or needs that automatically support each other. The catch is that you've got to get them operating.

The Quincunx (150 degrees)

⚻ This aspect joins two signs that don't share a quality, element, or gender, which makes it difficult for them to communicate with each other. It's frustrating. For that reason, this aspect has always been considered to require an adjustment in the way the two planets are used. Planets in quincunx often feel pushed, forced, or obligated to perform. They seem to correspond to health issues.

The Opposition (180 degrees)

☍ When two planets are opposed, they work against each other. For example, you may want to do something, and if you have two opposing planets you may struggle with two very different approaches to getting the job done. If Mars and Neptune are opposing, you may struggle between getting a job done the quick, easy way or daydreaming about all the creative possibilities open to you. It's as if the two are standing across from one another with their arms folded, involved in a debate, neither willing to concede an inch. They can break out of their standoff only by first becoming aware of one another and then compromising. This aspect is the least difficult of the traditionally known "hard" aspects because planets "at odds" with one another can come to some sort of compromise.

Transits

While your horoscope (natal chart) reflects the exact position of planets at the time of your birth, the planets, as you know, move on. They are said to be "transiting." We interpret a transit as a planet in its "today" position making an aspect to a planet in your natal chart. Transiting planets represent incoming influences and events that your natal planets will be asked to handle. The nature of the transiting planet describes the types of situations that will arise, and the nature of your natal planet tells which "piece" of you you're working on at the moment. When a planet transits through a house or aspects a planet in your chart, you will have opportunities for personal growth and change. Every transit you experience adds knowledge to your personality.

Sun Transit

A Sun transit points to the places in your chart where you'll want special attention, pats on the back, and appreciation. Here's where you want to shine. These are often times of public acclaim, when we're recognized, congratulated, or applauded for what we've done. Of course, the ultimate Sun transit is our birthday, the day when we're all secretly sure that we should be treated like royalty.

Moon Transit

When the Moon touches one of the planets in our natal chart, we react from an emotional point of view. A Moon transit often corresponds to the highs and lows we feel that last only a day or two. Our instincts are on high during a Moon transit and we're more liable to sense what's going on around us than to consciously know something.

Mercury Transit

Transiting Mercury creates activity in whatever area of life it visits. The subject is communication of all kinds, so conversation, letters, and quick errands take up our time now. Because of Mercury's love of duality, events will often occur in twos—as if Hermes the trickster were having some fun with us—and we're put in the position of having to do at least two things at once.

Venus Transit

Transiting Venus brings times when the universe gives us a small token of warmth or affection or a well-deserved break. These are often sociable, friendly periods when we do more than our usual share of mingling and are more interested in good food and cushy conditions than anything resembling work. A Venus transit also shows a time when others will give us gifts. Since Venus rules money, this transit can show when we'll receive financial rewards.

Mars Transit

Mars transiting a house can indicate high-energy times. You're stronger and restless, or perhaps cranky, angry, accident-prone, or violent. When Mars happens along, it's best to work or exercise hard to use up this considerable energy. Make yourself "too tired to be mad." These are ideal times to initiate projects that require a hard push of energy to begin.

Jupiter Transit

Under this transit you're in the mood to travel, take a class, or learn something new about the concerns of any house or planet Jupiter visits. You ponder the big questions. You grow under a Jupiter transit, sometimes even physically. Now is the time to take chances or risk a shot at the title. During a Jupiter transit you're luckier, bolder, and a lot more likely to succeed. This transit provides opportunities. Be sure to take advantage of them.

Saturn Transit

When Saturn comes along, we see things as they truly are. These are not traditionally great times, but they are often times when your greatest rewards appear. When Saturn transits a house or planet, he checks to see if the structure is steady and will hold up. You are then tested, and if you pass, you receive a symbolic certificate of some kind—and sometimes a real one, like a diploma. We will always be tested, but if we fail, life can feel very difficult. Firming up our lives is Saturn's mission. This is a great time to tap into Saturn's willpower and self-discipline to stop doing something. It is not traditionally a good time to begin new ventures, though.

Uranus Transit

The last thing in the world you'd ever expect to happen is exactly what you can expect under a Uranus transit. This is the planet of last-minute plan changes, reversals, and shock effects. So if you're feeling stuck in your present circumstances, when a Uranus transit happens along you won't be stuck for long. "Temporary people" often enter your life at these times, folks whose only purpose is to jolt you out of your present circumstances by appearing to provide exactly what you were sorely missing. That done, they disappear, leaving you with your life in a shambles. When these people arrive, enjoy them and allow them to break you out of your rut—just don't get comfortable.

Neptune Transit

A Neptune transit is a time when the universe asks only that you dream and nothing more. Your sensitivity heightens to the point that harsh sounds can actually make you wince. Compassion deepens, and psychic moments are common. A Neptune transit inspires divine discontent. You sigh, wish, feel nostalgic, and don't see things clearly at all. At the end of the transit, you realize that everything about you is different, that the reality you were living at the beginning of the transit has been gradually eroded or erased right from under your feet, while you stood right there upon it.

Pluto Transit

A Pluto transit is often associated with obsession, regeneration, and inevitable change. Whatever has gone past the point of no return, whatever is broken beyond repair, will pass from your life now. As with a Saturn transit, this time is not known to be wonderful, but when circumstances peel away everything from us and we're forced to see ourselves as we truly are, we do learn just how strong we are. Power struggles often accompany Pluto's visit, but being empowered is the end result of a positive Pluto transit. The secret is to let go, accept the losses or changes, and make plans for the future.

Retrograde Planets

Retrograde literally means "backward." Although none of the planets ever really throw their engines in reverse and move backward, all of them, except the Sun and Moon, appear to do so periodically from our perspective here on Earth. What's happening is that we're moving either faster or slower than the planet that's retrograde, and since we have to look over our shoulder to see it, we refer to it as retrograde.

Mercury Retrograde: A Communication Breakdown

The way retrograde planets seem to affect our affairs varies from planet to planet. In Mercury's case, it means often looking back at Mercury-ruled things—communications, contracts, and so on. Keep in mind that Mercury correlates with Hermes, the original trickster, and you'll understand how cleverly disguised some of these errors can be. Communications become confused or are delayed. Letters are lost or sent to Auckland instead of Oakland, or they end up under the car seat for three weeks. We sign a contract or agreement and find out later that we didn't have all the correct information and what we signed was misleading in some way. We try repeatedly to reach someone on the telephone but can never catch them, or our communications devices themselves break down or garble information in some way. We feel as if our timing is off, so short trips often become more difficult. We leave the directions at home or write them down incorrectly. We're late for appointments due to circumstances beyond our control, or we completely forget about them.

Is there a constructive use for this time period? Yes. Astrologer Erin Sullivan has noted that the ratio of time Mercury spends moving retrograde (backward) and direct (forward) corresponds beautifully with the amount of time we humans spend awake and asleep—about a third of our lives. So this period seems to be a time to take stock of what's happened over the past three months and assimilate our experiences.

A good rule of thumb with Mercury retrograde is to try to confine activities to those that have "re" attached to the beginning of a word, such as reschedule, repair, return, rewrite, redecorate, restore, replace, renovate, or renew.

Retrogrades of the Other Planets

With Venus retrograde every eighteen months for six weeks, relationships and money matters are delayed or muddled.

With Mars retrograde for eleven weeks and then direct for twenty-two months, actions initiated are often rooted in confusion or end up at cross-purposes to our original intentions. Typically under a Mars retrograde, the aggressor or initiator of a battle is defeated.

Jupiter retrogrades for four months and is direct for nine months. Saturn retrogrades for about the same amount of time. Each of the outer planets—Uranus, Neptune, and Pluto—stays retrograde for about six or seven months of every year. In general, remember that actions ruled by a particular planet quite often need to be repeated or done over when that planet is retrograde. Just make sure that whatever you're planning is something you don't mind doing twice.

Moon Void-of-Course

The Moon orbits Earth in about twenty-eight days, moving through each of the signs in about two days. As she passes through the thirty degrees of each sign, she visits with the planets in order by forming angles, or aspects, with them. Because she moves one degree in just two to two and a half hours, her influence on each planet lasts only a few hours. As she approaches the late degrees of the sign she's passing through, she eventually forms what will be her final aspect to another planet before leaving the sign. From this point until she actually enters the new sign, she is referred to as being "void-of-course" (v/c).

The Moon symbolizes the emotional tone of the day, carrying feelings of the sign she's "wearing" at the moment. She rules instincts. After she has contacted each of the planets, she symbolically "rests" before changing her costume, so her instincts are temporarily on hold. It's during this time that many people feel fuzzy, vague, or scattered. Plans or decisions do not pan out. Without the instinctual knowing the Moon provides as she touches each planet, we tend to be unrealistic or exercise poor judgment. The traditional definition of the void-of-course Moon is that "nothing will come of this," and it seems to be true. Actions initiated under a void-of-course Moon are often wasted, irrelevant, or incorrect—usually because information needed to make a sound decision is hidden or missing or has been overlooked.

Now, although it's not a good time to initiate plans when the Moon is void, routine tasks seem to go along just fine. However, this period is really ideal for what the Moon does best: reflection. It's at this time that we can assimilate what has occurred over the past few days. Use this time to meditate, ponder, and imagine. Let your conscious mind rest and allow yourself to feel.

On the lighter side, remember that there are other good uses for the void-of-course Moon. This is the time period when the universe seems to be most open to loopholes. It's a great time to make plans you don't want to fulfill or schedule things you don't want to do. In other words, like the saying goes, "To everything, there is a season." Even void-of-course Moons.

The Moon's Influence

As the Moon goes along her way, she magically appears and disappears, waxing to full from the barest sliver of a crescent just after she's new, then waning back to her invisible new phase again. The four quarters—the New Moon, the second quarter, the Full Moon, and the fourth quarter—correspond to the growth cycle of every living thing.

The Quarters

First Quarter

This phase begins when the Moon and the Sun are conjunct one another in the sky. At the beginning of the phase, the Moon is invisible, hidden by the brightness of the Sun as they travel together. The Moon is often said to be in her "dark phase" when she is just new. The New Moon can't actually be seen until 5½ to 12 hours after its birth. Toward the end of the first-quarter phase, as the Moon pulls farther away from the Sun and begins to wax toward the second quarter stage, a delicate silver crescent appears. This time corresponds to all new beginnings; this is the best time to begin a project.

Second Quarter

The second quarter begins when the Moon has moved 90 degrees away from the Sun. At this point the waxing Moon rises at about noon and sets at about midnight. It's at this time that she can be seen in the western sky during the early evening hours, growing in size from a crescent to her full beauty. This period corresponds to the development and growth of life, and with projects that are coming close to fruition.

Third Quarter

This phase begins with the Full Moon, when the Sun and Moon are opposite each other in the sky. It's now that the Moon can be seen rising in the east at sunset, a bit later each night as this phase progresses. This time corresponds to the culmination of plans and to maturity.

Fourth Quarter

This phase occurs when the Moon has moved 90 degrees past the full phase. She is decreasing in light, rises at midnight, and can be seen now in the eastern sky during the late evening hours. She doesn't reach the highest point in the sky until very early in the morning. This period corresponds to "disintegration"—a symbolic "drawing back" to reflect on what's been accomplished. It's now time to reorganize, clear the boards, and plan for the next New Moon stage.

The Moon Through the Signs

The signs indicate how we'll do things. Since the Moon rules the emotional tone of the day, it's good to know what type of mood she's in at any given moment. Here's a thumbnail sketch to help you navigate every day by cooperating with the Moon no matter what sign she's in.

Aries

The Moon in Aries is bold, impulsive, and energetic. It's a period when we feel feisty and maybe a little argumentative. This is when even the meekest aren't afraid to take a stand to protect personal feelings. Since Aries is the first sign of the zodiac, it's a natural starting point for all kinds of projects, and a wonderful time to channel all that "me first" energy to initiate change and new beginnings. Just watch out for a tendency to be too impulsive and stress-oriented.

Taurus

☽♉ The Moon in Taurus is the Lady at her most solid and sensual, feeling secure and well rooted. There's no need to stress or hurry—and definitely no need to change anything. We tend to resist change when the Moon is in this sign, especially change that's not of our own making. We'd rather sit still, have a wonderful dinner, and listen to good music. Appreciating the beauty of the earth, watching a sunset, viewing some lovely art, or taking care of money and other resources are Taurus Moon activities.

Gemini

☽♊ This mutable air sign moves around so quickly that when the Moon is here we're a bit more restless than usual, and may find that we're suddenly in the mood for conversation, puzzles, riddles, and word games. We want two—at least two—of everything. Now is a great time for letter writing, phone calls, or short trips. It's when you'll find the best shortcuts, and when you'll need to take them, too. Watch for a tendency to become a bit scattered under this fun, fickle Moon.

Cancer

☽♋ The Moon in this cardinal water sign is at her most nurturing. Here the Moon's concerns turn to home, family, children, and mothers, and we respond by becoming more likely to express our emotions and to be sympathetic and understanding toward others. We often find ourselves in the mood to take care of someone, to cook for or cuddle our dear ones. During this time, feelings run high, so it's important to watch out for becoming overly sensitive, dependent, or needy. Now is a great time to putter around the house, have family over, and tend to domestic concerns.

Leo

☽ ♌ The Leo Moon loves drama with a capital *D*. This theatrical sign has long been known for its big entrances, love of display, and need for attention. When the Moon is in this sign, we're all feeling a need to be recognized, applauded, and appreciated. Now, all that excitement, pride, and emotion can turn into melodrama in the blink of an eye, so it's best to be careful of overreacting or being excessively vain during this period. It's a great time to take in a show (or star in one), be romantic, or express your feelings for someone in regal style.

Virgo

☽ ♍ The Moon is at her most discriminating and detail-oriented in Virgo, the sign most concerned with fixing and fussing. This Moon sign puts us in the mood to clean, scour, sort, troubleshoot, and help. Virgo, the most helpful of all the signs, is also more health conscious, work-oriented, and duty bound. Use this period to pay attention to your diet, hygiene, and daily schedules.

Libra

☽ ♎ The Libra Moon is most oriented toward relationships and partnerships. Since Libra's job is to restore balance, however, you may find yourself in situations of emotional imbalance that require a delicate tap of the scales to set them right. In general, this is a social, polite, and friendly time, when others will be cooperative and agree more easily to compromise. A Libra Moon prompts us to make our surroundings beautiful, or to put ourselves in situations where beauty is all around us. This is a great time to decorate, shop for the home, or visit places of elegant beauty.

Scorpio

☽ ♏ Scorpio is the most intense sign, and when the Moon is here, she feels everything to the *n*th degree—and needless to say, we do, too. Passion, joy, jealousy, betrayal, love, and desire can take center stage in our lives now, as our emotions deepen to the point of possible obsession. Be careful of a tendency to become secretive or suspicious, or to brood over an offense that was not intended.

Now is a great time to investigate a mystery, do research, "dig"—both figuratively and literally—and allow ourselves to become intimate with someone.

Sagittarius

☽ ♐ The Moon is at her most optimistic and willing to let go of things in Sagittarius. Jupiter, the planet of long-distance travel and education of the higher mind, makes this a great time to take off for adventure or attend a seminar on a topic you've always been interested in—say, philosophy or religion. This is the sign with the gift of prophecy and wisdom. When the Moon is in this sign, spend time outdoors, be spontaneous, and laugh much too loudly; just watch for a tendency toward excess, waste, and overdoing.

Capricorn

☽ ♑ The Moon is at her most organized, practical, and businesslike in Capricorn. She brings out the dutiful, cautious, and pessimistic side of us. Our goals for the future become all-important. Now is the time to tend to the family business, act responsibly, take charge of something, organize any part of our lives that has become scattered or disrupted, set down rules and guidelines, or patiently listen and learn. Watch for the possibility of acting too businesslike at the expense of others' emotions.

Aquarius

☽ ♒ The Aquarius Moon brings out the rebel in us. This is a great time to break out of a rut, try something different, and make sure everyone sees us for the unique individuals we are. This sign is ruled by Uranus, so personal freedom and individuality are more important than anything now. Our schedules become topsy-turvy, and our causes become urgent. Watch for a tendency to become fanatical, act deliberately rebellious without a reason, or break tradition just for the sake of breaking it.

Pisces

☽ ♓ When the Moon slips into this sign, sleep, meditation, prayer, drugs, or alcohol is often what we crave to induce a trancelike state that will allow us to escape from the harshness of reality. Now is when we're most susceptible to emotional assaults of any kind, when we're feeling dreamy, nostalgic, wistful, or impressionable. It's also when we're at our most spiritual, when our boundaries are at their lowest, when we're compassionate, intuitive, and sensitive to those less fortunate. This is the time to attend a spiritual group or religious gathering.

2023 Eclipse Dates

April 20

Solar Eclipse at 29° ♈ 50'

(12:13 a.m. EDT)

May 5

Lunar Eclipse at 14° ♏ 58'

(1:34 p.m. EDT)

October 14

Solar Eclipse at 21° ♎ 08'

(1:55 p.m. EDT)

October 28

Lunar Eclipse at 5° ♉ 09'

(4:24 p.m. EDT)

2023 Retrograde Planets

Planet	Begin	Eastern	Pacific	End	Eastern	Pacific
Uranus	8/24/22	9:54 am	**6:54 am**	1/22	5:59 pm	**2:59 pm**
Mars	10/30/22	9:26 am	**6:26 am**	1/12	3:56 pm	**12:56 pm**
Mercury	12/29/22	4:32 am	**1:32 am**	1/18	8:12 am	**5:12 am**
Mercury	4/21	4:35 am	**1:35 am**	5/14	11:17 pm	**8:17 pm**
Pluto	5/1	1:09 pm	**10:09 am**	10/10	9:10 pm	**6:10 pm**
Saturn	6/17	1:27 pm	**10:27 am**	11/4	3:03 am	**12:03 am**
Neptune	6/30	5:07 pm	**2:07 pm**	12/6	8:20 am	**5:20 am**
Venus	7/22	9:33 pm	**6:33 pm**	9/3	9:20 pm	**6:20 pm**
Mercury	8/23	3:59 pm	**12:59 pm**	9/15	4:21 pm	**1:21 pm**
Uranus	8/28	10:39 pm	**7:39 pm**	1/26/24		**11:35 pm**
				1/27/24	2:35 am	
Jupiter	9/4	10:10 am	**7:10 am**	12/30	9:40 pm	**6:40 pm**
Mercury	12/12		**11:09 pm**	1/1/24	10:08 pm	**7:08 pm**
	12/13	2:09 am				

2023 New and Full Moons

- ○ Full Moon, 16 ♋ 22, January 6, 6:08 p.m. EST
- ● New Moon, 1 ♒ 33, January 21, 3:53 p.m. EST
- ○ Full Moon, 16 ♌ 41, February 5, 1:29 p.m. EST
- ● New Moon, 1 ♓ 22, February 20, 2:06 a.m. EST
- ○ Full Moon, 16 ♍ 40, March 7, 7:40 a.m. EST
- ● New Moon, 0 ♈ 50, March 21, 1:23 p.m. EDT
- ○ Full Moon, 16 ♎ 07, April 6, 12:34 a.m. EDT
- ● New Moon/Solar Eclipse, 29 ♈ 50, April 20, 12:13 a.m. EDT
- ○ Full Moon/Lunar Eclipse, 14 ♏ 58, May 5, 1:34 p.m. EDT
- ● New Moon, 28 ♉ 25, May 19, 11:53 a.m. EDT
- ○ Full Moon, 13 ♐ 18, June 3, 11:42 p.m. EDT
- ● New Moon, 26 ♊ 43, June 18, 12:37 a.m. EDT
- ○ Full Moon, 11 ♑ 19, July 3, 7:39 a.m. EDT
- ● New Moon, 24 ♋ 56, July 17, 2:32 p.m. EDT
- ○ Full Moon, 9 ♒ 16, August 1, 2:32 p.m. EDT
- ● New Moon, 23 ♌ 17, August 16, 5:38 a.m. EDT
- ○ Full Moon, 7 ♓ 25, August 30, 9:36 p.m. EDT
- ● New Moon, 21 ♍ 59, September 14, 9:40 p.m. EDT
- ○ Full Moon, 6 ♈ 00, September 29, 5:58 a.m. EDT
- ● New Moon/Solar Eclipse, 21 ♎ 08, October 14, 1:55 p.m. EDT
- ○ Full Moon/Lunar Eclipse, 5 ♉ 09, October 28, 4:24 p.m. EDT
- ● New Moon, 20 ♏ 44, November 13, 4:27 a.m. EST
- ○ Full Moon, 4 ♊ 51, November 27, 4:16 a.m. EST
- ● New Moon, 20 ♐ 40, December 12, 6:32 p.m. EST
- ○ Full Moon, 4 ♋ 58, December 26, 7:33 p.m. EST

2023 Planetary Phenomena

Information on Uranus and Neptune assumes the use of a telescope. Resource: *Astronomical Phenomena for the Year 2023*, prepared jointly with Her Majesty's Nautical Almanac Office of the United Kingdom Hydrographic Office and the United States Naval Observatory's Nautical Almanac Office. The dates are expressed in Universal Time and must be converted to your Local Mean Time. (See the World Map of Time Zones on page 193.)

Planets Visible in Morning and Evening

Planet	Morning	Evening
Mercury	Jan. 13 – March 7 May 11 – June 24 Sept. 14 – Oct. 8 Dec. 29 – Dec. 31	Jan. 1 – Jan. 2 March 26 – April 23 July 9 – Aug. 30 Nov. 5 – Dec. 17
Venus	Aug. 18 – Dec. 31	Jan. 1 – Aug. 8
Mars		Jan. 1 – Sept. 30
Jupiter	April 26 – Nov. 3	Jan. 1 – March 29 Nov. 3 – Dec. 31
Saturn	March 6 – Aug. 27	Jan. 1 – Jan. 30 Aug. 27 – Dec. 31

Mercury

Mercury can only be seen low in the east before sunrise or low in the west after sunset.

Venus

Venus is a brilliant object in the evening sky from the beginning of the year until the beginning of the second week of August, when it becomes too close to the Sun for observation. In the third week of August it reappears in the morning sky, where it stays until the end of the year.

Mars
Mars can be seen for more than half the night through late March. Its eastward elongation gradually decreases until it can be see in the evening sky until the end of September. From the beginning of October until the end of the year, it is too close to the Sun for observation.

Jupiter
Jupiter can be seen at the beginning of the year in the evening sky. From late March it becomes too close to the Sun for observation. It reappears in the morning sky in late April, and its westward elongation gradually increases until November 3. From early November it can be seen for more than half the night.

Saturn
Saturn can be seen in the evening sky from the beginning of the year. In late January it becomes too close to the Sun for observation until early March, when it reappears in the morning sky. Its westward elongation gradually increases until August 27, when it is visible throughout the night.

Uranus
From early February until mid-April, Uranus can be seen only in the evening sky. It then becomes too close to the Sun for observation, reappearing at the start of June in the morning sky.

Neptune
Neptune is visible at the beginning of the year in the evening sky. In late February it becomes too close to the Sun for observation and reappears in early April in the morning sky. In late December it can be seen only in the evening sky.

DO NOT CONFUSE Mercury with Venus at the start of January, when Venus is the brighter object, and with Jupiter in late March, when Jupiter is the brighter object.

2023 Weekly Forecasts

by Michelle Perrin, aka Astrology Detective

Overview of 2023

The year 2023 marks a major turning point, with three major planets changing signs, including Pluto. Due to this planet's elliptical orbit, it takes Pluto anywhere from 9 to 30 years to transit a sign, making it the orb that defines generations and major eras of history. Saturn is also marking a major transition, when it makes the last stop in its 29-year journey of the zodiac by entering Pisces, the last astrological sign. This will be the culmination of one cycle before starting an entirely new one when it enters Aries in mid-2025. Finally, Jupiter starts its yearlong transit of pragmatic, industrious Taurus.

Jupiter transits Taurus once every 12 years. This time around it enters the sign on May 16, 2023, and exits on May 25, 2024. Taurus is a hardworking sign, so this makes it an especially auspicious time to go after solid goals that will help build firm foundations for the future. Taurus is ruled by the planet of art and pleasure, Venus, so it is also a positive time for artists and artisans. There may be a tendency to pamper oneself through pricey material items. While a little indulgence is okay, try not to overdo it.

Saturn enters Pisces on March 7, stripping off the rose-colored glasses through which this sign likes to view the world. Saturn's transit through Aquarius created almost cultlike vibes that increased collective divisions in society, while technology-driven social media allowed the proliferation of propagandist messages on a wide array of subjects, leading to a type of mass brainwashing. Saturn in Pisces is much more reflective and personal. Increasing numbers of people may decide to unplug from the internet and tune back in to the universe. Additionally, this may usher in a time when we can finally analyze all the changes and pain society went through during the Covid pandemic, allowing us to ponder the true meaning of being alive, as opposed to merely existing. Pisces is the last sign of the zodiac, so its wisdom and enlightenment provide a culmination of the entire astrological journey.

Saturn represents deep thought and seriousness, allowing us to bring humanity back to a place of common sense after many years of heightened emotions.

This period will be like waking up with a hangover after an unhinged binge, dealing with remorse and regret, but also the desire to make right whatever has gone wrong. As a society, we have been in a state of decay for quite a while, particularly in terms of basic civility and courtesy. We now have to regain a sense of responsibility in order to pick up the pieces and set things back on the right course, which will happen by choice or force once Saturn enters Aries in 2025.

Saturn in Pisces marks endings of cycles. The years 1935–38 saw the final years before the beginning of a new globally interconnected world driven by technology with the advent of World War II in 1939. Likewise, the years 1964–66 bookended this era before 1967's Summer of Love completely transformed society yet again. Saturn's last transit of Pisces in 1993–96 marked the last truly "human" years prior to the mass adoption of the internet, when the online world became inextricably intertwined with real life.

Last but certainly not least, Pluto enters Aquarius on March 23, where it will remain until June 11, when it transits back into Capricorn. Pluto won't occupy Aquarius for the long haul until 2024, so we can consider this a sneak preview of what's to come. Pluto's change of sign is by far the most important planetary shift of the decade.

Pluto's entry into Capricorn in 2008 was felt immediately with the global Great Recession. During Pluto in Capricorn, cracks began to show in the facades of Big everything: Big Media, Big Business, Big Government, and Big Tech proved themselves to be largely out of touch, while also becoming increasingly authoritarian, censorious, and unjust to compensate and maintain a firm grip on their lapsing powers.

In the previous Pluto in Capricorn era, which took place in 1762–77, the British government levied many unfair taxes on the American colonies, causing increasing unrest and skirmishes, leading to the signing of the Declaration of Independence in 1776. There has been a lot of talk of this momentous date with the US Pluto return that occurred in 2022, but it must be remembered that it was at the beginning of the

Revolutionary War, not the end. Most of the fighting for freedom occurred during the last Pluto in Aquarius period, which spanned from 1777 to 1797. While the American conflict ended in 1783, it was soon followed by the French Revolution, which lasted from 1789 to 1799. In fact, this entire period ushered in an era known as the Age of Revolution, where citizens around the world were emboldened and inspired by the American success story and fought for their own independence against tyranny. This should be of no surprise to astrology lovers, as Aquarius is famous for representing renegades, rebels, and liberation.

What will this mean to the United States? According to some polls taken in 2021, between 40 and 50 percent of Americans agreed to some extent that it would be better for the US to break apart. There are very firm, obvious divergences in core ideologies across clear-cut geographical dividing lines. Could it be time for the US to change to a different form of government, perhaps one more like that of the European Union, where the states would have greater individual sovereignty but there would still be freedom of movement of goods and people across all borders? No matter what happens, this period will be of utmost importance to countries like France, the United States, Haiti, and Ireland, which were gripped by revolutionary atmospheres and witnessed major struggles for self-determination the last time Pluto was in Aquarius. With Pluto's entry into Aquarius coinciding with Saturn's ending of a 29-year cycle, change toward a more just society is definitely in the stars.

January 1–8

The start of 2023 is overflowing with powerful, loving vibes. If you are single, don't go rushing off at the stroke of midnight on New Year's Eve, as Prince(ss) Charming may not appear on your radar until the wee hours of January 1. Fun, spontaneity, and emotional warmth await everyone on this festive holiday, so make sure to spend it surrounded by people you care about or by going to a party where you can make new acquaintances. A motivated, can-do attitude prevails early in the week, making it an excellent time to set New Year's resolutions and get new business or creative projects off the ground. Everyone is flexible, open to new ideas, and willing to try new things. Energies grind to a halt at Friday's Full Moon, which ushers in a weekend that could be filled with suspicion, power plays, manipulations, and hurt feelings. If any drama flares up, try to extricate yourself as soon as possible.

Advice to get you through the week: Stop ruminating and start brainstorming. By projecting your intelligence and charm outward to improve the world around you, you will also bolster your feelings of inner confidence and self-worth.

Top astrological event of the week: *Friday:* Full Moon in Cancer opposite Mercury in Capricorn: It's possible that scheming people will be revealed when the truth about past actions comes to light.

January 9–15

Get out and go for your dreams on Monday. The universe is filled with enthusiasm, confidence, and charm, guaranteeing that doors will magically open. You may need to deal with the resentment of the local busybody, but don't listen to their criticism or let them hold you back. The most important aspect of the week is Mars turning direct in Gemini on Thursday. The planet of dynamic action has been in retrograde motion since October 30, placing the world in an extended holding pattern. It may have been hard to advance projects or move things forward, but luckily the energies now shift significantly to kick off the new year with energetic, positive vibes. If you have had a difficult time sticking to resolutions, things will get much easier. It may be hard to tear yourself away from your work on Friday, but log off and enjoy the evening. Saturday is an auspicious time to volunteer to make your community a better place, but the vibe shifts in the evening, when a more anxious atmosphere takes over.

Advice to get you through the week: Reach out and network with old friends and colleagues early in the week so you can get your ducks in a row and hit the ground running on Thursday, when plans speed into action. Spend the weekend with low-key, kindhearted friends, because self-absorbed divas may be on ego overdrive.

Top astrological event of the week: *Thursday:* Mars direct in Gemini: The New Year starts now. After two months of stagnation and stalled situations, it's full steam ahead.

January 16–22

The week could get off to a grumpy start, filled with anxiety over controlling authoritarians who keep everyone around them walking on eggshells. Luckily the energies shift on Tuesday, when a sense of personal autonomy and power returns. There is a feeling of fate and destiny in the air on Tuesday and Wednesday, so break out the dating app and start swiping or plan an in-person rendezvous. Mercury has been retrograde since December 29, so the past few weeks may have seen a lot of crossed wires, technical glitches, online shopping problems, and travel delays. From Wednesday, clarity will return, with Friday being an inspired day for brainstorming and problem-solving. This is the best weekend of the year so far. Powerful, loving vibes abound, making it an optimal period to spend with friends, partners, family, or potential suitors. The New Moon in Aquarius on Saturday is pushing everyone to get out of their comfort zone and explore new horizons.

Advice to get you through the week: Avoid signing contracts, making important decisions, or finalizing negotiations until Wednesday, when Mercury ends its retrograde station. After this date, all personal planets will be direct for the first time since late October, and the pace of life will fully start to flow again. Singles could meet their soul mate, so be on the lookout.

Top astrological event of the week: *Saturday:* New Moon in Aquarius in conjunction with Pluto in Capricorn, sextiling Jupiter in Aries and trining Mars in Gemini: This is a day bursting with passion, confidence, and enthusiasm—perfect for a date.

January 23–29

After the hustle and bustle of the past few weeks, this is a really mellow week, defined by gentle, fleeting transits. Instead of feeling like big things are swirling around you, the vibes will be subtle and cozy, gently inching you toward certain actions. The entire workweek is auspicious for team endeavors, negotiations, pitching new clients, brainstorming, and doing tasks that require a lot of concentration. Assignments of all types can be done without any sense of tedium or drudgery. Venus enters starry-eyed Pisces on Thursday, where it will remain until February 20. This entire period will be infused with a sweet sense of sentimental bliss and a courtly approach to love, making it auspicious for singles and couples alike. A spontaneous, enthusiastic weekend is in the cards. Try not to make too many firm plans in advance, but instead let yourself go with the flow in order to explore and discover the world.

Advice to get you through the week: Things will be relatively quiet and easygoing at work, so try to get caught up on any backlogs you may have. Turn your thoughts to romance at the weekend. Do something spontaneous to add some spice and excitement to your love life.

Top astrological event of the week: *Sunday:* Sun in Aquarius trine Mars in Gemini: Who says you can't paint the town red on a Sunday evening? With this enthusiastic, buoyant energy, it would be a shame to sit at home.

January 30–February 5

This is another chill, laid-back workweek. After a lazy start on Monday, things quickly rev up, fueling everyone with an abundance of enthusiasm and inspiration. Whether you're working alone or in a team, the entire week is opportune for creative, out-of-the-box thinking, combined with the logical determination to get things done. Energies may suddenly spin out of control at the weekend, starting on Friday evening, when an angsty, rebellious streak surges out of nowhere. This could lead to power struggles and behind-the-scenes manipulations on Saturday, causing disputes, harsh words, and hurt feelings by the evening. On Sunday, individual desires could be stymied, and the only choices available may be to submit and obey or be shunned. Try to stay away from aggressive, domineering types when socializing.

Advice to get you through the week: With calm, dreamy energies prevailing throughout the workweek, it is an auspicious time to pitch idealistic projects to bosses and clients, as they will be more open to suggestions than usual. You may want to pursue solitary pursuits over the weekend in order to avoid the madness of crowds.

Top astrological event of the week: *Sunday:* Full Moon in Leo square Uranus in Taurus: The ideals of the collective trump those of the individual in a tussle for power.

February 6–12

It may be hard to drag yourself to work on Monday, but you'll get into the swing of things by the afternoon. Allow your thoughts to meander organically instead of trying to view the world through cold, hard logic. Hypercritical vibes could lead to energy depletion and hurt feelings on Tuesday, but the evening promises ebullient socializing, so say yes to any last-minute invitations. You could feel like Cinderella when the clock strikes midnight later that night, and a sudden storybook romance could sweep you off your feet, making this a perfect date night for singles and couples alike. The end of the week is defined by strong Mercurial vibes. On Friday, your mental acuity is off the charts; you'll know exactly what to say to impress bosses and clients at work. Mercury moves into Aquarius early Saturday morning and immediately gets drawn into a square with the Moon in the fellow fixed sign of Scorpio. Emotional smothering could brush up against the need for personal space and sentimental detachment, leading to power games throughout the day as everyone struggles to get their way.

Advice to get you through the week: A dreamy, artistic approach to mental tasks is perfect early in the week, while a quick-witted, chatty demeanor will help you make your mark on Friday.

Top astrological event of the week: *Friday:* Mercury conjunct Pluto in Capricorn: Set about problem-solving complex issues at work. Your ingenuity will impress the higher-ups.

February 13–19

Be wary of people who try to kill you with kindness on Monday; sometimes the easiest way to control others is not with an iron fist, but a velvet glove. Valentine's Day starts out on an optimistic, joyous note, but by after-dinner drinks things could get testy, with petty arguments breaking out. If single, you might experience fleeting feelings of solitude, but Sunday is an excellent day to seek a new suitor, so set your sights on the weekend to start turning things around. Colleagues may not be receptive to criticism on Wednesday, so put off giving feedback until Friday, when the vibes are much more positive, favoring both communication and teamwork. Thursday starts out on a highly productive note, but make sure you don't bite off more than you can chew or you could lose steam by midafternoon. An upbeat weekend promises wonderful times for connecting with friends and family on Saturday, while on Sunday you may choose to stay in bed all day with your one and only. The passionate vibes will help consolidate feelings of love and togetherness.

Advice to get you through the week: You may want to schedule your Valentine's Day festivities for the weekend, when the energies are more relaxed and you'll have more time to enjoy each other's company.

Top astrological event of the week: *Wednesday:* Venus conjunct Neptune in Pisces square the Moon in Sagittarius: This is a day overflowing with dreamy, romantic sentiments, though they could get bruised by gung-ho, emotionally insensitive people.

February 20–26

This is a vibrant week, bursting with a sense of excitement in the air. From the first day of the week, there is a feeling of turning a corner and starting something new, thanks to the New Moon, along with Venus's entrance into Aries. Tuesday is a time when a creative, seat-of-your-pants approach will get you further than well-thought-out plans. Passion and love abound in equal measure on Wednesday, on both a personal and a universal level. Use this time to swipe for a suitor, pep up an existing relationship, or help out doing volunteer work to make the world a better place. Uplifting vibes finish out the workweek, making it easy to complete all tasks. This overall period is so mild and productive that by the time Saturday rolls around, you may be left with nothing to do, filling you with a sense of anxiety and foreboding. However, the energies quickly shift again on Sunday, which is an excellent day to spend with the people you truly care about.

Advice to get you through the week: The week's positive, enthusiastic energies will put the necessary wind in your sails, allowing you to tackle work projects with ease. Dare to try new things, go after your goals, and revamp your love life.

Top astrological event of the week: *Monday:* New Moon in Pisces: This lone wolf New Moon sits next to Saturn in Aquarius, without forming any other aspects, making it an excellent day to focus on romance and commitment.

February 27–March 5

February closes out with a week overflowing with productivity and romance. March has a lot of astrological doozies in store, making it a busy, jam-packed month, so enjoy this moment of calm and harmony while you can. Monday, Tuesday, and Thursday are excellent days for getting things done, especially if you are working with a team. The first day of the workweek promotes dynamic engagement, while the second day boosts work requiring focus and intellectual elbow grease. There's a tendency to bite off more that you can chew on Wednesday, leading to exhaustion. Instead of socializing, it may be better to stay at home to relax, recharge your batteries, and go to bed early. Thursday is one of the best date nights of the entire year for everyone. If you are single, your instincts are spot-on, allowing you to make wise choices when selecting a partner. Clashes with bosses are possible on Friday, so put off pitches, critiques, and delicate negotiations to another day. Saturday is bursting with excitement and love; plan a daytime date so you can connect in a more chivalrous, courtly manner. The energetic vibes continue on Sunday, making it a great day for sports and getting in shape. By Sunday evening you may be ready to turn in early to recover from the week's enthusiastic energies.

Advice to get you through the week: Opportunities for romance abound on Thursday, so schedule time for dates or looking for a new suitor online.

Top astrological event of the week: *Thursday:* Venus conjunct Jupiter in Aries: Get out and enjoy the exhilaration of romance. If you are single, approach dates with a spirit of pure fun, devoid of any awkward sentimentality.

March 6–12

A large number of planets are shifting signs in March, opening up a new chapter for society and the individual. These major changes start on Tuesday when Saturn enters Pisces, ushering in a time of reflection and enhanced wisdom for all. Saturn's two-year transit through this sign is explored in greater depth in the introduction, but this week, Saturn's shift occurs at Tuesday's Full Moon in Virgo, forming a loose square with Mars and trining Uranus. This major event shakes things up quite suddenly, forcing everyone to ditch outmoded actions and change course. Friday's energy of determination and ambition is not conducive to teamwork, which could cause headaches for managers who have to navigate all the drama. However, it is also a highly productive day, allowing you to plow through tasks so your weekend is free of any workplace worries. Saturday and Sunday are both highly romantic. Try to do something spontaneous with your sweetie on Saturday; the sense of adventure will increase feelings of love and joy. Sunday, however, has gentler, more low-key vibes, when some cuddles and cozy conversations are all that is needed to increase your bond.

Advice to get you through the week: If you have been swept away by toxic ideologies or group dynamics in the past two years, it is time to step back and reflect on what is really going on. A sort of deprogramming may be necessary to return to reality.

Top astrological event of the week: *Tuesday:* Saturn enters Pisces: This is one of the month's two major transits. Last time Saturn changed signs was in 2020, during the height of the global health crisis, which ushered in worldwide lockdowns and increased authoritarianism. Things could start to get back to a new normal, but what exactly this "new normal" is could lead to an existential crisis of sorts.

March 13–19

A tendency to flee from reality could lead to misguided actions during the workweek. Confusing energies prevail from Monday to Friday, due to either incompetence or outright manipulation. No matter the cause, it would be best to put off any major decisions until the last week of the month, if possible. Wednesday offers a bit of relief thanks to gently artistic vibes, making it an excellent time for creative projects or seeking romance. Thursday could be quite stressful; everyone may be feeling overworked and exhausted, leading to snappiness and petty disputes. By happy hour on Friday, everyone is ready to unwind and relax, ensuring an evening of good cheer. These positive vibes continue into the weekend. Saturday evening is a great time to catch up socially with close friends, while Sunday is bursting with enthusiasm, confidence, and romance.

Advice to get you through the week: If you get inundated with work, keep your eyes on the weekend, when relaxation is ensured. Try not to get caught up in squabbles or other people's chaos.

Top astrological event of the week: *Tuesday:* Mars in Gemini square Neptune in Pisces, which is also part of a lunar T-square that draws in a Sagittarius Moon, along with the Sun and Mercury in Pisces: This could be a highly manipulative, confusing day. Look out for smooth talkers who are trying to guilt you into doing something against your better instincts.

March 20–26

This week is marked by three planetary shifts, including Pluto's game-changing entry into Aquarius on Thursday. The last time Pluto changed signs was back in 2008, ushering in an era of economic insecurity and intense politicization. For a deep dive on all things Pluto, be sure to read the introduction. The Sun enters Aries, the first sign of the zodiac, on Monday, marking the first day of spring and the astrological new year! It's a perfect time to celebrate, thanks to the day's powerful, confident, and enthusiastic vibes. Mars is the third planet to change signs this week, zooming into Cancer on Saturday. Cancer's feminine energy takes a bit of the edge off warrior-like Mars, and promotes domestic issues such as family, fertility, and sprucing up the home. All these shifts create an almost dreamlike atmosphere, as can be witnessed by Tuesday's New Moon and an ultra-romantic Friday, when you could quickly be swept off your feet by someone new.

Advice to get you through the week: Allow yourself to drift along with the week's ever-changing vibes. This would be an excellent time to open new chapters in your own life, especially in the domestic sphere.

Top astrological event of the week: *Thursday:* Pluto enters Aquarius: This is the granddaddy of all transits, and hands down the most important planetary shift of the year, if not the decade.

March 27–April 2

All the planetary shifts of the past few weeks have brought about a renewed enthusiasm for life, creating a desire for adventure and trying new things. The entire week is bursting with positive energy. Thanks to a can-do attitude, there is practically nothing you can't do. Wednesday and Thursday promote teamwork and getting things done. After such a vibrant workweek, you should reward yourself by sleeping in on Saturday; the morning's lazy energy isn't conducive to much else. After a low-energy lunch on Sunday, a boost of revved-up energy returns midafternoon. Wednesday and Thursday are the best date nights of the week, so dare to set up a spontaneous rendezvous.

Advice to get you through the week: If there is anything you have dreamed of doing for a long time, it's time to set the wheels in motion and launch your own business or creative endeavor.

Top astrological event of the week: *Thursday:* Venus conjunct Uranus in Taurus: This is a memorable day for romance. If single, you may spontaneously meet an exciting suitor who whisks you off your feet and into their heart.

April 3–9

The week could start out on a petty note, with everyone scrambling to impress the boss so that their ideas will win. Thankfully, a sense of teamwork and harmony returns midweek, so that the proper decisions can be made and implemented. Wednesday is an opportune moment to tackle tasks of a mental nature, as concentration and focus are guaranteed. There may be a tendency, however, to bite off more than you can chew, forcing you to finally concentrate on creating a better work-life balance at Thursday's Full Moon. Being chained to a desk could be sheer drudgery on Friday, as the day's dynamic vibes are much more conducive to movement, creativity, and interaction with other human beings. If you try to provide the most perfect Easter experience ever, you may end up with nothing but stress. On the other hand, if you take things easy, you will be able to enjoy relaxing times bonding with your guests and family.

Advice to get you through the week: This week the focus is on the importance of togetherness, as opposed to the attainment of individual ego goals.

Top astrological event of the week: *Thursday:* Full Moon in Libra opposite Jupiter in Aries: Forget about diplomacy. When it comes to achieving your goals, you'll need to stand up and fight for them.

April 10–16

This is a laid-back week, filled with a bounty of gentle, positive vibes. You'll be ready to jump into the thick of things with enthusiasm and confidence at the start of the week. Tuesday's powerful trine between Venus and Pluto makes it an excellent day for networking and forging new contacts. Venus enters Gemini on this same day, ushering in an auspicious period for written and verbal communications until May 7. You may need to come up with sudden solutions to deal with unforeseen changes on Wednesday, so stay flexible. If you try to tackle everything by yourself on Thursday, you may feel crushed under the burden. It would be much better to deal with things as a team, so don't be afraid to ask for help. Friday is a lazy day, when everyone will be waiting for the end of the workweek. Saturday is bursting with fun and good times, while Sunday is better for solitary pursuits or single-person sports, such as bicycling or climbing.

Advice to get you through the week: Pool your resources with others at work; it will make all tasks easier to finish.

Top astrological event of the week: *Tuesday:* Sun conjunct Jupiter in Aries: Everyone will be bursting with confidence and a zest for life. Take a chance on the road less traveled.

April 17–23

An otherworldly sense of electricity and expectation pervades the first three days of the week, as is often the case during the period immediately preceding an eclipse. You may feel like you are walking in a dream landscape of extreme potential; something is taking shape in the ether, but it has yet to fully form. When the Solar Eclipse detonates on Thursday, it brings the confidence to stand up to bullies and construct solid, more stable structures for the future. Events that arise at the eclipse will urge us to push the pause button so we can better review certain situations and implement more radical, idealistic changes instead of just going full steam ahead with the status quo. With Mercury turning retrograde on Friday, it is an excellent time to clear out old work before taking on new projects. Saturday is quite a lazy day, so put off chores to another time. Sunday is a wonderful time to spend with loved ones, bonding over deep, thought-provoking conversations.

Advice to get you through the week: Make sure your foundations are sturdy before building new frameworks.

Top astrological event of the week: *Thursday:* New Moon Solar Eclipse in Aries in square aspect with Pluto: Rebel spirits will fight back against authoritarian control. Thanks to a loose sextile with Saturn, this is an excellent period to start building local structures and independent networks outside of the mainstream.

April 24–30

On Monday there is a tendency to escape into a dreamworld as a means of coping with stress. If you insist on putting things off or denying they even exist, you may need to pay the piper later in the week when you fall behind in your tasks, leading to sudden setbacks with unhappy bosses and colleagues, which could temporarily bruise your ego. Tuesday's vibes are incredibly productive, so plow through as much work as possible on that day, especially if you have a deadline approaching. Energies lighten considerably and immediately at the weekend, so schedule a TGIF with friends to lift your spirits. Push yourself outside your comfort zone on Saturday by trying new, adventurous things. You don't need to do a lot of research or planning in advance; spontaneity will make the day even more exciting. Sunday's laid-back vibes are conducive to socializing and catching up with old friends.

Advice to get you through the week: Don't allow molehills to grow into mountains. Try to stay on top of all of your responsibilities.

Top astrological event of the week: *Thursday:* Lunar T-square between the Moon in Leo opposite Pluto in Aquarius and square the Sun in Taurus: Sometimes it's easier to obey than to go your own way. Tough decisions must be made that may require selling out—but that choice is yours and yours alone.

May 1–7

The workweek is likely to be filled with tension, confusion, and shifting sands, but the energy improves dramatically at the weekend, so try to soldier through all office politics by staying detached from any drama. This won't be easy to do, due to Mercury's retrograde motion and several disharmonious aspects to murky Neptune. Emotion trumps logic at this time, making it easy to be manipulated by people who only have their own interests in mind. Luckily, Venus is making several harmonious aspects, so seek counsel from tried-and-true people you know have your back; after all, there is safety in numbers. This is especially true at Friday's unpredictable Lunar Eclipse. Saturday is an excellent day for sports, catching up on chores, and enjoying art. Spending time with people you love will recharge your batteries and dispel the muddled energy from earlier in the week.

Advice to get you through the week: It may be hard to take firm action at this time due to the proliferation of confusing vibes. Sometimes it's better to wait things out. Seek advice only from those you know you can trust.

Top astrological event of the week: *Friday:* Lunar Eclipse in Scorpio opposite Uranus and Mercury retrograde in Taurus: This volatile energy could lead to sudden fights based on incorrect assumptions, creating an emotional break. Try to stay calm and put off confrontations to another day.

May 8–14

Monday kicks off with a repeat of last week's suspicious, devious vibes, but luckily things turn around quickly on Tuesday, when logical thinking, confidence, and self-esteem make a sudden comeback. Wednesday is filled with positive, ethereal energy, making it a perfect day for creative visualization, but it may be hard to work up the energy to put plans into practice. Don't force yourself; instead, let your imagination wander to conjure up the solutions you need and can implement at a later date. Friday could start off with feelings of anxiety due to workplace uncertainties, but the evening's loving vibes make it perfect for dating, romance, and socializing. If you are single, Saturday is a five-star day for matchmaking. You will have the shrewdness and wisdom to find a reliable partner who is also gentle and kind. Those already in a couple may want to take things to the next level or make long-term plans for the future. Mercury turns direct on Mother's Day, clearing up the fog and confusion of the past few weeks while promising a warm and cheerful day for all.

Advice to get you through the week: Put off the grunt work to another time and instead focus on creative thinking and true love.

Top astrological event of the week: *Saturday:* Venus in Cancer trine Saturn in Pisces: This weekend is infused with romance. Couples should think about building a future together, while singles could meet a new suitor that will morph into a stable relationship.

May 15–21

This is a week of extremes, filled with powerful cosmic vibes that bounce from challenging to downright exhilarating on an almost daily basis. The week gets off to a positive, gung-ho start, making it an excellent time for productivity and inspiration. When Jupiter shifts signs from energetic, fun Aries to pragmatic, workaholic Taurus on Tuesday (more on this in the intro), it sets the stage for Wednesday, when people's career ambitions run high. The workplace could quickly morph into a viper's den of ruthless competition. In order to keep your spot in the pecking order, you will need to stand up with courage and confidence. This is a day when wallflowers will definitely go unnoticed. Luckily, the universe quickly does a 180. Thursday promotes teamwork at the job and romance in your private life, while Friday's invigorating New Moon is a perfect time to create a long-term business plan so you can go after your goals. Plans made at this time can slowly blossom into success in the upcoming year. The mood swings yet again on Saturday, a time when individual members of friendship groups or families could butt heads, leading to petty squabbles and machinations to achieve control. You may want to lie low on this day and save your socializing for Sunday, when the Sun enters Gemini, promising an ebullient, chatty good time for all.

Advice to get you through the week: If things seem difficult, hang tight; the energies will turn around by the next day.

Top astrological event of the week: *Tuesday/Wednesday:* Jupiter enters Taurus and squares Pluto in Aquarius: This rare aspect is fraught with tension and stubbornness. People will not be in the mood for compromise, leading to stand-offs.

May 22–28

Mars's entry into Leo last week on the 20th will be triggering a lot of repeating, disharmonious fixed-sign energies in the upcoming month and a half, pitting authority, groups, and the individual against each other. Authoritarianism can come from both the charismatic leader and the decentralized mob, creating treacherous waters for the solitary human to navigate. This tendency will be evident on Tuesday and Wednesday, when the collective hive mind fights to take control, leading to clampdowns by rulers as well as rebellion by renegades. Sometimes the best way to deal with difficult situations is just to opt out. You don't need to waste your energy on other people's drama. Luckily, the workweek is bookended by extremely positive vibes. Monday is a highly productive day, while unexpected romance is in store on Friday—singles should keep their eyes open! Saturday and Sunday are pretty lazy days, so don't beat yourself up if all you want to do is sit around and read a book or chat with friends.

Advice to get you through the week: True autonomy comes from going your own way instead of trying to win the war.

Top astrological event of the week: *Tuesday:* Mars in Leo square Jupiter in Taurus: Disputes lingering from last week could erupt into major conflagrations. Keep your personal fire wall enabled.

May 29–June 4

After the intense rollercoaster ride of the past few weeks, things hit a more even-keeled plateau. No one is really in the mood to work on Monday. Luckily, it's Memorial Day, and even if you must clock in today, try to make some time to enjoy the festivities. The holiday is defined by a jovial, upbeat atmosphere. If you decide to travel for the long weekend, you will be up for adventure, so dare to go off the beaten path. Keep your private life private to avoid becoming the victim of a gossip campaign at the office on Wednesday. Even though you are feeling productive on Thursday, avoid taking on too many obligations or you could face burnout by Friday morning. Ethereal, fairy-tale energies abound on Friday evening. It will be difficult to resist falling in love, so whether single or in a couple, schedule a romantic rendezvous. Saturday's Full Moon kills the vibe for work and responsibility while ramping up the desire for fun and adventure, so schedule your day to reflect this.

Advice to get you through the week: Let the holiday spirit continue throughout the week. If single, use Memorial Day get-togethers to search for a new suitor.

Top astrological event of the week: *Friday:* Venus in Cancer trine Neptune in Pisces, as part of a Grand Lunar Trine with the Moon in Scorpio: This is a time for healing after a tense few weeks. Spend the evening socializing with friends and family or going out on a date.

June 5–11

Venus enters Leo on Monday, triggering the fixed-sign energies alluded to in previous weeks. Venus and Mars in Leo are forming a stubborn T-square with Jupiter in Taurus and Pluto in Aquarius, which comes to a head this week on Wednesday. During the first days of the week, people might be aggressive and overly sensitive, ready to fly off the handle at the slightest provocation. There may be a feeling of walking on eggshells, especially around controlling, domineering types. Try to keep your nose down and concentrate on your work. Put off meetings or negotiations until Friday, if possible, when harmonious, generous vibes abound. Sunday is another emotionally volatile day, when people's feelings could get easily hurt. Escape through your mind by either creating or taking in art, watching a movie, or burying yourself in work. Pluto also retrogrades back into Capricorn on this day, helping to tone down the intense, headstrong fixed-sign vibes of recent weeks.

Advice to get you through the week: This isn't the best period for teamwork or group activities. Detach from the crowd to focus on your own projects and self-improvement.

Top astrological event of the week: *Sunday:* Pluto retrograde reenters Capricorn: After giving us a sneak peak of the upcoming era, Pluto dips back into Capricorn, resurrecting issues regarding the economy and big government.

June 12–18

Emotions continue to run high this week, especially on Wednesday. Try to avoid delicate subjects or confrontational situations on this day. The best day to tackle such topics is Monday, when everyone will be willing to play ball with a can-do, confident attitude. Thursday could be a gloomy, ponderous day; if you are feeling slightly melancholic or anxiety-ridden, know that this energy will pass by Friday afternoon, which is flowing with delicately optimistic and nurturing vibes. Yet another highly romantic Saturday is in store, when online dating could be especially fruitful. Sunday's Cancer Moon is trine Saturn—the planet signifying the father—making this a highly moving and loving Father's Day.

Advice to get you through the week: Get things done early in the week, as low spirits may hinder enthusiasm and productivity later on.

Top astrological event of the week: *Sunday:* New Moon in Gemini square Neptune in Pisces, then Cancer Moon trine Saturn in Pisces: This is an auspicious day for tackling physical chores such as gardening, cleaning, and home maintenance. Thinking could be cloudy, so put off work of an intellectual nature.

June 19–25

Monday is defined by a harmonious sextile between liberating Jupiter and restrictive Saturn—a perfect astrological configuration to commemorate Juneteenth. This aspect represents the strength that comes from overcoming and emancipating yourself from tyranny and regaining your own locus of control. It is a perfect day to move forward together, constructing a more positive future while never forgetting the past. Tuesday follows in these vibes, with a freewheeling mood that provides an escape route from control freaks. Wednesday is a vibrant day that is ideal for networking and socializing. It may seem hard to keep up with Thursday's constantly changing atmosphere, but Mars is providing an extra boost of energy to help. Sunday features some draining, confusing vibes that could lead to mental exhaustion. Seek advice from trusted, authoritative sources.

Advice to get you through the week: Celebrate freedom. This is an auspicious time to join a volunteer organization so you can help make the world a better place.

Top astrological event of the week: *Wednesday:* Sun enters Cancer, the Summer Solstice: Summer is finally here! The Sun slides into Cancer without making any major aspects, so you can enjoy the season's laid-back vibes without any other stresses.

June 26–July 2

Monday's bull-in-a-china-shop energy could result in rash actions, leading to accidents or irreversible mishaps at work. Slow down and take a more methodical approach for everyone's safety and security. Tuesday is a perfect time to arrange a date, while Wednesday's highly productive vibes will help you tackle all workplace responsibilities without breaking a sweat; schedule important presentations and interviews on this day. That pesky fixed-sign energy returns on Thursday with a lunar T-square, igniting disputes out of nowhere, with no one in the mood to compromise. By Friday, a more levelheaded vibe returns. The evening promises delightful opportunities for socializing, but you may want to call it an early night because exhaustive energies arise close to midnight. Canadian readers will enjoy a jovial, gregarious Canada Day on Saturday, but don't worry if you live somewhere else; the heavens will be showering these positive vibes down on everyone, regardless of location. People may be a bit flaky on Sunday, so try to schedule outings only with reliable friends and family.

Advice to get you through the week: The week's scattershot energies are a bit all over the place, so take advantage of the positive aspects and lie low on days with more challenging ones.

Top astrological event of the week: *Wednesday:* Sun in Cancer trine Saturn in Pisces, part of a Lunar Grand Trine with Mercury in Cancer and the Moon in Scorpio: This vibrant day is conducive to teamwork and group problem-solving. Whether at work or in your personal life, there is no reason to go it alone; tap into the hive mind to find the best solutions.

July 3–9

With the July 4th holiday coming up on Tuesday, Monday's energies will be prodding everyone to switch off from thinking about work and career and shift their focus to family. Independence Day itself will be filled with spontaneity and emotional closeness, so make sure to spend it with those you love. On Wednesday, it will be back to the grind; don't be surprised if you have a pile-up of tasks waiting for you that accumulated over the holiday. Mars will be exiting Leo early next week, making Thursday the last time the red planet is triggered by challenging fixed-sign aspects. Get through this obstinate energy in stride, knowing it will soon start to dissipate. Friday is a highly productive time, perfect for getting serious about your career trajectory. If you are looking for a new job, schedule an interview or send out your résumé. For all others, this is an auspicious day for reaching out to clients, making pitches, and networking. The weekend is up for anything, from socializing to creativity. Be spontaneous and go where your heart leads. Saturday brunch and Sunday evening are ideal for dating.

Advice to get you through the week: Outside of a bullheaded, uncooperative Thursday, the rest of the week offers a wide array of opportunities for inspiration and connection.

Top astrological event of the week: *Monday:* Full Moon in Capricorn opposite Mercury in Cancer and trine Jupiter in Taurus: If you have been going down a one-way street with blinders on career-wise, it's time to take a new approach. By giving up outworn attitudes, you can turn a corner professionally.

July 10–16

Energies could be tense on Monday. It may not be the best time to approach bosses with an innovative new idea, as they may shoot it down merely to affirm their authority. The evening's vibes are much more positive, however. While Monday is typically a day for relaxing at home, getting out and socializing could prove to be invigorating. Mars exits Leo on the first day of the week, but have no fear: Mercury enters this fiery, exciting sign on Tuesday, promising a creative, confident, and mentally inspired period until the end of the month. Tuesday is a fertile day in terms of work, allowing you to plow through a huge number of tasks. Wednesday's ultra-confident vibes promote spontaneity and dating. You'll be able to express your true self without any awkwardness or shyness; just be careful not to project your emotional insecurities onto your partner. A lunar T-square on Thursday is a time when innovation stands off against the status quo. Hold off on proposing new ideas until Friday, when the vibes are much more spontaneous and pioneering. Schedule a TGIF, as the evening's mood is upbeat and cheerful. Saturday evening and Sunday brunch offer excellent opportunities for socializing and blowing off steam.

Advice to get you through the week: Put work on the back burner and focus on enjoying your evenings and weekends hanging out with friends and loved ones.

Top astrological event of the week: *Tuesday:* Mercury enters Leo: The next few weeks will be defined by mental bravery and an optimistic outlook on life. Dare to think different.

July 17–23

While Monday's New Moon is bursting with inspiration and creativity, the downside is that everyone will be fighting to get their ideas heard by the higher-ups all at once, leading to a slightly cut-throat atmosphere. These vibes persist on Wednesday, so you may want to keep your cards close to your chest to avoid being kneecapped. A gentler atmosphere that promotes teamwork prevails on Thursday morning, but by the afternoon everyone will be back to brownnosing in order to achieve their ambitions for the rest of the workweek. On Friday you may just want to call it a day early and stay home that evening, as the week's Darwinian edge spills over into social life. While the weekend offers moments of spontaneity and good cheer, it's also a period of cloudy, delusional thinking, especially in terms of romance. Put off major decisions regarding your love life until early September if possible.

Advice to get you through the week: Things could get ruthless in the workplace. You will need to walk a fine line between staying out of the line of fire and making sure you are not shunned out of the spotlight.

Top astrological event of the week: *Saturday:* Venus retrograde in Leo: Put off nonessential cosmetic procedures until early December to avoid unwanted results. Instead, raid your closet. You can revamp your look by reintroducing old items you haven't worn in a while.

July 24–30

The week starts off with cooperative vibes but by Tuesday afternoon quickly devolves into the ego-driven atmosphere that pervaded last week. Wednesday starts out highly productive, but you could soon get overwhelmed if you take on too many tasks; learn when to say no. People could resurrect emotionally hurtful issues from the past on Thursday and Friday, opening old wounds and triggering negative thought patterns. Tap into your inner strength or escape into a film to pull you through. Things turn around in time for the weekend. Saturday is an excellent date night for both couples and singles, while Sunday is a perfect time for adventure sports or urban explorations; dare to venture off into new territories.

Advice to get you through the week: Try not to get sucked into a psychological rabbit hole during the workweek. Keep your sights fixed on weekend fun.

Top astrological event of the week: *Friday:* Mercury enters Virgo: Mercury joins Mars in level-headed Virgo. The energies shift from adding flair and glamour to your world to pragmatically navigating reality.

July 31–August 6

The week starts off with innovative, empowering vibes. Prioritize your work schedule to get approval on projects on Monday, as the upcoming days could be fraught with tension. Tuesday's energies are highly ambitious, with a tendency to bite off more than one can chew while trampling over everyone else in order to reach one's own goals—an approach that won't go down well with management. Still, it's a great day to go after your career goals by scheduling interviews and negotiations or laying the groundwork for entrepreneurial endeavors. An emotionally volatile atmosphere prevails on Wednesday, especially when it comes to teamwork and romance. It's not the best night for a first date. By Thursday, bosses may start to crack down on renegades who are trying to implement actions and decisions without getting the okay from the proper authorities. Luckily, positive vibes return for the weekend. Friday evening is an excellent time for romance, while Saturday promises ebullient outings with friends. You may want to stay away from arrogant, difficult people on Sunday, as egos inflate out of control.

Advice to get you through the week: This isn't the best time to fight against the status quo, as your ideas are likely to be nixed. Instead of fighting city hall, focus on wining and dining over the weekend.

Top astrological event of the week: *Tuesday:* Aquarius Full Moon T-square with Jupiter in Taurus: If you are part of a suffocating group dynamic, this Full Moon will give you the courage to go your own way and express your true identity.

August 7–13

The early part of the week is filled with a lot of contradictory energy, making it a time when challenging and harmonious aspects commingle and balance each other out. It's best to focus on working on projects independently on Monday. Avoid seeking the advice or approval of higher-ups, as they may thwart your actions just to feel in control. The same goes for Tuesday, when ingenuity, creativity, and innovation are off the charts. If you share your revolutionary ideas, however, the world may not be ready for them, leading to feelings of defeat. Keep your ideas to yourself until you can refine them. Wednesday is a lazy day when it comes to getting things done, but the mind is a-popping, making it a great day for conjuring up visionary ideas and conversation. With Venus retrograde squaring Uranus, accidents and unwanted results could occur when undergoing nonessential beauty treatments and plastic surgery, so try to reschedule appointments. On Thursday it will be hard to find other people who have your back; luckily, you don't need their support, as self-confidence gets a major boost. Energies turn completely positive in time for the weekend. Saturday is an excellent time to tackle chores, while Sunday is a five-star day for socializing, dating, and catching up with loved ones.

Advice to get you through the week: It's best not to externalize your locus of control. Avoid seeking validation about your endeavors from others. Instead, tap into your own feelings of self-worth and let your inner compass be your guide.

Top astrological event of the week: *Sunday:* The Sun conjunct Venus in Leo: This is a day filled with confidence and self-esteem. Pamper yourself and celebrate your inner light. It's one of the best date nights of the month.

August 14–20

The energies at Wednesday's New Moon are so strong that they dominate and are reinforced throughout the rest of the workweek. The New Moon takes place in glamorous, playful, and exciting Leo, while squaring off against Uranus in ultra-pragmatic Taurus. Why do so many people think worthwhile things are serious and boring, while superficial, fun things are foolish? An enthusiasm for living and creative expression butts up against a killjoy status quo at this New Moon. Living well is the best revenge, so embrace joy and levity, and integrate these forces into your life. To counterbalance the frivolity, Mars is trining Uranus the same day, forming a loose Grand Trine in the hardworking earth signs, making it an auspicious period for business matters and getting entrepreneurial projects off the ground. All in all, the week has a work hard, play hard vibe to it, infusing all facets of life with exuberance and power. The weekend is quite mellow. If you are painting the town red on Friday, your beer goggles may push you toward an ill-considered hookup come closing time in the wee hours of Saturday morning. Try to resist temptation to avoid regrets the day after.

Advice to get you through the week: Enjoy fashion, art, and fun for their own sake. At the same time, put your full force into making your work dreams come true, as ambitious, productive energies are in abundance.

Top astrological event of the week: *Wednesday:* Mars in Virgo trine Uranus in Taurus: It will be easy to implement change today, as you will be able to sway any who express resistance to your cause almost immediately.

August 21–27

While the week starts off on a stressful note, the energies lighten considerably by Thursday evening. Emotionally painful memories and traumas from the past could come bubbling up to the surface on Tuesday, draining you of your vital energy. It is best to stay away from triggers. If you have any deceivers or manipulators in your circle, it is time to move away from their toxicity once and for all. On Wednesday, Mercury turns retrograde in Virgo, one of its rulers, shutting down the planet's tendency to overthink things. Decision-making may be off, so try to rely on gut instinct instead until mid-September. Two midweek lunar T-squares give off slightly challenging energies. Emotions could be hurt quite easily on Wednesday, so refrain from giving or asking for advice or constructive criticism, especially regarding creative projects or personal beauty. On Thursday, nosy, judgmental attitudes are likely to prevail, so steer clear of any busybodies in your life. Thursday evening, however, ushers in a gorgeous trine between Mars and Pluto, making it one of the best date nights of the year. New encounters at this time will have a fated, soul-mate quality to them, so get out on the prowl. Mars helps you overcome any shyness, giving you the courage to approach a new suitor. As for the weekend, Saturday starts off on a lazy note but becomes more productive by midafternoon. Mars enters super social Libra on Sunday, marking the start of a festive period when it will be easy to make new acquaintances. Forget about work and chores and start networking while having fun.

Advice to get you through the week: Try not to take things to heart at the beginning of the week. Self-confidence makes a comeback on Thursday, and the weekend holds many opportunities for merry-making and human connection.

Top astrological event of the week: *Thursday:* Mars in Virgo trine Pluto in Capricorn: Mars makes a farewell harmonious aspect to Pluto before it moves into Libra on Sunday. Energies will soon turn to socializing and fun, so get as much work done today as possible.

August 28–September 3

An abundance of energy and ambition jump-starts the week, making Monday an excellent time to impress bosses or apply for a new job. Energies soon take a downward shift. Tuesday could be a slightly moody day, filled with reminiscences of past loves and friendships. FOMO will be strong, so refrain from stalking successful friends on social media to avoid feelings of useless resentment. Wednesday's Full Moon sits close to Saturn in Pisces, creating yet more melancholic vibes. It's time to ditch childlike fairy-tale visions of the world and instead embrace personal responsibility and a realistic approach to life. Thursday is filled with electricity and the opportunity for change, as long as you don't overthink things. Whether you're single or in a couple, Saturday is an excellent time for romance. This is the last day before Venus ends its retrograde motion, so if there is someone from your past who got away, it's now or never to try to reconnect. Tackle chores on Sunday afternoon; once Venus turns direct on Sunday evening, a sense of self-esteem concerning personal beauty comes bouncing back. It's finally full steam ahead for cosmetic procedures, although it may be best to schedule them between September 15 and October 7—Mercury will no longer be retrograde then, while Venus will still be in fabulous Leo, guaranteeing the best conditions for a complete makeover.

Advice to get you through the week: Stop looking over your shoulder early in the week. There is no reason to compare yourself to others since they are on a completely different life path.

Top astrological event of the week: *Sunday:* Venus direct in Leo: The time has finally arrived when you can implement a new beauty regimen and update your look. Schedule a cosmetic procedure, get a haircut, or change your hair color. It's time for a new you from the outside in.

September 4–10

This week is dominated by a number of buoyant aspects between the Sun and Mercury in Virgo and Jupiter in Taurus. The summer holidays are over and it's time to get back to work. Luckily, the stars are here to help you achieve your goals and obtain success! Even though Monday is Labor Day and many people have the day off, don't let the day's excellent communicative vibes go to waste. This is a productive time to make pitches, send off your résumé, draft a business plan, or catch up on work emails. Try to sneak off from the day's festivities to take constructive steps toward a business goal, if only for an hour. Wednesday is bursting with auspicious professional vibes and is an excellent day for brainstorming, teamwork, and getting things done. Confidence and enthusiasm abound in equal measure, so dare to make your move. Spend happy times catching up with family or sprucing up your home on Saturday. Control freaks might huff and puff until they have their way on Sunday, so make your escape by taking in a film or working on an artistic project.

Advice to get you through the week: This is an extremely auspicious period for professional advancement. There is no time like the present to go for your goals.

Top astrological event of the week: *Friday:* The Sun in Virgo trine Jupiter in Taurus: This is yet another five-star day for anything related to career or finance. Amazing opportunities can blossom from the tiniest seeds, so keep your eyes open.

September 11–17

Positive career vibes continue this week. While you might feel a bit overwhelmed by the sheer amount of work you have to do and the rate at which it builds up, by Thursday you'll have the physical and mental stamina to tackle anything you put your mind to. This day's extremely industrious New Moon bestows confidence and opportunity. It is an especially auspicious time for job seeking, interviews, or pitching new clients. The workweek ends with Mercury turning direct on Friday; clarity returns and all the setbacks and delays of recent weeks will finally dissipate. The week is equally auspicious for love, with Monday and Saturday dishing up passion and sweet courtly sentiment in equal measure. If you go out with a new suitor on Saturday night, by closing time you may feel pressured to take things to the next level intimately, without really wanting to. To get to know each other at a slower pace, try to arrange group dates so you won't be put into awkward one-on-one situations. Otherwise, tell your date that your chariot will turn into a pumpkin if you don't slip out by midnight.

Advice to get you through the week: Whether you are searching for new prospects in love or career, the week is bursting with exciting energy.

Top astrological event of the week: *Thursday:* New Moon in Virgo trine Uranus in Taurus: Sudden opportunities arise from nowhere; stay alert so you can pounce as soon as you get the chance.

September 18–24

This week the mood bounces back and forth between confusion and clarity. Monday starts things off at peak performance, making it easy to concentrate and brainstorm. On Tuesday there could be a fox in the henhouse. Petty gossip and innuendo could lead to sudden hurt feelings and stubborn disputes, which could largely be due to someone manipulating things behind the scenes. Be wary of any information that comes to light today that paints somebody in a bad light, as smear campaigns abound. Wednesday is much more positive. Its dreamy, schmoozy atmosphere makes it the perfect time to move and shake. However, work that requires deep focus and solitude may seem like a chore, so schedule things accordingly. Thursday is another day when ambitions pay off. Courage and confidence provide the boost needed to show the world what you've got. Schedule a happy hour with friends, colleagues, or a new date. The bewildering vibes return on Friday, when competent individuals could be targeted for takedown by resentful types; stay alert and watch your back. The weekend's positive vibes promote socializing and vibrant conversations on Saturday, while Sunday's Grand Lunar Trine in the earth signs opens the gateway to success. Even though it's the weekend, you could impress people with influence by putting in some overtime to problem-solve and finish projects.

Advice to get you through the week: Be careful who you trust. Make a beeline for the exit when the office gossip enters the room.

Top astrological event of the week: *Thursday:* Sun in Virgo trine Pluto in Capricorn: Hard work won't go unnoticed by higher-ups. Approach bosses about a raise or promotion.

September 25–October 1

There is an overload of innovative, visionary ideas on Monday, so put your thinking cap on and don't be afraid to think outside the box. Wednesday is better for networking and expanding your contact circle, while Thursday promotes creativity. The waters on Tuesday and Friday are a bit more delicate to navigate. There is no room for compromise, leading to volatile vibes and touchy emotions. Rationality and emotional detachment face off against smothering compassion, with no middle ground. Try to avoid triggering conversations and keep things as light as possible. Try to work on your own rather than in a team. Sudden disputes with a love interest could stir up slightly anxious vibes at the start of the weekend, so Friday is not the best day to schedule a date. Saturday is much more promising in terms of romance, although you may want to schedule a daytime rendezvous, as the evening ushers in vibes where everyone wants to be in driver's seat. Both Saturday and Sunday are great times to catch up with friends and bask in the joy of good conversation. Saturday afternoon provides an auspicious opportunity to plan for your long-term future. Inspired ideas will put you on the right track.

Advice to get you through the week: Don't bend over backward trying to please people who play the victim card, as they will never be satisfied and will only demand more and more of your emotional capital.

Top astrological event of the week: *Friday:* Full Moon in Aries: This lone wolf Full Moon is not making any major aspects to other planets. It's a good time to tone down your competitive, purely ego-driven tendencies so you can become a better team player.

October 2–8

The first week of October floats along with mostly positive vibes until things turn a bit more tense at the weekend, when power struggles and arguments could flare. If you can balance logic and creativity on Monday, you can make powerful breakthroughs that are innovative and visionary. You will gain greater insights by tapping into your own subconscious rather that pooling brainpower in a team. Tuesday is yet another five-star day to look for a job or approach an existing employer for a boost in wages or job level. Wednesday and Thursday are productive and energetic, although there is a tendency to idle away the hours daydreaming on Thursday. Overall, 2023 has an incredible preponderance of weekends filled with positive vibes, so it's good to count those blessings when dealing with the angry energies that will be present on this particular Saturday and Sunday. Back away quickly at the first sign of drama, and do not allow yourself to get sucked into other people's bad moods or psychological toxicity. Escaping into art and work can provide some relief from the tension. After a super extended stay in Leo, Venus finally bids adieu to this sign on Sunday. A bit of glamour will fade from the world, being replaced by a renewed vigor to eat a nutritious diet and get fit from the inside out instead of the outside in.

Advice to get you through the week: The weekend is potentially a power keg of explosive energies. Steer clear of domineering people who have a tendency to bully and need to be the center of attention.

Top astrological event of the week: *Sunday:* Mars in Libra square Pluto in Capricorn: This could be a tense day filled with aggressive energy. Control freaks will be able to squash opposition rather quickly, so avoid getting dragged into useless disputes.

October 9–15

After a slightly grumpy start, the week quickly gains momentum, invigorated by a dynamic Mars and electric Solar Eclipse. You may need to don a thick skin on Tuesday, as judgmental, resentful people will be in the mood to bulldoze over the kind, beautiful souls of the world simply to alleviate their own self-hatred. Don't take their words and actions to heart. Generous, emotionally upbeat vibes return on Wednesday, while Thursday is a no-nonsense day that is all about getting things done; there is no room for pipe dreams and idling. If you jump on every opportunity and work your hustle, your efforts won't go unnoticed by the powers that be. Mars enters its traditional ruler of Scorpio the same day, ushering in six weeks of intense, slow-burning passion that will surely heat up the cool autumn months. Friday is an excellent day to prove your loyalty by having the backs of those you love—and those who truly care about you will do the same. If you need help, do not be afraid to reach out, as support may be closer than you think. A frothy New Moon in Libra on Saturday is bursting with excitement and flair. There is a feeling of anticipation in the air—a corner is being turned, opening out to expanding new vistas filled with fascinating new things to discover, free from the baggage of the past. Sunday afternoon is perfect for sports or fitness, while the evening is all about love, romance, and dating.

Advice to get you through the week: Once we get past Tuesday, the rest of the week is bursting with exhilarating, dynamic energies and inspiration.

Top astrological event of the week: *Saturday:* Solar Eclipse in Libra: This eclipse lies close to Mercury opposite Chiron. You can move on from past hurts by surrounding yourself with positive, uplifting people who bring joy to your world.

October 16–22

The week starts off with lazy, languid energy and doesn't really kick into gear until Friday. You may feel like dialing it in at work early in the week, so you may want to keep a low profile if you slack off a little. Invigorated, inspired vibes return by Thursday afternoon, making it an excellent day for tackling duties, problem-solving, or schmoozing with clients. During the daytime, Friday offers excellent conditions for teamwork and laying the groundwork for new projects. TGIF happy hours will bring feelings of joy and togetherness, but you may want to call it an early night, as an aura of petty competition and devious manipulation may start to creep in after dinner. Group outings could be challenging this weekend, as domineering people insist on making single-handed decisions and expecting others to follow, leading to division and resentment. When it comes to romance, avoid scheduling a date on Wednesday. Meeting for early evening cocktails on Friday could provide fun moments of flirtation, but you will want to bounce by dinnertime to avoid the night's more challenging aspects. Saturday is a bit of a mixed bag, as the early evening is dreamy and fated, while egos could start to clash around midnight; it would be better to cut dates short to avoid these stressful vibes. Sunday afternoon, however, is an excellent time to plan for the future.

Advice to get you through the week: Take it easy this week. Put off the hard work to another time and enjoy the romantic vibes of Saturday evening.

Top astrological event of the week: *Sunday:* Mercury in Scorpio trine Saturn in Pisces: This shrewd aspect will help you make proper decisions concerning long-term difficult situations.

October 23–29

The Sun enters Scorpio on Monday, joining Mercury and Mars. After an extroverted period of early fall frivolity, the nights lengthen and we enter the deeper, more mysterious Scorpio season. The focus shifts to the noble pursuits of personal loyalty and the seductive bonds of passion, as well as the more destructive forces that can be unleashed by unbridled, intensely felt emotion. Tuesday is one of the best days of the month. Its extraordinarily productive vibes make it easy to focus and concentrate on any task at hand. Inspiration can be found in almost anything, creating a renewed enthusiasm for living and widening one's horizons. Wednesday's unhurried, dreamy energies are perfect for creativity and art; put off the mundane worries of the workaday world to another day. There's nothing much else going on until the weekend, so enjoy the calm, relaxing days. Things are shaken up at a volcanic Lunar Eclipse, which can be felt on both Saturday and Sunday. Arguments could erupt out of nowhere, blocking out the sunlight and scattering fallout over the entire immediate vicinity. Try to diffuse tense situations as soon as they arise. These are definite days of reckoning, when long-suppressed emotions finally come to light so they can be dealt with and put to rest.

Advice to get you through the week: It is the best of times; it is the worst of times. Enjoy the delicate vibes of the workweek, as conflicts may have to be addressed once the weekend rolls around.

Top astrological event of the week: *Saturday/Sunday:* Lunar Eclipse close to Jupiter and opposite the Sun, Mercury, and Mars: Saturday's Lunar Eclipse is a bit of a doozy. These energies are echoed on Sunday, making the entire two-day period feel super intense. It may be difficult to let things go and move on. Alternatively, you may be tempted to burn bridges so you can never go back.

October 30–November 5

There will be lots of treats in store this Halloween. If you have children or young relatives, tender memories can be made this holiday season. Instead of buying a store-bought costume, create something handmade together—the more fantastical the better. For the child-free, just because you are all grown up doesn't mean you have to miss out on all the fun. Throw a party or attend one with friends. If single, a trick-or-treat date night could jump-start a new relationship. People may be exhausted and lazy the morning after all the festivities, but a productive spirit returns in the afternoon and lasts for the rest of the workweek. Visionary vibes proliferate on Friday, with everyone jockeying for their ideas to be implemented, which could lead to arguments. Truly talented individuals could be targeted to get them out of the way. Luckily, a sense of teamwork returns by the afternoon and everyone can make peace. Singles could be mesmerized by a fascinating Svengali. Be aware that cloudy thinking could keep you from realizing that you are being sold a false set of goods. Avoid getting too close to a new suitor until you carry out a thorough background check to make sure their story checks out. It may be better to put off dating this weekend to avoid being duped. Negative thoughts could be roused from their slumber on Saturday, leading to stubborn arguments and finger-pointing on Sunday.

Advice to get you through the week: Treats will be overflowing on Halloween, but you may have to deal with an onslaught of tricks by the weekend. Stay away from emotionally volatile people.

Top astrological event of the week: *Friday:* Sun in Scorpio opposite Jupiter in Taurus: Egos could clash in a big way between the true believers and the individualists.

November 6–12

Monday starts off with highly romantic vibes, so focus your thoughts on the softer side of life. Singles could meet their soul mate if they get out there and mingle, while couples should schedule time together to strengthen their bonds. It's a bit of a lazy day as far as work is concerned, so put off deadlines to another day to avoid the stress. The upbeat vibes continue until Friday. Tuesday is filled with mirth and gregariousness, making it an excellent time to increase your circle of social and work contacts. Wednesday's exuberant vibes create a gung-ho, can-do attitude, where you can achieve anything you put your mind to. It is an excellent day to brainstorm and plan for the future. Venus, the planet of love and creativity, moves into Libra, one of its rulers, midweek, opening the heart even further to *amour*. Thursday is a lovingly sweet date night, but starting Friday, the rest of the week's energies get rather tense, so gather your rosebuds while you can. People may have different visions of how to complete a task or project on Friday, leading to petty standoffs at work as everyone jockeys for control. The weekend's energies are a bit intense on Saturday, which is filled with rash, reckless energy. Avoid hooking up with someone on a whim; you may later regret it. Sunday is a good time to catch up on sleep and rest, as exhaustion may quickly set in.

Advice to get you through the week: The week's dreamy, romantic energies could lead you to jump into things too quickly with a new suitor on Saturday. Hit the brakes and take things slow.

Top astrological event of the week: *Saturday:* Mars in Scorpio opposite Uranus in Taurus: This skittish energy is accident-prone, so pay extra-close attention when on the road or traveling.

November 13–19

If you can make it past Monday, the rest of the week is a breeze, filled with confidence, magnetism, and a healthy sense of idealism. Monday's New Moon is a different matter. It could be easy to get swept away by delusions and illusions, leading to impulsive actions. Avoid signing on the dotted line or hastily joining causes or groups on this day. Rationality and teamwork are favored on Tuesday and Wednesday, while Thursday is perfect for projects that require concentration. It will be easy to make new contacts at this time, so get out and start networking. Thursday isn't the best date night, however, as people could become emotionally touchy over the smallest thing. On Friday and Saturday, the compassionate people of the world win out, making these days extra promising for volunteer work or implementing social change that is real and not simply performative. On a personal level, use these days to make your personal or professional dreams come true. Saturday is also an excellent time to integrate a new exercise and fitness plan into your daily routine, as it has a good chance of sticking and becoming a long-term habit. Sunday's vibe promotes romance, art, and ideas. Read a good book, watch a documentary, or go on a date to a museum.

Advice to get you through the week: Use your life energy to make the entire world pulse at a higher vibration.

Top astrological event of the week: *Monday:* New Moon conjunct Mars in Scorpio opposite Uranus in Taurus: This is a truly wildcard day when absolutely anything could happen, with the potential for things to spin out of control quite easily. Seek peace instead of escalating conflicts.

November 20–26

Thanksgiving week is here, featuring the potential for overindulgence and strained familial relationships and a plethora of opportunities for socializing and catching up with old friends. The week gets off to a bit of a sluggish start on Monday, but things start zooming along nicely by the afternoon, when hard work will impress people with influence. If you want to approach your boss for a promotion, raise, or boost in benefits, Tuesday is one of the most auspicious days of the year to do so. It is also a perfect day for job interviews, pitching clients, and sending out your résumé, so focus on going after your ambitions today. The Sun enters festive Sagittarius on Wednesday and is joined by Mars on Friday, promising a holiday season overflowing with good cheer and plenty of opportunities for mingling. This is a very extroverted, upbeat day. Feelings of shyness will dissipate, making it easy to approach people and strike up a conversation. Thanksgiving may seem like a lot of work for little payoff. Judgmental relatives may try to rain on the parades of their more free-wheeling kin. Things slow down on Saturday after the excitement of Thanksgiving. It's a great time to just lounge around; don't feel like you need to take part in even more celebrations. This may also be the last chance for controlling family members to cause disruption before people go their own way on Sunday, so try to avoid any negative people among your relations. Finish out the week on Sunday by relaxing and going to sleep early to recharge your batteries.

Advice to get you through the week: Thanksgiving could feature a few family squabbles. Luckily, the Sun and Mars bring enough positivity and enthusiasm to turn things around quickly and mitigate any disputes.

Top astrological event of the week: *Saturday:* Mars in Sagittarius square Saturn in Pisces: An overload of food, hobnobbing, and shopping over the long Thanksgiving weekend may leave everyone exhausted and in need of a good sleep on Sunday night.

November 27–December 3

Monday's Full Moon will push you to distance yourself from any close-minded killjoys in your world. Thanks to the Thanksgiving holidays, you probably know exactly who they are. If you take steps to do this now, you will be able to freely and joyfully express your true self over the upcoming year. It may be hard to get back into the swing of things at work, as thinking may be cloudy on Monday and Tuesday, so put off important decisions until later in the week. Wednesday and Thursday are upbeat days that are perfect for clearing out a backlog of tasks and thinking on your feet. No matter how good your intentions, bosses could be on a rampage on Friday. Put off sharing your visions and pitches to avoid hurt feelings and baseless rejection. Friday evening, however, is a different story. The weekend roars to life with highly social vibes. Hang out with friends or plan a passionate evening with your sweetie. Saturday offers both merriment and productivity—the choice is yours. It's also an excellent day for making long-term plans with your romantic partner. Sunday's energy is more volatile, so avoid bossy people who might try to run roughshod over your ideas and desires.

Advice to get you through the week: All in all, this is a very productive week in terms of work, while Friday evening offers plenty of joy and fun.

Top astrological event of the week: *Monday:* Mercury in Sagittarius square Neptune in Pisces: Avoid getting sucked into ideological debates with people who have a religious-like zeal instead of an open mind.

December 4–10

The week starts off by sending mixed messages. A Lunar Grand Trine favors extroversion and communications, while a Lunar T-square makes all work of a mundane nature quite tedious. Try to schedule dynamic projects and meetings today to accentuate the positive and eliminate the negative, as the old song goes. Tuesday is asking us to swallow our pride; if we can get out of the way of our own egos and learn to work together as a team, the whole will definitely be greater than the sum of its parts. This is also an excellent day for spontaneous romance. Doing something unexpected and unplanned can bring couples closer together. For singles, a casual or dating relationship could morph into something long-term—you'll never know if you don't ask. Thinking is not on-target on Wednesday. You'll need to keep extra aware to avoid making ill-advised decisions based on fudged data. Alternatively, someone may be manipulating or guilt-tripping you into doing something that is not in your own best interest. It's better to wait until Thursday to make any firm commitments, as logic and insight will be on overdrive that day. If you are in a new relationship or courtship, you may want to keep things discreet, as judgmental friends may want to try to trip up a good thing. If it's good enough for you, you don't need to worry about anyone else. Sunday is a lazy day. Luckily, it's the weekend, so spend a cozy afternoon lounging around at home.

Advice to get you through the week: Work transparently in a team at the office, but when it comes to romance, be as private as possible.

Top astrological event of the week: *Thursday:* Mercury in Capricorn trine Jupiter in Taurus: This is an excellent day for problem-solving, brainstorming, and finding innovative solutions to workplace challenges.

December 11–17

Mercury turns retrograde on Wednesday and won't resume direct motion until New Year's Day. Try to do all online Christmas shopping before this day, as shipping may be delayed. Do not spend more than you have in case payments are late in arriving during the retrograde period. This motion promotes getting in touch with old friends, family, colleagues, and loved ones who have dropped off the radar and bringing them back into your life. If you are single, you may even decide to reach out to the one who got away. Monday and Thursday are great for online dating, while the New Moon on Tuesday offers passion and action. This turbocharged Moon will help you get everything organized for the holidays before Mercury turns retrograde midweek.

You'll also be able to clear out a backlog of tasks on Wednesday. On Thursday, a group brainstorming session will assist in problem-solving and making decisions. It will be easy to clash with bosses on Friday, so avoid delicate subjects or negotiations. Saturday's nebulous vibes could lead you to feel suspicious about the true motivations of a loved one. Take a detached, wait-and-see approach instead of confronting things head-on, as clarity will return on January 1. On Sunday you'll have the stamina and superpowers to get caught up on domestic tasks and finish preparations for the holidays.

Advice to get you through the week: Before Mercury turns retrograde on Wednesday, finalize travel plans for the holidays and finish all online shopping.

Top astrological event of the week: *Tuesday:* New Moon in Sagittarius: This is a perfect day for scheduling events and activities for the holiday season. Dare to think outside the box and venture outside your comfort zone by planning a short weekend trip.

December 18–24

The workweek gets off to a mentally productive start. Kick off your Monday by catching up on emails, communications, and a backlog of tasks. Tuesday's dreamy energy is best put to use on utopian, creative projects. Try to set your ego aside as you pursue humanitarian and artistic goals. The winter solstice occurs on Thursday, ushering in a period of extended daylight in the Northern Hemisphere. Romantic partners could be unreliable today, leading to hurt feelings; it is definitely not the best date night. Friday's extremely productive vibes will allow you to finish all work and holiday preparations so you can enjoy the long holiday weekend without any job-related deadlines hanging over your head. This is also a very social day, both personally and professionally. Stay away from daytime dates on Saturday, as the evening's vibes are much more romantic and harmonious. You'll be as busy as an elf at Santa's workshop on Christmas Eve. Get friends and family together to deck the halls, bake cookies, and trim the tree, if that's part of your tradition. With the day's industrious vibes, you may want to prep and cook meals in advance so you can spend the actual holiday relaxing and socializing.

Advice to get you through the week: The week abounds with cheerful, industrious energy so you can happily take care of whatever needs to get done for the holidays.

Top astrological event of the week: *Friday:* Sun conjunct Mercury in Sagittarius: Make sure to send out holiday greetings to past work colleagues and bosses. They could prove to be useful contacts in the future.

December 25–31

The end of 2023 closes with a Christmas miracle, as the holiday's energies are bursting with love and good cheer. Even if you don't celebrate this observance, you can still partake in the harmonious astrological vibes. After the merriment of Christmas Day, exhaustion quickly sets in, so you may want to go to sleep early. Tuesday's Full Moon extends the upbeat, generous mood. Tap into your inner confidence and leadership skills to put an end to any long-standing family feuds so you can start the year on a more stable note. Wednesday is a five-star day to socialize with friends, while Thursday is a bit of a mixed bag. On the one hand, there is an abundance of love and creativity, thanks to a Lunar Grand Trine, but on the other, you might have a lot of ideas you want to get off the ground without knowing where to start. Once Mercury turns direct on January 1, you'll finally know exactly what to do to move forward. For now, put work on the back burner and focus on romance, family, and friends. Thursday and Friday are especially auspicious days to search for a suitor. Emotions run high in the daytime on New Year's Eve, but luckily, a super festive atmosphere returns in time for the countdown to 2024.

Advice to get you through the week: Forget about work and duties and enjoy the holiday period seeking romance and mirth. The universe is leaving an abundance of life-expanding presents under the tree, especially for singles in search of "the one."

Top astrological event of the week: *Monday:* Venus in Scorpio trine Neptune: If all you want for Christmas is peace on earth and goodwill to all, you'll certainly receive your wish. The day's loving vibes promise a harmonious time around the tree. If you are single, treat yourself to some swipes on a dating app; you may receive the gift of true love.

About the Astrologer

Michelle Perrin, aka Astrology Detective, has built a reputation as one of the world's most trusted and sought-after astrologers for more than ten years. Her work has appeared in some of the most influential titles online and in print, making her one of the few astrologers who has garnered respect from both a mass audience and the astrological community. Her horoscopes have appeared on the websites for Canada's W Dish and Slice TV Networks, Tarot.com's Daily Horoscope site, and *Dell Horoscope* magazine, among others. Her writings have also been featured in *The Mountain Astrologer*, the leading trade journal for the astrological community, and astrology.com. She is also a long-term contributor to Llewellyn's annual *Moon Sign Book* and *Moon Sign Datebook*. Her website is www.astrologydetective.com or follow her at https://www.instagram.com/hashtaghoroscopes/.

Finding Opportunity Periods

by Jim Shawvan

There are times when the most useful things you can do are ordinary tasks such as laundry, cooking, listening to music, reading, learning, or meditating. There are other times when the universe opens the gates of opportunity. Meetings, decisions, or commitments during these "Opportunity Periods" can lead to new and positive developments in your life. Most people are unaware of these subtle changes in the energies, so they wind up doing laundry when they could be signing an important contract, or they go out to try to meet a new sweetheart when the energies for such a thing are totally blocked.

I developed the Opportunity Periods system over more than thirty years, as I tested first one hypothesis and then another in real life. In about 1998, when I studied classical astrology with Lee Lehman, the system got some added zing, including William Lilly's idea that the Moon when void-of-course in the signs of the Moon and Jupiter "performeth somewhat." The signs of the Moon and Jupiter are Taurus, Cancer, Sagittarius, and Pisces. For those who want to understand the details of the system, they are explained here. If you simply want to use the system, all the information you need is on the calendar pages (you don't need to learn the technicalities).

An Opportunity Period (OP) is a period in which the aspects of the transiting Moon to other transiting planets show no interference with the free flow of decision and action.

Opportunity Periods apply to everyone in the world all at once; although, if the astrological influences on your own chart are putting blocks in your path, you may not be able to use every OP to the fullest. Nevertheless, you are always better off taking important actions and making crucial decisions during an Opportunity Period.

Signs of the Moon and Jupiter
Taurus: the Moon's exaltation
Cancer: the Moon's domicile and Jupiter's exaltation
Sagittarius: Jupiter's fiery domicile
Pisces: Jupiter's watery domicile

Steps to Find Your Opportunity Periods

Under Sun's Beams
Step 1: Determine whether the Moon is "under Sun's beams"; that is, less than 17 degrees from the Sun. If it is, go to step 7. If not, continue to step 2.

Moon Void-of-Course
Step 2: Determine when the Moon goes void-of-course (v/c). The Moon is said to be void-of-course from the time it makes the last Ptolemaic aspect (conjunction, sextile, square, trine, or opposition) in a sign until it enters the next sign.

In eight of the twelve signs of the zodiac, Moon-void periods are NOT Opportunity Periods. In the other four signs, however, they are! According to seventeenth-century astrologer William Lilly, the Moon in the signs of the Moon and Jupiter "performeth somewhat." Lee Lehman says that she has taken this to the bank many times—and so have I.

Stressful or Easy Aspect
Step 3: Determine whether the aspect on which the Moon goes void is a stressful or an easy aspect. Every square is stressful, and every trine and every sextile is easy. Conjunctions and oppositions require judgment according to the nature of the planet the Moon is aspecting, and according to your individual ability to cope with the energies of that planet. For example, the Moon applying to a conjunction of Jupiter, Venus, or Mercury is easy, whereas, for most purposes, the Moon applying to a conjunction of Saturn, Mars, Neptune, Pluto, or Uranus is stressful. However, if you are a person for whom Uranus or Pluto is a familiar and more or less comfortable energy, you may find that the period before the Moon's conjunction to that planet is an Opportunity Period for you. (Since this is true for relatively few people, such periods are not marked as OPs in this book.)

Oppositions can work if the Moon is applying to an opposition of Jupiter, Venus, Mercury, or the Sun (just before the Full Moon). The Moon applying to a conjunction with the Sun (New Moon) presents a whole set of issues on its own. See step 7.

Easy Equals Opportunity

Step 4: If the aspect on which the Moon goes void is an easy aspect, there is an Opportunity Period before the void period. If the aspect on which the Moon goes void is a stressful aspect, there is no Opportunity Period preceding the void period in that sign. To determine the beginning of the Opportunity Period, find the last stressful aspect the Moon makes in the sign. The Opportunity Period runs from the last stressful aspect to the last aspect (assuming that the last aspect is an easy one). If the Moon makes no stressful aspects at all while in the sign, then the Opportunity Period begins as soon as the Moon enters the sign, and ends at the last aspect.

When Is an Aspect Over?

Step 5: When is an aspect over? There are three different answers to this question, and I recommend observation to decide. I also recommend caution.

- An aspect is over (in electional astrology) as soon as it is no longer exact. For example, if the Moon's last stressful aspect in a sign is a square to Saturn at 1:51 p.m., the Opportunity Period (if there is one) would be considered to begin immediately. This is the way the Opportunity Periods are shown in this book.

- Lee Lehman says an aspect is effective (for electional purposes) until it is no longer partile. An aspect is said to be partile if the two planets are in the same degree numerically. For example, a planet at 0° Aries 00' 00" is in partile trine to a planet at 0° Leo 59' 59", but it is not in partile conjunction to a planet at 29° Pisces 59' 59", even though the orb of the conjunction is only one second of arc ($1/3{,}600$) of a degree.

- An aspect is effective until the Moon has separated from the exact aspect by a full degree, which takes about two hours. This is the most cautious viewpoint. If you have doubts about the wisdom of signing a major contract while the Moon is still within one degree of a nasty aspect, then for your own peace of mind you should give it two hours, to get the one-degree separating orb.

Translating Light and Translating Darkness

Step 6: One should avoid starting important matters when the Moon is translating light from a stressful aspect with a malefic planet to an ostensibly easy aspect with another malefic planet—or even a series of such aspects uninterrupted by any aspects to benefic planets. I refer to this as "translating darkness." Translation of light is a concept used primarily in horary astrology, and it is discussed in great detail in books and on websites on that subject. For example, the Moon's last difficult aspect is a square to Saturn, and there is an apparent Opportunity Period because the Moon's next aspect is a trine to Mars, on which the Moon goes void-of-course. The problem is this: the Moon is translating light from one malefic to another, and this vitiates what would otherwise be an Opportunity Period. The same would be true if the sequence were, for example, Moon square Saturn, then Moon trine Mars, then Moon sextile Neptune—an unbroken series of malefics.

For the purpose of this system, we may regard all of the following planets as malefics: Mars, Saturn, Uranus, Neptune, and Pluto. I can almost hear the howls of protest from the folks who believe there is no such thing as a malefic planet or a bad aspect. On the level of spiritual growth, that is doubtless true, but this book is meant to be used to make your everyday life easier. Anyone who urges others to suffer more than absolutely necessary in the name of spirituality is indulging in great spiritual arrogance themselves.

New Moon, Balsamic Phase, and Cazimi Notes

Step 7: Here are some notes on the period around the New Moon: waxing, waning, Balsamic, under beams, combust, and Cazimi.

As it separates from conjunction with the Sun (New Moon) and moves toward opposition (Full Moon), the Moon is said to be waxing, or increasing in light. Traditionally the period of the waxing Moon is considered favorable for electional purposes.

Then after the Full Moon, as the Moon applies to a conjunction with the Sun, the Moon is said to be waning, or decreasing in light. Traditionally this period is regarded as a poor choice for electional purposes, and the closer the Moon gets to the Sun, the worse it is said to be. In practice, I find that problems seem to occur only as the Moon gets very close to the Sun.

When the Moon is applying to a conjunction with the Sun (New Moon) and is less than 45 degrees away from the Sun, the Moon is said to be in its Balsamic phase. This phase is associated with giving things up and is considered especially unfavorable for starting things you wish to increase.

Any planet within 17 degrees of the Sun is said to be under Sun's beams. Traditionally this weakens the planet, particularly for electional and horary purposes.

Any planet within 8 degrees of the Sun is said to be combust. Traditionally this weakens the planet even more, particularly in electional and horary work.

Any planet whose center is within 17 minutes of arc of the center of the Sun in celestial longitude is said to be Cazimi. Oddly, this is considered the highest form of accidental dignity. In other words, a planet is thought to be weak when under Sun's beams, weaker still when combust, but—surprisingly—very powerful and benefic when Cazimi!

The average speed of the Moon is such that it remains Cazimi for about an hour; that is, half an hour before and half an hour after the exact conjunction with the Sun (New Moon). Other things being equal, you can use the Cazimi Moon to start something if you really want it to succeed.

However, please do not attempt to use the Cazimi Moon at the time of a Solar Eclipse, nor if the Moon is moving from the Cazimi into a stressful aspect. Cazimi is powerful, but it cannot override the difficulties shown by a Solar Eclipse, nor those shown by, say, the Moon's application to a square of Saturn.

If you really need to start something around the time of the New Moon, and you cannot use the Cazimi, it is a good idea to wait until the first Opportunity Period after the Moon has begun waxing. Even if the Moon is still under Sun's beams at that time, it is better than starting the new project while the Moon is still waning. However, if you can reasonably do so, it is best to wait for the first Opportunity Period after the Moon is no longer under Sun's beams; that is, after the Moon has separated from the Sun by at least 17 degrees. For the principles to use at that time, see step 2.

About the Astrologers

Paula Belluomini, CAP ISAR, began studying astrology as a teenager while living in Brazil. Growing up, she became fascinated with the movement of the stars and was passionate about learning how their positions affected life on Earth. She immersed herself in all the literature she could find on the subject, and moved to Southern California in the 1990s to continue her studies through independent coursework.

Paula completed the steps required to become a Certified Astrological Professional (CAP) by the International Society for Astrological Research (ISAR) in 2015, and participated in several astrological conferences promoted by ISAR and UAC. She was introduced to Jim Shawvan's Opportunity Periods system in Anaheim (ISAR 2003), and has followed his work ever since.

Paula's main areas of expertise and interest include modern astrology with predictive techniques, relationship analysis, and relocational astrology, as well as electional, mundane, and traditional astrology. More recently, horary astrology has piqued her interest because of its practicality and ability to answer questions in a more objective way.

In addition to providing astrology consulting services, Paula writes articles and posts about current astrological events, gives lectures about specific topics, participates in research and study groups, and continues educating herself on the stars.

Aside from astrology, Paula has a degree in marketing and is an experienced graphic and web designer who often creates artwork with astrological themes. For more information, please visit her website at astropaula.com.

Jim Shawvan developed the system of Opportunity Periods over a period of three decades, out of his interest in electional astrology—the art of picking times for important actions such as getting married, opening a business, or incorporating a company (or even matters of only medium importance). Jim began the study of astrology in 1969. He taught classes in predictive astrology and lectured numerous times to the San Diego Astrological Society and other astrological groups and conferences.

Jim's articles appeared in *The Mountain Astrologer* and other publications. He predicted the delay in the results of the US presidential election of 2000, and in early 2001 he predicted that, in response to anti-American terrorism, the US would be at war in Afghanistan in the first two years of George W. Bush's presidency.

Jim studied cultural anthropology and structural linguistics at Cornell University, and later became a computer programmer and systems analyst. From 1989 to 1997 he was the technical astrologer at Neil Michelsen's Astro Communications Services, handling the most difficult questions and orders. He held the Certified Astrological Professional certificate issued by the International Society for Astrological Research (ISAR). Jim passed away in 2019 and is greatly missed.

Business Guide

Collections

Try to make collections on days when your Sun is well aspected. Avoid days when Mars or Saturn are aspected. If possible, the Moon should be in a cardinal sign: Aries, Cancer, Libra, or Capricorn. It is more difficult to collect when the Moon is in Taurus or Scorpio.

Employment, Promotion

Choose a day when your Sun is favorably aspected or the Moon is in your tenth house. Good aspects of Venus or Jupiter are beneficial.

Loans

Moon in the first and second quarters favors the lender; in the third and fourth it favors the borrower. Good aspects of Jupiter or Venus to the Moon are favorable to both, as is Moon in Leo, Sagittarius, Aquarius, or Pisces.

New Ventures

Things usually get off to a better start during the increase of the Moon. If there is impatience, anxiety, or deadlock, it can often be broken at the Full Moon. Agreements can be reached then.

Partnerships

Agreements and partnerships should be made on a day that is favorable to both parties. Mars, Neptune, Pluto, and Saturn should not be square or opposite the Moon. It is best to make an agreement or partnership when the Moon is in a mutable sign, especially Gemini or Virgo. The other signs are not favorable, with the possible exception of Leo or Capricorn. Begin partnerships when the Moon is increasing in light, as this is a favorable time for starting new ventures.

Public Relations

The Moon rules the public, so this must be well aspected, particularly by the Sun, Mercury, Uranus, or Neptune.

Selling

Selling is favored by good aspects of Venus, Jupiter, or Mercury to the Moon. Avoid aspects to Saturn. Try to get the planetary ruler of your product well aspected by Venus, Jupiter, or the Moon.

Signing Important Papers

Sign contracts or agreements when the Moon is increasing in a fruitful sign. Avoid days when Mars, Saturn, Neptune, or Pluto are afflicting the Moon. Don't sign anything if your Sun is badly afflicted.

Calendar Pages

How to Use Your *Daily Planetary Guide*

Both Eastern and Pacific times are given in the datebook. The Eastern times are listed in the left-hand column. The Pacific times are in the right-hand column in bold typeface. Note that adjustments have been made for Daylight Saving Time. The void-of-course Moon is listed to the right of the daily aspect at the exact time it occurs. It is indicated by "☽ v/c." On days when it occurs for only one time zone and not the other, it is indicated next to the appropriate column and then repeated on the next day for the other time zone. Note that the monthly ephemerides in the back of the book are shown for midnight Greenwich Mean Time (GMT). Opportunity Periods are designated by the letters "OP." See page 77 for a detailed discussion on how to use Opportunity Periods.

Symbol Key

Planets/ Asteroids	☉	Sun	♃	Jupiter
	☽	Moon	♄	Saturn
	☿	Mercury	♅	Uranus
	♀	Venus	♆	Neptune
	♂	Mars	♇	Pluto
	⚷	Chiron		
Signs	♈	Aries	♎	Libra
	♉	Taurus	♏	Scorpio
	♊	Gemini	♐	Sagittarius
	♋	Cancer	♑	Capricorn
	♌	Leo	♒	Aquarius
	♍	Virgo	♓	Pisces
Aspects	☌	Conjunction (0°)	△	Trine (120°)
	⚹	Sextile (60°)	⚻	Quincunx (150°)
	□	Square (90°)	☍	Opposition (180°)
Motion	℞	Retrograde	D	Direct
Moon Phases	●	New Moon	◐	2nd Quarter
	○	Full Moon	◑	4th Quarter

DECEMBER 2022

Mercury Note: Mercury goes retrograde on Thursday, December 29, 2022, and remains so until January 18, 2023, after which it will still be in its Storm until January 24. Projects initiated during this entire period may not work out as planned. It's best to use this time for reviews, editing, escrows, and so forth.

26 Mon
1st ≈
Hanukkah ends
Kwanzaa begins
Boxing Day (Canada & UK)

☽≈ □ ♅ ♉	2:35 am	
☽≈ ☌ ♄≈	1:19 pm **10:19 am**	☽ v/c
☽ enters ♓		**11:34 pm**

27 Tue
1st ≈

☽ enters ♓	2:34 am	
☽♓ ⚹ ☉♑	12:23 pm **9:23 am**	
☽♓ □ ♂Ⅱ	6:54 pm **3:54 pm**	

28 Wed
1st ♓

OP: After Moon conjoins Neptune today until v/c Moon today or on Thursday. Mercury is moving slowly, but you can use this excellent time for creative ideas, fun, social activities, and mind expansion.

♀♑ ⚹ ♆♓	3:32 am **12:32 am**	
☽♓ ⚹ ♅♉	4:02 am **1:02 am**	
☽♓ ☌ ♆♓	5:05 pm **2:05 pm**	
☽♓ ⚹ ♀♑	6:25 pm **3:25 pm**	
☽♓ ⚹ ☿♑	7:43 pm **4:43 pm**	
☽♓ ⚹ ♇♑	**10:21 pm**	☽ v/c

29 Thu
1st ♓
☽ 2nd Quarter 8 ♈ 18
Mercury retrograde

☽♓ ⚹ ♇♑	1:21 am	☽ v/c
☿℞	4:32 am **1:32 am**	
☽ enters ♈	5:36 am **2:36 am**	
☽♈ ☌ ♃♈	7:11 am **4:11 am**	
☿♑ ☌ ♀♑	8:58 am **5:58 am**	
☽♈ □ ☉♑	8:21 pm **5:21 pm**	
☽♈ ⚹ ♂Ⅱ	10:17 pm **7:17 pm**	
☽♈ ☌ ⚷♈	**11:55 pm**	

December 2022 • January

☽♈ ☌ ♆♈	2:55 am
☉♑ ⚻ ♂♊	6:21 pm **3:21 pm**
☽♈ ⚹ ♄♒	9:52 pm **6:52 pm**
☽♈ □ ☿♑	**10:00 pm**

Fri 30
2nd ♈

☽♈ □ ☿♑	1:00 am
☽♈ □ ♀♑	5:59 am **2:59 am**
☽♈ □ ♇♑	7:44 am **4:44 am** ☽ v/c
☽ enters ♉	12:08 pm **9:08 am**
♀♑ ☌ ♇♑	**9:25 pm**

Sat 31
2nd ♈
New Year's Eve

♀♑ ☌ ♇♑	12:25 am
☽♉ △ ☉♑	8:42 am **5:42 am**
☽♉ ☌ ♅♉	4:52 pm **1:52 pm**
☿♑ ⚹ ♆♓	**10:44 pm**

Sun 1
2nd ♉
New Year's Day
Kwanzaa ends

Eastern Standard Time (EST) plain / **Pacific Standard Time (PST) bold**

DECEMBER 2022	JANUARY	FEBRUARY
S M T W T F S	S M T W T F S	S M T W T F S
1 2 3	1 2 3 4 5 6 7	1 2 3 4
4 5 6 7 8 9 10	8 9 10 11 12 13 14	5 6 7 8 9 10 11
11 12 13 14 15 16 17	15 16 17 18 19 20 21	12 13 14 15 16 17 18
18 19 20 21 22 23 24	22 23 24 25 26 27 28	19 20 21 22 23 24 25
25 26 27 28 29 30 31	29 30 31	26 27 28

January

2 Mon
2nd ♉

OP: After Moon squares Saturn until Moon enters Gemini. (Taurus is one of the four signs in which the v/c Moon is a good thing. See page 77.) This is a favorable time for trade and artistic projects, but with Mercury retrograde, use it for projects you started before the holidays.

☿♑ ⚹ ♆♓	1:44 am	
☽♉ □ ♄≈	7:15 am	**4:15 am**
☽♉ △ ☿♑	7:30 am	**4:30 am**
☽♉ ⚹ ♆♓	7:53 am	**4:53 am**
☉♑ □ ♅♈	11:02 am	**8:02 am**
☽♉ △ ♀♑	5:16 pm	**2:16 pm** ☽ v/c
♀ enters ≈	9:09 pm	**6:09 pm**
☽ enters ♊	9:44 pm	**6:44 pm**
☽♊ △ ♀≈	9:48 pm	**6:48 pm**
☽♊ ⚹ ♃♈		**9:37 pm**

3 Tue
2nd ♊

☽♊ ⚹ ♃♈	12:37 am	
☽♊ ☌ ♂♊	2:47 pm	**11:47 am**
☽♊ ⚹ ♅♈	9:22 pm	**6:22 pm**
☽♊ ⚻ ☉♑		**9:30 pm**

4 Wed
2nd ♊

☽♊ ⚻ ☉♑	12:30 am	
♀≈ ⚹ ♃♈	4:08 am	**1:08 am**
☽♊ ⚻ ☿♑	2:10 pm	**11:10 am**
☽♊ △ ♄≈	6:54 pm	**3:54 pm**
☽♊ □ ♆♓	7:08 pm	**4:08 pm** ☽ v/c

5 Thu
2nd ♊

☽♊ ⚻ ♀♑	4:50 am	**1:50 am**
☽ enters ♋	9:15 am	**6:15 am**
☉♑ △ ♅♉	11:43 am	**8:43 am**
☽♋ □ ♃♈	12:50 pm	**9:50 am**
☽♋ ⚻ ♀≈	4:16 pm	**1:16 pm**

January

☽⊗ □ ♂♈	9:24 am **6:24 am**
☽⊗ ⚹ ♅♉	3:30 pm **12:30 pm**
☽⊗ ☍ ☉♑	6:08 pm **3:08 pm**
☽⊗ ☍ ☿♑	8:36 pm **5:36 pm**

Fri 6
2nd ♋
○ Full Moon 16 ♋ 22

☽⊗ △ ♆♓	7:30 am **4:30 am**
☽⊗ ⚻ ♄♒	7:42 am **4:42 am**
☉♑ ☌ ☿♑	7:57 am **4:57 am**
☽⊗ ☍ ♀♑	5:23 pm **2:23 pm** ☽ v/c
☽ enters ♌	9:40 pm **6:40 pm**
☽♌ △ ♃♈	**11:00 pm**

Sat 7
3rd ♋

☽♌ △ ♃♈	2:00 am
☽♌ ☍ ♀♒	11:52 am **8:52 am**
☽♌ ⚹ ♂♊	2:19 pm **11:19 am**
☿♑ △ ♅♉	6:23 pm **3:23 pm**
☽♌ △ ♂♈	10:03 pm **7:03 pm**

Sun 8
3rd ♌

Eastern Standard Time (EST) plain / Pacific Standard Time (PST) bold

DECEMBER 2022	JANUARY	FEBRUARY
S M T W T F S	S M T W T F S	S M T W T F S
1 2 3	1 2 3 4 5 6 7	1 2 3 4
4 5 6 7 8 9 10	8 9 10 11 12 13 14	5 6 7 8 9 10 11
11 12 13 14 15 16 17	15 16 17 18 19 20 21	12 13 14 15 16 17 18
18 19 20 21 22 23 24	22 23 24 25 26 27 28	19 20 21 22 23 24 25
25 26 27 28 29 30 31	29 30 31	26 27 28

January

9 Mon
3rd ♌

☽♌ ⊼ ☿♑	3:05 am	**12:05 am**
☽♌ □ ♅♉	4:02 am	**1:02 am**
♀♒ △ ♂♊	10:22 am	**7:22 am**
☽♌ ⊼ ☉♑	12:26 pm	**9:26 am**
☽♌ ⊼ ♆♓	8:13 pm	**5:13 pm**
☽♌ ☍ ♄♒	8:52 pm	**5:52 pm** ☽ v/c

10 Tue
3rd ♌

☽♌ ⊼ ♇♑	6:09 am	**3:09 am**
☽ enters ♍	10:15 am	**7:15 am**
☽♍ ⊼ ♃♈	3:17 pm	**12:17 pm**
☽♍ □ ♂♊		**11:36 pm**

11 Wed
3rd ♍

☽♍ □ ♂♊	2:36 am	
☿♑ □ ⚷♈	3:49 am	**12:49 am**
☽♍ ⊼ ♀♒	7:25 am	**4:25 am**
☽♍ △ ☿♑	9:58 am	**6:58 am**
☽♍ ⊼ ⚷♈	10:32 am	**7:32 am**
☽♍ △ ♅♉	4:17 pm	**1:17 pm**

12 Thu
3rd ♍
Mars direct
OP: After Moon opposes Neptune until v/c Moon. This is a great opportunity to be productive and review ongoing projects.

☽♍ △ ☉♑	6:08 am	**3:08 am**
☽♍ ☍ ♆♓	8:21 am	**5:21 am**
☽♍ ⊼ ♄♒	9:25 am	**6:25 am**
♀♒ ✶ ⚷♈	1:46 pm	**10:46 am**
♂D		3:56 pm **12:56 pm**
☽♍ △ ♇♑	6:06 pm	**3:06 pm** ☽ v/c
☽ enters ♎	9:56 pm	**6:56 pm**

90

January

Fri 13
3rd ♎

☽☌♃♈	3:34 am	**12:34 am**
☉♑✶♆♓	9:11 am	**6:11 am**
☽△♂♊	1:46 pm	**10:46 am**
☽□☿♑	4:55 pm	**1:55 pm**
☽☌♄♈	9:30 pm	**6:30 pm**
☽△♀♒		**9:58 pm**
☽⚻♅♉		**11:54 pm**

Sat 14
3rd ♎
◐ 4th Quarter 24 ♎ 38

☽△♀♒	12:58 am	
☽⚻♅♉	2:54 am	
☽⚻♆♓	6:22 pm	**3:22 pm**
☽△♄♒	7:47 pm	**4:47 pm**
♀♒□♅♉	8:22 pm	**5:22 pm**
☽□☉♑	9:10 pm	**6:10 pm**

Sun 15
4th ♎

☽□♀♑	3:40 am	**12:40 am** ☽ v/c
☽ enters ♏	7:08 am	**4:08 am**
☽♏⚻♃♈	1:07 pm	**10:07 am**
☽♏⚻♂♊	10:08 pm	**7:08 pm**
☽♏✶☿♑	10:47 pm	**7:47 pm**

Eastern Standard Time (EST) plain / **Pacific Standard Time (PST) bold**

DECEMBER 2022							**JANUARY**							**FEBRUARY**						
S	M	T	W	T	F	S	S	M	T	W	T	F	S	S	M	T	W	T	F	S
				1	2	3	1	2	3	4	5	6	7				1	2	3	4
4	5	6	7	8	9	10	8	9	10	11	12	13	14	5	6	7	8	9	10	11
11	12	13	14	15	16	17	15	16	17	18	19	20	21	12	13	14	15	16	17	18
18	19	20	21	22	23	24	22	23	24	25	26	27	28	19	20	21	22	23	24	25
25	26	27	28	29	30	31	29	30	31					26	27	28				

January

Mercury Note: Mercury goes direct on Wednesday, January 18, but remains in its Storm, moving slowly, until January 24.

---

16 Mon
4th ♏
Martin Luther King Jr. Day

☽♏ ⚻ ⚷♈	5:21 am	**2:21 am**
☽♏ ☍ ♅♉	10:17 am	**7:17 am**
☽♏ □ ♀♒	2:09 pm	**11:09 am**
☽♏ △ ♆♓		**9:48 pm**
☿♑ ⚻ ♂♊		**10:42 pm**
☽♏ □ ♄♒		**11:27 pm**

---

17 Tue
4th ♏

OP: After Moon squares Saturn on Monday or today until v/c Moon today. This short OP offers early birds a chance to focus on letting go of unnecessary thoughts and possessions.

☽♏ △ ♆♓	12:48 am	
☿♑ ⚻ ♂♊	1:42 am	
☽♏ □ ♄♒	2:27 am	
☽♏ ✶ ☉♑	7:36 am	**4:36 am**
☽♏ ✶ ♀♑	9:27 am	**6:27 am** ☽ v/c
☽ enters ♐	12:33 pm	**9:33 am**
☽♐ △ ♃♈	6:41 pm	**3:41 pm**
☽♐ ☍ ♂♊		**11:39 pm**

---

18 Wed
4th ♐
Mercury direct

☽♐ ☍ ♂♊	2:39 am	
☿ D	8:12 am	**5:12 am**
☽♐ △ ⚷♈	9:13 am	**6:13 am**
☉♑ ☌ ♀♑	9:44 am	**6:44 am**
☽♐ ⚻ ♅♉	1:42 pm	**10:42 am**
☽♐ ✶ ♀♒	10:05 pm	**7:05 pm**

---

19 Thu
4th ♐

☽♐ □ ♆♓	3:17 am	**12:17 am**
☽♐ ✶ ♄♒	5:09 am	**2:09 am** ☽ v/c
☽ enters ♑	2:11 pm	**11:11 am**
☽♑ □ ♃♈	8:29 pm	**5:29 pm**

January

Fri 20
4th ♑
Sun enters Aquarius

☉ enters ♒	3:30 am	**12:30 am**
☽♑ ☌ ☿♑	3:30 am	**12:30 am**
☽♑ ☍ ♂Ⅱ	3:42 am	**12:42 am**
☽♑ □ ⚷♈	9:45 am	**6:45 am**
☽♑ △ ♅♉	1:55 pm	**10:55 am**
☿♑ ☍ ♂Ⅱ	8:06 pm	**5:06 pm**

Sat 21
4th ♑
● New Moon 1 ♒ 33

OP: **This Cazimi Moon is usable ½ hour before and ½ hour after the Sun-Moon conjunction.** If you have something important to start around now, this is a great time to do it.

☽♑ ⚹ ♆♓	3:01 am	**12:01 am**
☽♑ ☌ ♀♑	10:52 am	**7:52 am** ☽ v/c
☽ enters ♒	1:29 pm	**10:29 am**
☽♒ ☌ ☉♒	3:53 pm	**12:53 pm**
☽♒ ⚹ ♃♈	8:09 pm	**5:09 pm**

Sun 22
1st ♒
Lunar New Year (Rabbit)
Uranus direct

☽♒ △ ♂Ⅱ	3:02 am	**12:02 am**
☽♒ ⚹ ⚷♈	8:46 am	**5:46 am**
☽♒ □ ♅♉	12:49 pm	**9:49 am**
♀♒ ☌ ♄♒	5:13 pm	**2:13 pm**
♅ D		5:59 pm **2:59 pm**

Eastern Standard Time (EST) plain / **Pacific Standard Time (PST) bold**

DECEMBER 2022	JANUARY	FEBRUARY
S M T W T F S	S M T W T F S	S M T W T F S
1 2 3	1 2 3 4 5 6 7	1 2 3 4
4 5 6 7 8 9 10	8 9 10 11 12 13 14	5 6 7 8 9 10 11
11 12 13 14 15 16 17	15 16 17 18 19 20 21	12 13 14 15 16 17 18
18 19 20 21 22 23 24	22 23 24 25 26 27 28	19 20 21 22 23 24 25
25 26 27 28 29 30 31	29 30 31	26 27 28

January

Mercury Note: Mercury finally leaves its Storm on Wednesday. Look over your notes on any ideas that occurred to you while Mercury was retrograde or slow. How do they look now?

23 Mon
1st ≈

☽≈ ☌ ♄≈	4:25 am	**1:25 am**
☽≈ ☌ ♀≈	5:19 am	**2:19 am** ☽ v/c
☽ enters ♓	12:36 pm	**9:36 am**
☽♓ □ ♂Ⅱ		**11:56 pm**

24 Tue
1st ♓

OP: After Moon squares Mars on Monday or today until Moon enters Aries on Wednesday. Wait two hours after the square for balance. Use this time to meditate and sharpen your intuition as Mercury is picking up speed.

☽♓ □ ♂Ⅱ	2:56 am	
☽♓ ⚹ ☿♑	4:59 am	**1:59 am**
☽♓ ⚹ ♅♉	12:43 pm	**9:43 am**
☉≈ ⚹ ♃♈	8:30 pm	**5:30 pm**
☽♓ ☌ ♆♓		**11:42 pm**

25 Wed
1st ♓

☽♓ ☌ ♆♓	2:42 am	
☽♓ ⚹ ♀♑	11:12 am	**8:12 am** ☽ v/c
☽ enters ♈	1:48 pm	**10:48 am**
☽♈ ☌ ♃♈	10:18 pm	**7:18 pm**
☽♈ ⚹ ☉≈	11:59 pm	**8:59 pm**

26 Thu
1st ♈

☽♈ ⚹ ♂Ⅱ	5:40 am	**2:40 am**
☽♈ □ ☿♑	10:08 am	**7:08 am**
☽♈ ☌ ⚷♈	11:17 am	**8:17 am**
♀ enters ♓	9:33 pm	**6:33 pm**

FRI 27
1st ♈

☿♑ □ ⚷♈ 5:42 am **2:42 am**
☽♈ ⚹ ♄♒ 10:13 am **7:13 am**
☽♈ □ ♇♑ 4:01 pm **1:01 pm** ☽ v/c
☽ enters ♉ 6:42 pm **3:42 pm**
☽♉ ⚹ ♀♓ 8:56 pm **5:56 pm**

SAT 28
1st ♉
◐ 2nd Quarter 8 ♉ 26

☽♉ □ ☉♒ 10:19 am **7:19 am**
☽♉ △ ☿♑ 8:44 pm **5:44 pm**
☽♉ ☌ ♅♉ 10:37 pm **7:37 pm**

SUN 29
2nd ♉

☽♉ ⚹ ♆♓ 3:02 pm **12:02 pm**
☽♉ □ ♄♒ 7:03 pm **4:03 pm**
☉♒ △ ♂♊ 8:45 pm **5:45 pm**
☿♑ △ ♅♉ 9:16 pm **6:16 pm**
☽♉ △ ♇♑ **9:52 pm** ☽ v/c

OP: After Moon squares Saturn today until Moon enters Gemini on Monday. If you enjoy staying up late on Sunday nights, this is a great chance to begin a new project.

Eastern Standard Time (EST) plain / **Pacific Standard Time (PST) bold**

DECEMBER 2022

S	M	T	W	T	F	S
				1	2	3
4	5	6	7	8	9	10
11	12	13	14	15	16	17
18	19	20	21	22	23	24
25	26	27	28	29	30	31

JANUARY

S	M	T	W	T	F	S
1	2	3	4	5	6	7
8	9	10	11	12	13	14
15	16	17	18	19	20	21
22	23	24	25	26	27	28
29	30	31				

FEBRUARY

S	M	T	W	T	F	S
			1	2	3	4
5	6	7	8	9	10	11
12	13	14	15	16	17	18
19	20	21	22	23	24	25
26	27	28				

30 MON
2nd ♉

☽♉ △ ♇♑	12:52 am		☽ v/c
☽ enters ♊	3:35 am	**12:35 am**	
☽♊ □ ♀♓	12:24 pm	**9:24 am**	
☽♊ ✶ ♃♈	3:01 pm	**12:01 pm**	
☽♊ ☌ ♂♊	11:27 pm	**8:27 pm**	
☽♊ △ ☉♒		**10:24 pm**	

31 TUE
2nd ♊

OP: After Moon squares Neptune today or on Wednesday until v/c Moon on Wednesday. It's the perfect time to connect with others and strengthen your mind. Night owls only!

☽♊ △ ☉♒	1:24 am		
☽♊ ✶ ⚷♈	4:25 am	**1:25 am**	
☽♊ ⚻ ☿♑	12:27 pm	**9:27 am**	
☽♊ □ ♆♓		**11:21 pm**	

1 WED
2nd ♊

☽♊ □ ♆♓	2:21 am		
☽♊ △ ♄♒	6:58 am	**3:58 am**	☽ v/c
☽♊ ⚻ ♇♑	12:33 pm	**9:33 am**	
☉♒ ✶ ⚷♈	2:27 pm	**11:27 am**	
☽ enters ♋	3:11 pm	**12:11 pm**	

2 THU
2nd ♋

GROUNDHOG DAY

IMBOLC

☽♋ □ ♃♈	3:55 am	**12:55 am**	
☽♋ △ ♀♓	7:15 am	**4:15 am**	
☽♋ □ ⚷♈	4:49 pm	**1:49 pm**	
☽♋ ⚻ ☉♒	7:12 pm	**4:12 pm**	
☽♋ ✶ ♅♉	9:27 pm	**6:27 pm**	

February

☽⊗ ☌ ☿ ♑	7:09 am	**4:09 am**
☽⊗ △ ♆ ♓	3:02 pm	**12:02 pm**
☽⊗ ⚻ ♄ ≈	8:09 pm	**5:09 pm**
☉≈ □ ♅ ♉	9:50 pm	**6:50 pm**
☽⊗ ☌ ♀ ♑		**10:19 pm** ☽ v/c

Fri 3
2nd ♋

☽⊗ ☌ ♀ ♑	1:19 am	☽ v/c
☽ enters ♌	3:48 am	**12:48 am**
☽♌ △ ♃ ♈	5:34 pm	**2:34 pm**
♀♓ □ ♂ ♊	10:29 pm	**7:29 pm**
☽♌ ✶ ♂ ♊		**11:35 pm**
☽♌ ⚻ ♀ ♓		**11:58 pm**

Sat 4
2nd ♋

☽♌ ✶ ♂ ♊	2:35 am	
☽♌ ⚻ ♀ ♓	2:58 am	
☽♌ △ ♃ ♈	5:39 am	**2:39 am**
☽♌ □ ♅ ♉	10:08 am	**7:08 am**
☽♌ ☍ ☉≈	1:29 pm	**10:29 am**
☽♌ ⚻ ☿ ♑		**11:37 pm**

Sun 5
2nd ♌
○ Full Moon 16 ♌ 41

Eastern Standard Time (EST) plain / **Pacific Standard Time (PST) bold**

JANUARY								FEBRUARY								MARCH					
S	M	T	W	T	F	S	S	M	T	W	T	F	S	S	M	T	W	T	F	S
1	2	3	4	5	6	7				1	2	3	4				1	2	3	4
8	9	10	11	12	13	14	5	6	7	8	9	10	11	5	6	7	8	9	10	11
15	16	17	18	19	20	21	12	13	14	15	16	17	18	12	13	14	15	16	17	18
22	23	24	25	26	27	28	19	20	21	22	23	24	25	19	20	21	22	23	24	25
29	30	31					26	27	28					26	27	28	29	30	31	

February

6 Mon
3rd ♌

☽ ♌ ⊼ ☿ ♑	2:37 am	
☽ ♌ ⊼ ♆ ♓	3:44 am	**12:44 am**
☽ ♌ ☍ ♄ ♒	9:15 am	**6:15 am** ☽ v/c
☿ ♑ ⚹ ♆ ♓	1:26 pm	**10:26 am**
☽ ♌ ⊼ ♀ ♑	1:56 pm	**10:56 am**
☽ enters ♍	4:14 pm	**1:14 pm**

7 Tue
3rd ♍

☽ ♍ ⊼ ♃ ♈	6:51 am	**3:51 am**
☽ ♍ □ ♂ ♊	4:05 pm	**1:05 pm**
☽ ♍ ⊼ ⚷ ♈	5:58 pm	**2:58 pm**
☽ ♍ ☍ ♀ ♓	10:01 pm	**7:01 pm**
☽ ♍ △ ♅ ♉	10:16 pm	**7:16 pm**
♀ ♓ ⚹ ♅ ♉		**9:29 pm**

8 Wed
3rd ♍

OP: After Moon opposes Neptune today until v/c Moon today or on Thursday. Wait two hours after the opposition for clarity. This OP is good for anything, including creativity, romance, or practical matters.

♀ ♓ ⚹ ♅ ♉	12:29 am	
☽ ♍ ⊼ ☉ ♒	6:58 am	**3:58 am**
☽ ♍ ☍ ♆ ♓	3:40 pm	**12:40 pm**
☽ ♍ △ ☿ ♑	9:30 pm	**6:30 pm**
☽ ♍ ⊼ ♄ ♒	9:32 pm	**6:32 pm**
☽ ♍ △ ♀ ♑		**10:40 pm** ☽ v/c

9 Thu
3rd ♍

☽ ♍ △ ♀ ♑	1:40 am	☽ v/c
☽ enters ♎	3:47 am	**12:47 am**
☽ ♎ ☍ ♃ ♈	7:02 pm	**4:02 pm**

February

Fri 10
3rd ♎

☽︎ ⚺ △ ♂ ♊	4:25 am	**1:25 am**
☽︎ ⚺ ☍ ⚸ ♈	5:05 am	**2:05 am**
☽︎ ⚺ ⚻ ♅ ♉	9:08 am	**6:08 am**
☿ ♑ ☌ ♀ ♑	12:16 pm	**9:16 am**
☽︎ ⚺ ⚻ ♀ ♓	3:18 pm	**12:18 pm**
☽︎ ⚺ △ ☉ ♒	10:39 pm	**7:39 pm**
☽︎ ⚺ ⚻ ♆ ♓		**11:04 pm**

Sat 11
3rd ♎

☽︎ ⚺ ⚻ ♆ ♓	2:04 am	
☿ enters ♒	6:22 am	**3:22 am**
☽︎ ⚺ △ ♄ ♒	8:07 am	**5:07 am**
☽︎ ⚺ ☐ ♀ ♑	11:41 am	**8:41 am** ☽︎ v/c
♂ ♊ ⚹ ⚸ ♈	1:02 pm	**10:02 am**
☽︎ enters ♏	1:34 pm	**10:34 am**
☽︎ ♏ ☐ ☿ ♒	2:27 pm	**11:27 am**

Sun 12
3rd ♏

☽︎ ♏ ⚻ ♃ ♈	5:07 am	**2:07 am**
☽︎ ♏ ⚻ ⚸ ♈	1:57 pm	**10:57 am**
☽︎ ♏ ⚻ ♂ ♊	2:28 pm	**11:28 am**
☽︎ ♏ ☍ ♅ ♉	5:43 pm	**2:43 pm**

Eastern Standard Time (EST) plain / **Pacific Standard Time (PST) bold**

		JANUARY				
S	M	T	W	T	F	S
1	2	3	4	5	6	7
8	9	10	11	12	13	14
15	16	17	18	19	20	21
22	23	24	25	26	27	28
29	30	31				

		FEBRUARY				
S	M	T	W	T	F	S
			1	2	3	4
5	6	7	8	9	10	11
12	13	14	15	16	17	18
19	20	21	22	23	24	25
26	27	28				

		MARCH				
S	M	T	W	T	F	S
			1	2	3	4
5	6	7	8	9	10	11
12	13	14	15	16	17	18
19	20	21	22	23	24	25
26	27	28	29	30	31	

February

13 Mon
3rd ♏
◐ 4th Quarter 24 ♏ 40

☽♏ △ ♀♓	5:16 am	**2:16 am**
☽♏ △ ♆♓	9:49 am	**6:49 am**
☽♏ □ ☉♒	11:01 am	**8:01 am**
☽♏ □ ♄♒	3:53 pm	**12:53 pm**
☽♏ ⚹ ♇♑	6:52 pm	**3:52 pm** ☽ v/c
☽ enters ♐	8:31 pm	**5:31 pm**

14 Tue
4th ♐
Valentine's Day

☽♐ ⚹ ☿♒	3:39 am	**12:39 am**
☽♐ △ ♃♈	11:56 am	**8:56 am**
☽♐ △ ⚷♈	7:34 pm	**4:34 pm**
☽♐ ☍ ♂♊	9:06 pm	**6:06 pm**
☽♐ ⚻ ♅♉	10:59 pm	**7:59 pm**

15 Wed
4th ♐

OP: After Moon squares Venus today until Moon enters Capricorn today or on Thursday. This is a unique time to open up, work with groups, and establish long-lasting connections.

♀♓ ☌ ♆♓	7:25 am	**4:25 am**
☽♐ □ ♆♓	2:06 pm	**11:06 am**
☽♐ □ ♀♓	2:43 pm	**11:43 am**
☽♐ ⚹ ☉♒	7:03 pm	**4:03 pm**
☽♐ ⚹ ♄♒	8:06 pm	**5:06 pm** ☽ v/c
☽ enters ♑		**9:00 pm**

16 Thu
4th ♑

OP: After Moon squares Jupiter today until v/c Moon on Friday. Use this Last Quarter Moon OP to wrap up ongoing projects and accomplish goals.

☽ enters ♑	12:00 am	
☉♒ ☌ ♄♒	11:48 am	**8:48 am**
☽♑ □ ♃♈	3:11 pm	**12:11 pm**
☽♑ □ ⚷♈	9:46 pm	**6:46 pm**
☽♑ ⚻ ♂♊		**9:12 pm**
☽♑ △ ♅♉		**9:55 pm**

FRI 17
4th ♑

☽♑ ⚻ ♂♊ 12:12 am
☽♑ △ ♅♉ 12:55 am
☽♑ ⚹ ♆♓ 3:16 pm **12:16 pm**
☽♑ ⚹ ♀♓ 8:06 pm **5:06 pm**
☿♒ ⚹ ♃♈ 9:13 pm **6:13 pm**
☽♑ ☌ ♇♑ 11:18 pm **8:18 pm** ☽ v/c
☽ enters ♒ **9:35 pm**

SAT 18
4th ♑
SUN ENTERS PISCES

☽ enters ♒ 12:35 am
☽♒ ⚹ ♃♈ 3:51 pm **12:51 pm**
☉ enters ♓ 5:34 pm **2:34 pm**
☽♒ ☌ ☿♒ 5:35 pm **2:35 pm**
☽♒ ⚹ ⚷♈ 9:42 pm **6:42 pm**
☽♒ □ ♅♉ **9:42 pm**
☽♒ △ ♂♊ **10:01 pm**

SUN 19
4th ♒
● New Moon 1 ♓ 22 (Pacific)

☽♒ □ ♅♉ 12:42 am
☽♒ △ ♂♊ 1:01 am
♀♓ ⚹ ♇♑ 12:05 pm **9:05 am**
☽♒ ☌ ♄♒ 9:00 pm **6:00 pm** ☽ v/c
☽ enters ♓ 11:56 pm **8:56 pm**
☽♓ ☌ ☉♓ **11:06 pm**
♀ enters ♈ **11:56 pm**

Eastern Standard Time (EST) plain / **Pacific Standard Time (PST) bold**

JANUARY

S	M	T	W	T	F	S
1	2	3	4	5	6	7
8	9	10	11	12	13	14
15	16	17	18	19	20	21
22	23	24	25	26	27	28
29	30	31				

FEBRUARY

S	M	T	W	T	F	S
			1	2	3	4
5	6	7	8	9	10	11
12	13	14	15	16	17	18
19	20	21	22	23	24	25
26	27	28				

MARCH

S	M	T	W	T	F	S
			1	2	3	4
5	6	7	8	9	10	11
12	13	14	15	16	17	18
19	20	21	22	23	24	25
26	27	28	29	30	31	

February

20 Mon
4th ♓
● New Moon 1 ♓ 22 (Eastern)
Presidents' Day

☽♓ ☌ ☉♓	2:06 am	
♀ enters ♈	2:56 am	
☿♒ ⚹ ⚷♈	11:59 am	**8:59 am**
☽♓ ⚹ ♅♉		**9:20 pm**
☽♓ □ ♂♊		**10:44 pm**

21 Tue
1st ♓
Mardi Gras (Fat Tuesday)
OP: After Moon conjoins Neptune today until Moon enters Aries today or on Wednesday. This is the time to take part in the arts, have fun, expand your mind, or even indulge your romantic side.

☽♓ ⚹ ♅♉	12:20 am	
☽♓ □ ♂♊	1:44 am	
☽♓ ☌ ♆♓	2:52 pm	**11:52 am**
☿♒ □ ♅♉	5:22 pm	**2:22 pm**
☽♓ ⚹ ♇♑	11:06 pm	**8:06 pm** ☽ v/c
☽ enters ♈		**9:14 pm**

22 Wed
1st ♓
Ash Wednesday

☽ enters ♈	12:14 am	
☽♈ ☌ ♀♈	4:26 am	**1:26 am**
☿♒ △ ♂♊	3:14 pm	**12:14 pm**
☽♈ ☌ ♃♈	5:48 pm	**2:48 pm**
☽♈ ☌ ⚷♈	10:56 pm	**7:56 pm**

23 Thu
1st ♈

☽♈ ⚹ ♂♊	4:44 am	**1:44 am**
☽♈ ⚹ ☿♒	6:03 am	**3:03 am**
☽♈ ⚹ ♄♒		**10:06 pm**
☽♈ □ ♇♑		**11:22 pm** ☽ v/c

☽♈ ⚹ ♄♒	1:06 am			**Fri 24** 1st ♈
☽♈ □ ♇♑	2:22 am		☽ v/c	
☽ enters ♉	3:29 am	**12:29 am**		
☽♉ ⚹ ☉♓	2:02 pm	**11:02 am**		

☽♉ ☌ ♅♉	7:25 am	**4:25 am**	**Sat 25** 1st ♉
☽♉ □ ☿♒	7:16 pm	**4:16 pm**	
☽♉ ⚹ ♆♓		**9:15 pm**	

☽♉ ⚹ ♆♓	12:15 am			**Sun 26** 1st ♉
☽♉ □ ♄♒	8:45 am	**5:45 am**		
☽♉ △ ♇♑	9:42 am	**6:42 am**	☽ v/c	
☽ enters ♊	10:48 am	**7:48 am**		

OP: After Moon squares Saturn until Moon enters Gemini. This is a promising time for innovative, transformative work. Get up early so you can catch it!

Eastern Standard Time (EST) plain / **Pacific Standard Time (PST) bold**

JANUARY

S	M	T	W	T	F	S
1	2	3	4	5	6	7
8	9	10	11	12	13	14
15	16	17	18	19	20	21
22	23	24	25	26	27	28
29	30	31				

FEBRUARY

S	M	T	W	T	F	S
			1	2	3	4
5	6	7	8	9	10	11
12	13	14	15	16	17	18
19	20	21	22	23	24	25
26	27	28				

MARCH

S	M	T	W	T	F	S
			1	2	3	4
5	6	7	8	9	10	11
12	13	14	15	16	17	18
19	20	21	22	23	24	25
26	27	28	29	30	31	

February • March

27 Mon
1st ♊
◐ 2nd Quarter 8 ♊ 27

☽♊ □ ☉♓	3:06 am	**12:06 am**
☽♊ ⚹ ♀♈	3:24 am	**12:24 am**
☽♊ ⚹ ♃♈	9:08 am	**6:08 am**
☽♊ ⚹ ⚷♈	1:30 pm	**10:30 am**
☽♊ ☌ ♂♊	11:21 pm	**8:21 pm**

28 Tue
2nd ♊

OP: After Moon squares Neptune until v/c Moon. Wait two hours after the square. The waxing Moon favors continuous growth, and this OP is good for clarity, communication, connections, etc.

☽♊ □ ♆♓	10:46 am	**7:46 am**
☽♊ △ ☿♒	2:27 pm	**11:27 am**
☽♊ △ ♄♒	8:07 pm	**5:07 pm** ☽ v/c
☽♊ ⚻ ♀♑	8:40 pm	**5:40 pm**
☽ enters ♋	9:40 pm	**6:40 pm**

1 Wed
2nd ♋

☽♋ △ ☉♓	8:10 pm	**5:10 pm**
☽♋ □ ♀♈	9:50 pm	**6:50 pm**
☽♋ □ ♃♈	10:04 pm	**7:04 pm**
♀♈ ☌ ♃♈		**9:36 pm**
☽♋ □ ⚷♈		**10:41 pm**

2 Thu
2nd ♋

♀♈ ☌ ♃♈	12:36 am	
☽♋ □ ⚷♈	1:41 am	
☽♋ ⚹ ♅♉	5:03 am	**2:03 am**
☿♒ ☌ ♄♒	9:34 am	**6:34 am**
☿ enters ♓	5:52 pm	**2:52 pm**
☽♋ △ ♆♓	11:23 pm	**8:23 pm**

March

Fri 3
2nd ♋

- ☽♋ ⚻ ♄♒ 9:19 am **6:19 am**
- ☽♋ ☍ ♀♑ 9:22 am **6:22 am** ☽ v/c
- ☽ enters ♌ 10:16 am **7:16 am**
- ♀♈ ☌ ⚷♈ 12:48 pm **9:48 am**
- ☽♌ ⚻ ☿♓ 1:01 pm **10:01 am**

Sat 4
2nd ♌

- ☽♌ △ ♃♈ 11:56 am **8:56 am**
- ☽♌ ⚻ ☉♓ 2:27 pm **11:27 am**
- ☽♌ △ ⚷♈ 2:38 pm **11:38 am**
- ☽♌ △ ♀♈ 5:28 pm **2:28 pm**
- ☽♌ □ ♅♉ 5:54 pm **2:54 pm**

Sun 5
2nd ♌

- ☽♌ ⚹ ♂♊ 4:26 am **1:26 am**
- ☽♌ ⚻ ♆♓ 12:06 pm **9:06 am**
- ☽♌ ⚻ ♀♑ 9:54 pm **6:54 pm**
- ☽♌ ☍ ♄♒ 10:18 pm **7:18 pm** ☽ v/c
- ☽ enters ♍ 10:38 pm **7:38 pm**

Eastern Standard Time (EST) plain / **Pacific Standard Time (PST) bold**

	FEBRUARY							MARCH							APRIL					
S	M	T	W	T	F	S	S	M	T	W	T	F	S	S	M	T	W	T	F	S
			1	2	3	4				1	2	3	4							1
5	6	7	8	9	10	11	5	6	7	8	9	10	11	2	3	4	5	6	7	8
12	13	14	15	16	17	18	12	13	14	15	16	17	18	9	10	11	12	13	14	15
19	20	21	22	23	24	25	19	20	21	22	23	24	25	16	17	18	19	20	21	22
26	27	28					26	27	28	29	30	31		23	24	25	26	27	28	29
														30						

March

6 Mon
2nd ♍
Purim begins at sundown

☉ ⚹ ♅ ♉	8:42 am	**5:42 am**
☽♍ ☍ ☿ ♓	11:32 am	**8:32 am**
☽♍ ☌ ♃ ♈		**10:00 pm**
☽♍ ☌ ⚷ ♈		**11:46 pm**

7 Tue
2nd ♍
○ Full Moon 16 ♍ 40

☽♍ ☌ ♃ ♈	1:00 am	
☽♍ ☌ ⚷ ♈	2:46 am	
☽♍ △ ♅ ♉	5:51 am	**2:51 am**
☽♍ ☍ ☉ ♓	7:40 am	**4:40 am**
♄ enters ♓	8:35 am	**5:35 am**
☽♍ ☌ ♀ ♈	11:53 am	**8:53 am**
☽♍ □ ♂ ♊	6:06 pm	**3:06 pm**
☽♍ ☍ ♆ ♓	11:39 pm	**8:39 pm**

8 Wed
3rd ♍

☽♍ △ ♇ ♑	9:07 am	**6:07 am** ☽ v/c
☽ enters ♎	9:44 am	**6:44 am**
☽♎ ☌ ♄ ♓	9:58 am	**6:58 am**

9 Thu
3rd ♎

☽♎ ☌ ☿ ♓	8:10 am	**5:10 am**
☽♎ ☍ ♃ ♈	12:27 pm	**9:27 am**
☽♎ ☍ ⚷ ♈	1:20 pm	**10:20 am**
☽♎ ☌ ♅ ♉	4:15 pm	**1:15 pm**
☽♎ ☌ ☉ ♓	10:52 pm	**7:52 pm**

March

Fri 10
3rd ♎

☽♎ ☍ ♀♈	4:07 am	**1:07 am**
☽♎ △ ♂♊	6:00 am	**3:00 am**
☽♎ ⚻ ♆♓	9:30 am	**6:30 am**
☽♎ □ ♇♑	6:37 pm	**3:37 pm** ☽ v/c
☽ enters ♏	7:06 pm	**4:06 pm**
☽♏ △ ♄♓	7:51 pm	**4:51 pm**

Sat 11
3rd ♏

♀♈ ⚹ ♂♊	10:05 am	**7:05 am**
☿♓ ⚹ ♅♉	4:04 pm	**1:04 pm**
☽♏ ⚻ ♃♈	9:55 pm	**6:55 pm**
☽♏ ⚻ ⚷♈	9:58 pm	**6:58 pm**
☽♏ ☍ ♅♉		**9:43 pm**
♃♈ ☌ ⚷♈		**10:53 pm**
☽♏ △ ☿♓		**11:07 pm**

Sun 12
3rd ♏

DAYLIGHT SAVING TIME BEGINS AT 2:00 A.M.

OP: After Moon opposes Uranus on Saturday or today until v/c Moon today or on Monday. This is a good time to have meaningful conversations and process emotions during the waning phase of the Moon.

☽♏ ☍ ♅♉	12:43 am	
♃♈ ☌ ⚷♈	1:53 am	
☽♏ △ ☿♓	3:07 am	
☽♏ △ ☉♓	12:32 pm	**9:32 am**
☽♏ ⚻ ♄♓	4:43 pm	**1:43 pm**
☽♏ △ ♆♓	6:18 pm	**3:18 pm**
☽♏ ⚻ ♀♈	6:37 pm	**3:37 pm**
☽♏ ⚹ ♇♑		**11:58 pm** ☽ v/c

Eastern Standard Time (EST) becomes Eastern Daylight Time (EDT) March 12 (plain)
Pacific Standard Time (PST) becomes Pacific Daylight Time (PDT) March 12 (bold)

FEBRUARY	MARCH	APRIL
S M T W T F S	S M T W T F S	S M T W T F S
1 2 3 4	1 2 3 4	1
5 6 7 8 9 10 11	5 6 7 8 9 10 11	2 3 4 5 6 7 8
12 13 14 15 16 17 18	12 13 14 15 16 17 18	9 10 11 12 13 14 15
19 20 21 22 23 24 25	19 20 21 22 23 24 25	16 17 18 19 20 21 22
26 27 28	26 27 28 29 30 31	23 24 25 26 27 28 29
		30

March

13 Mon
3rd ♏

☽♏ ✶ ♀♍	2:58 am	☽ v/c
☽ enters ♐	3:21 am	**12:21 am**
☽♐ □ ♄♓	4:34 am	**1:34 am**

14 Tue
3rd ♐

● 4th Quarter 24 ♐ 13

OP: After Moon opposes Mars today until Moon enters Capricorn on Wednesday. A good Tuesday night that's better for play than for work, so have some fun with it!

☽♐ △ ⚷♈	5:16 am	**2:16 am**
☽♐ △ ♃♈	5:57 am	**2:57 am**
☽♐ ⊼ ♅♉	7:49 am	**4:49 am**
☽♐ □ ☿♓	5:38 pm	**2:38 pm**
♂♊ □ ♆♓	7:39 pm	**4:39 pm**
☽♐ □ ☉♓	10:08 pm	**7:08 pm**
☽♐ □ ♆♓	11:38 pm	**8:38 pm**
☽♐ ☍ ♂♊	11:45 pm	**8:45 pm**

15 Wed
4th ♐

☽♐ △ ♀♈	4:50 am	**1:50 am** ☽ v/c
☽ enters ♑	8:06 am	**5:06 am**
☽♑ ✶ ♄♓	9:41 am	**6:41 am**
☉♓ ☌ ♆♓	7:39 pm	**4:39 pm**

16 Thu
4th ♑

OP: After Moon squares Jupiter today until v/c Moon on Friday. This Last Quarter Moon OP is a productive time for practical matters, though it is best to avoid debates.

☽♑ □ ⚷♈	8:59 am	**5:59 am**
☽♑ □ ♃♈	10:17 am	**7:17 am**
☽♑ △ ♅♉	11:22 am	**8:22 am**
☿♓ ☌ ♆♓	1:13 pm	**10:13 am**
☉♓ □ ♂♊	2:10 pm	**11:10 am**
♀♈ □ ♀♑	3:59 pm	**12:59 pm**
♀ enters ♉	6:34 pm	**3:34 pm**
☿♓ □ ♂♊		**9:49 pm**
☽♑ ✶ ♆♓		**11:26 pm**

108

March

Fri 17
4th ♑
St. Patrick's Day

☿♓ □ ♂Ⅱ 12:49 am
☽♑ ⚹ ♆♓ 2:26 am
☽♑ ⚻ ♂Ⅱ 4:04 am **1:04 am**
☽♑ ⚹ ☿♓ 4:28 am **1:28 am**
☽♑ ⚹ ☉♓ 4:37 am **1:37 am**
☉♓ ☌ ☿♓ 6:45 am **3:45 am**
☽♑ ☌ ♀♑ 10:14 am **7:14 am** ☽ v/c
☽ enters ♒ 10:25 am **7:25 am**
☽♒ □ ♀♉ 11:50 am **8:50 am**
♀♉ ⚹ ♄♓ 6:25 pm **3:25 pm**

Sat 18
4th ♒

☽♒ ⚹ ⚷♈ 10:35 am **7:35 am**
☽♒ ⚹ ♃♈ 12:27 pm **9:27 am**
☽♒ □ ♅♉ 12:50 pm **9:50 am**
☿♓ ⚹ ♀♑ 11:24 pm **8:24 pm**
☿ enters ♈ **9:24 pm**

OP: After Moon squares Uranus today until v/c Moon on Sunday. This is a creative time that is perfect for innovative insights!

Sun 19
4th ♒

☿ enters ♈ 12:24 am
☽♒ △ ♂Ⅱ 6:33 am **3:33 am** ☽ v/c
☽ enters ♓ 11:12 am **8:12 am**
☽♓ ☌ ♄♓ 1:28 pm **10:28 am**
☽♓ ⚹ ♀♉ 4:54 pm **1:54 pm**

Eastern Daylight Time (EDT) plain / **Pacific Daylight Time (PDT) bold**

FEBRUARY	MARCH	APRIL
S M T W T F S	S M T W T F S	S M T W T F S
1 2 3 4	1 2 3 4	1
5 6 7 8 9 10 11	5 6 7 8 9 10 11	2 3 4 5 6 7 8
12 13 14 15 16 17 18	12 13 14 15 16 17 18	9 10 11 12 13 14 15
19 20 21 22 23 24 25	19 20 21 22 23 24 25	16 17 18 19 20 21 22
26 27 28	26 27 28 29 30 31	23 24 25 26 27 28 29
		30

March

20 Mon
4th ♓
Spring Equinox
Ostara
Sun enters Aries
International Astrology Day

☽♓ ⚹ ♅♉ 1:34 pm **10:34 am**
☉♓ ⚹ ♀♑ 4:12 pm **1:12 pm**
☉ enters ♈ 5:24 pm **2:24 pm**

21 Tue
4th ♓
● New Moon 0 ♈ 50

OP: This Cazimi Moon is usable ½ hour before and ½ hour after the Sun-Moon conjunction. Perfect for new beginnings. If you have something important to start around now, this is a great time to do it.

☽♓ ☌ ♆♓ 4:20 am **1:20 am**
☽♓ □ ♂♊ 8:55 am **5:55 am**
☽♓ ⚹ ♀♑ 11:58 am **8:58 am** ☽ v/c
☽ enters ♈ 12:01 pm **9:01 am**
☽♈ ☌ ☉♈ 1:23 pm **10:23 am**
☽♈ ☌ ☿♈ 9:34 pm **6:34 pm**

22 Wed
1st ♈
Ramadan begins at sundown

☽♈ ☌ ⚷♈ 1:05 pm **10:05 am**
☽♈ ☌ ♃♈ 4:17 pm **1:17 pm**

23 Thu
1st ♈

OP: After Moon sextiles Saturn today until v/c Moon on Saturday. This intense and long OP is suitable for anything you want to see grow, from finances to deep romance.

♀ enters ♒ 8:13 am **5:13 am**
☽♈ ⚹ ♂♊ 1:13 pm **10:13 am** ☽ v/c
☽ enters ♉ 2:42 pm **11:42 am**
☽♉ □ ♀♒ 2:42 pm **11:42 am**
☽♉ ⚹ ♄♓ 5:57 pm **2:57 pm**

Fri 24
1st ♉

☽♉ ☌ ♀♉	6:31 am	**3:31 am**
☽♉ ☌ ♅♉	7:52 pm	**4:52 pm**

Sat 25
1st ♉

♂ enters ♋	7:45 am	**4:45 am**
♂♋ ⚻ ♇♒	9:34 am	**6:34 am**
☽♉ ⚹ ♆♓	12:19 pm	**9:19 am** ☽ v/c
☽ enters ♊	8:42 pm	**5:42 pm**
☽♊ △ ♇♒	8:46 pm	**5:46 pm**
☽♊ □ ♄♓		**9:38 pm**

Sun 26
1st ♊

☽♊ □ ♄♓	12:38 am	
☽♊ ⚹ ☉♈	7:03 am	**4:03 am**
☿♈ ☌ ⚷♈	2:58 pm	**11:58 am**
☽♊ ⚹ ⚷♈		**10:41 pm**

Eastern Daylight Time (EDT) plain / **Pacific Daylight Time (PDT) bold**

FEBRUARY

S	M	T	W	T	F	S
			1	2	3	4
5	6	7	8	9	10	11
12	13	14	15	16	17	18
19	20	21	22	23	24	25
26	27	28				

MARCH

S	M	T	W	T	F	S
			1	2	3	4
5	6	7	8	9	10	11
12	13	14	15	16	17	18
19	20	21	22	23	24	25
26	27	28	29	30	31	

APRIL

S	M	T	W	T	F	S
						1
2	3	4	5	6	7	8
9	10	11	12	13	14	15
16	17	18	19	20	21	22
23	24	25	26	27	28	29
30						

March

27 Mon
1st ♊

☽♊ ✶ ⚷♈	1:41 am	
☽♊ ✶ ☿♈	3:39 am	**12:39 am**
☽♊ ✶ ♃♈	6:57 am	**3:57 am**
☽♊ □ ♆♓	9:39 pm	**6:39 pm** ☽ v/c
☿♈ ☌ ♃♈		**11:50 pm**

28 Tue
1st ♊
● 2nd Quarter 8 ♋ 09

☿♈ ☌ ♃♈	2:50 am	
☽ enters ♋	6:22 am	**3:22 am**
☽♋ ⊼ ♀≈	6:32 am	**3:32 am**
☽♋ ☌ ♂♋	9:19 am	**6:19 am**
☽♋ △ ♄♓	11:04 am	**8:04 am**
☽♋ □ ☉♈	10:32 pm	**7:32 pm**

29 Wed
2nd ♋

OP: After Moon squares Mercury today or on Thursday until Moon enters Leo on Thursday. The Moon in Cancer is usually conservative, but with Venus conjunct Uranus, it is a favorable opportunity to try something out of the ordinary.

☽♋ ✶ ♀♉	12:50 pm	**9:50 am**
☽♋ □ ⚷♈	1:09 pm	**10:09 am**
☽♋ ✶ ♅♉	3:40 pm	**12:40 pm**
☽♋ □ ♃♈	7:35 pm	**4:35 pm**
☽♋ □ ☿♈		**11:30 pm**

30 Thu
2nd ♋

☽♋ □ ☿♈	2:30 am	
☽♋ △ ♆♓	9:45 am	**6:45 am** ☽ v/c
♂♋ △ ♄♓	3:03 pm	**12:03 pm**
♀♉ ☌ ♅♉	6:26 pm	**3:26 pm**
☽ enters ♌	6:31 pm	**3:31 pm**
☽♌ ☍ ♀≈	6:46 pm	**3:46 pm**
☽♌ ⊼ ♄♓	11:51 pm	**8:51 pm**

March • April

☽♌ △ ☉♈	4:29 pm	**1:29 pm**	
☽♌ △ ☫♈		**11:02 pm**	

Fri 31
2nd ♌

☽♌ △ ☫♈	2:02 am		
☽♌ □ ♅♉	4:30 am	**1:30 am**	
☽♌ □ ♀♉	8:06 am	**5:06 am**	
☽♌ △ ♃♈	9:25 am	**6:25 am**	
☽♌ ⚻ ♆♓	10:28 pm	**7:28 pm**	
☽♌ △ ☿♈		**11:03 pm**	☽ v/c

Sat 1
2nd ♌
April Fools' Day

OP: After Moon squares Venus today until v/c Moon today or on Sunday. With the waxing Moon between benefic planets, this OP can be used for anything that piques your interest.

☽♌ △ ☿♈	2:03 am	☽ v/c	
☽ enters ♍	6:57 am	**3:57 am**	
☽♍ ⚻ ♀♒	7:16 am	**4:16 am**	
☽♍ ☍ ♄♓	12:44 pm	**9:44 am**	
☽♍ ⚹ ♂♋	3:08 pm	**12:08 pm**	

Sun 2
2nd ♌
Palm Sunday

Eastern Daylight Time (EDT) plain / **Pacific Daylight Time (PDT) bold**

FEBRUARY							**MARCH**							**APRIL**						
S	M	T	W	T	F	S	S	M	T	W	T	F	S	S	M	T	W	T	F	S
			1	2	3	4				1	2	3	4							1
5	6	7	8	9	10	11	5	6	7	8	9	10	11	2	3	4	5	6	7	8
12	13	14	15	16	17	18	12	13	14	15	16	17	18	9	10	11	12	13	14	15
19	20	21	22	23	24	25	19	20	21	22	23	24	25	16	17	18	19	20	21	22
26	27	28					26	27	28	29	30	31		23	24	25	26	27	28	29
														30						

April

3 Mon
2nd ♍

☽♍ ⚼ ☉♈ 9:49 am **6:49 am**
☿ enters ♉ 12:22 pm **9:22 am**
☽♍ ⚼ ⚷♈ 2:07 pm **11:07 am**
☿♉ □ ♀♒ 2:55 pm **11:55 am**
☽♍ △ ♅♉ 4:28 pm **1:28 pm**
☽♍ ⚼ ♃♈ 10:12 pm **7:12 pm**
☽♍ △ ♀♉ **11:04 pm**

4 Tue
2nd ♍

☽♍ △ ♀♉ 2:04 am
☽♍ ☍ ♆♓ 9:50 am **6:50 am** ☽ v/c
☽ enters ♎ 5:51 pm **2:51 pm**
☽♎ △ ♀♒ 6:13 pm **3:13 pm**
☽♎ ⚼ ☿♉ 10:16 pm **7:16 pm**
☽♎ ⚼ ♄♓ 11:54 pm **8:54 pm**

5 Wed
2nd ♎
○ Full Moon 16 ♎ 07 (Pacific)
Passover begins at sundown

☽♎ □ ♂♋ 4:12 am **1:12 am**
☿♉ ✶ ♄♓ 12:21 pm **9:21 am**
☉♈ ☌ ⚷♈ 6:18 pm **3:18 pm**
☽♎ ☍ ⚷♈ **9:07 pm**
☽♎ ☍ ☉♈ **9:34 pm**
☽♎ ⚼ ♅♉ **11:21 pm**

6 Thu
2nd ♎
○ Full Moon 16 ♎ 07 (Eastern)

☽♎ ☍ ⚷♈ 12:07 am
☽♎ ☍ ☉♈ 12:34 am
☽♎ ⚼ ♅♉ 2:21 am
☽♎ ☍ ♃♈ 8:43 am **5:43 am** ☽ v/c
☽♎ ⚼ ♀♉ 5:06 pm **2:06 pm**
☽♎ ⚼ ♆♓ 6:57 pm **3:57 pm**
☽ enters ♏ **11:29 pm**
☽♏ □ ♀♒ **11:54 pm**

April

Fri 7
3rd ♎
Good Friday

☽ enters ♏	2:29 am
☽♏ □ ♀♒	2:54 am
☽♏ △ ♄♓	8:44 am **5:44 am**
☽♏ ☍ ☿♉	1:53 pm **10:53 am**
♀♉ ⚹ ♆♓	1:58 pm **10:58 am**
☽♏ △ ♂♋	2:42 pm **11:42 am**
☿♉ ⚹ ♂♋	**11:29 pm**

Sat 8
3rd ♏

☿♉ ⚹ ♂♋	2:29 am
☽♏ ⚻ ♅♈	7:49 am **4:49 am**
☽♏ ☍ ♅♉	9:56 am **6:56 am**
☽♏ ⚻ ☉♈	12:27 pm **9:27 am**
☽♏ ⚻ ♃♈	4:51 pm **1:51 pm**
☽♏ △ ♆♓	**10:50 pm**

Sun 9
3rd ♏
Easter

☽♏ △ ♆♓	1:50 am
☽♏ ☍ ♀♉	5:09 am **2:09 am** ☽ v/c
☽ enters ♐	8:57 am **5:57 am**
☽♐ ⚹ ♀♒	9:23 am **6:23 am**
☽♐ □ ♄♓	3:21 pm **12:21 pm**
☽♐ ⚻ ♂♋	10:51 pm **7:51 pm**
☽♐ ⚻ ☿♉	**10:23 pm**

Eastern Daylight Time (EDT) plain / **Pacific Daylight Time (PDT) bold**

	MARCH								APRIL								MAY					
S	M	T	W	T	F	S	S	M	T	W	T	F	S	S	M	T	W	T	F	S
			1	2	3	4							1		1	2	3	4	5	6
5	6	7	8	9	10	11	2	3	4	5	6	7	8	7	8	9	10	11	12	13
12	13	14	15	16	17	18	9	10	11	12	13	14	15	14	15	16	17	18	19	20
19	20	21	22	23	24	25	16	17	18	19	20	21	22	21	22	23	24	25	26	27
26	27	28	29	30	31		23	24	25	26	27	28	29	28	29	30	31			
							30													

April

10 Mon
3rd ♐

☽ ♐ ⊼ ☿ ♉	1:23 am	
☽ ♐ △ ♆ ♈	1:28 pm	**10:28 am**
☽ ♐ ⊼ ♅ ♉	3:29 pm	**12:29 pm**
☽ ♐ △ ☉ ♈	9:48 pm	**6:48 pm**
☽ ♐ △ ♃ ♈	10:55 pm	**7:55 pm**
♀ enters ♊		**9:47 pm**

11 Tue
3rd ♐

♀ enters ♊	12:47 am	
♀ ♊ △ ♀ ♒	6:14 am	**3:14 am**
☽ ♐ □ ♆ ♓	6:48 am	**3:48 am** ☽ v/c
☽ enters ♑	1:33 pm	**10:33 am**
☽ ♑ ⊼ ♀ ♊	2:43 pm	**11:43 am**
☉ ♈ ☌ ♃ ♈	6:07 pm	**3:07 pm**
☽ ♑ ⚹ ♄ ♓	8:08 pm	**5:08 pm**

12 Wed
3rd ♑

☽ ♑ ☍ ♂ ♋	5:03 am	**2:03 am**
☽ ♑ △ ☿ ♉	9:35 am	**6:35 am**
☽ ♑ □ ♆ ♈	5:27 pm	**2:27 pm**
☽ ♑ △ ♅ ♉	7:24 pm	**4:24 pm**

13 Thu
3rd ♑

◐ 4th Quarter 23 ♑ 11

PASSOVER ENDS

OP: After Moon squares the Sun until v/c Moon. There is a short window of time to finish up ongoing projects during this Last Quarter Moon OP. It is the last chance before Mercury slows down and turns retrograde.

☽ ♑ □ ♃ ♈	3:20 am	**12:20 am**
☽ ♑ □ ☉ ♈	5:11 am	**2:11 am**
☽ ♑ ⚹ ♆ ♓	10:14 am	**7:14 am** ☽ v/c
☽ enters ♒	4:42 pm	**1:42 pm**
☽ ♒ ☌ ♀ ♒	5:11 pm	**2:11 pm**
☽ ♒ △ ♀ ♊	10:23 pm	**7:23 pm**

Mercury Note: Mercury enters its Storm (moving less than 40 minutes of arc per day) on Saturday, as it slows down before going retrograde. The Storm acts like the retrograde. Not favorable to start new projects—just follow through with the items that are already on your plate. Write down new ideas with date and time they occurred.

Fri 14

4th ≈

Orthodox Good Friday

☽≈ ⊼ ♂♋	9:47 am	**6:47 am**
♀♊ □ ♄♓	12:38 pm	**9:38 am**
☽≈ □ ☿♉	3:16 pm	**12:16 pm**
☽≈ ⚹ ⚷♈	8:14 pm	**5:14 pm**
☽≈ □ ♅♉	10:08 pm	**7:08 pm**

Sat 15

4th ≈

☽≈ ⚹ ♃♈	6:36 am	**3:36 am**
☽≈ ⚹ ☉♈	11:16 am	**8:16 am** ☽ v/c
☽ enters ♓	6:57 pm	**3:57 pm**
☽♓ ☌ ♄♓		**10:58 pm**

Sun 16

4th ♓

Orthodox Easter

☽♓ ☌ ♄♓	1:58 am	
☽♓ □ ♀♊	4:58 am	**1:58 am**
☽♓ △ ♂♋	1:49 pm	**10:49 am**
☽♓ ⚹ ☿♉	7:24 pm	**4:24 pm**
☽♓ ⚹ ♅♉		**9:25 pm**

OP: After Moon squares Venus today until Moon enters Aries on Monday. This OP is favorable for the arts, meditation, and connecting with others.

Eastern Daylight Time (EDT) plain / **Pacific Daylight Time (PDT) bold**

MARCH

S	M	T	W	T	F	S
			1	2	3	4
5	6	7	8	9	10	11
12	13	14	15	16	17	18
19	20	21	22	23	24	25
26	27	28	29	30	31	

APRIL

S	M	T	W	T	F	S
						1
2	3	4	5	6	7	8
9	10	11	12	13	14	15
16	17	18	19	20	21	22
23	24	25	26	27	28	29
30						

MAY

S	M	T	W	T	F	S
	1	2	3	4	5	6
7	8	9	10	11	12	13
14	15	16	17	18	19	20
21	22	23	24	25	26	27
28	29	30	31			

April

17 Mon
4th ♓

☽♓ ⚹ ♅♉	12:25 am		
☽♓ ☌ ♆♓	2:57 pm	**11:57 am**	☽ v/c
☽ enters ♈	9:09 pm	**6:09 pm**	
☽♈ ⚹ ♇♒	9:42 pm	**6:42 pm**	

18 Tue
4th ♈

☽♈ ⚹ ♀♊	11:47 am	**8:47 am**
☽♈ □ ♂♋	6:16 pm	**3:16 pm**
☽♈ ☌ ⚷♈		**10:25 pm**

19 Wed
4th ♈
Solar Eclipse | ● New Moon 29 ♈ 50 (Pacific)

☽♈ ☌ ⚷♈	1:25 am		
☽♈ ☌ ♃♈	1:27 pm	**10:27 am**	
☽♈ ☌ ☉♈		**9:13 pm**	☽ v/c
☽ enters ♉		**9:30 pm**	
☽♉ □ ♇♒		**10:04 pm**	

20 Thu
4th ♈
Solar Eclipse | ● New Moon 29 ♈ 50 (Eastern)
Sun enters Taurus

☽♈ ☌ ☉♈	12:13 am		☽ v/c
☽ enters ♉	12:30 am		
☽♉ □ ♇♒	1:04 am		
☉ enters ♉	4:14 am	**1:14 am**	
☽♉ ⚹ ♄♓	8:30 am	**5:30 am**	
☉♉ □ ♇♒	12:27 pm	**9:27 am**	
☽♉ ⚹ ♂♋		**9:37 pm**	

Mercury Note: Mercury goes retrograde on Friday, April 21, and remains so until May 14, after which it will still be in its Storm until May 24. Projects initiated during this entire period may not work out as planned. It's best to use this time for reviews, editing, escrows, and so forth.

Fri 21

1st ♉

Ramadan ends

Mercury retrograde

☽♉ ⚹ ♂♋ 12:37 am

☽♉ ☌ ☿♉ 4:05 am **1:05 am**

☿℞ 4:35 am **1:35 am**

☽♉ ☌ ♅♉ 8:09 am **5:09 am**

☽♉ ⚹ ♆♓ 11:41 pm **8:41 pm** ☽ v/c

OP: After Moon conjoins Uranus today until Moon enters Gemini on Saturday. Mercury is retrograde and we are now between two eclipses. It is best to focus and use this OP for practical matters.

Sat 22

1st ♉

Earth Day

☽ enters ♊ 6:11 am **3:11 am**

☽♊ △ ♇♒ 6:49 am **3:49 am**

☽♊ □ ♄♓ 3:00 pm **12:00 pm**

Sun 23

1st ♊

☽♊ ☌ ♀♊ 8:43 am **5:43 am**

☽♊ ⚹ ⚷♈ 1:47 pm **10:47 am**

☿♉ ⚹ ♂♋ 11:19 pm **8:19 pm**

Eastern Daylight Time (EDT) plain / **Pacific Daylight Time (PDT) bold**

MARCH

S	M	T	W	T	F	S
			1	2	3	4
5	6	7	8	9	10	11
12	13	14	15	16	17	18
19	20	21	22	23	24	25
26	27	28	29	30	31	

APRIL

S	M	T	W	T	F	S
						1
2	3	4	5	6	7	8
9	10	11	12	13	14	15
16	17	18	19	20	21	22
23	24	25	26	27	28	29
30						

MAY

S	M	T	W	T	F	S
	1	2	3	4	5	6
7	8	9	10	11	12	13
14	15	16	17	18	19	20
21	22	23	24	25	26	27
28	29	30	31			

April

24 Mon
1st ♊

☽♊ ⚹ ♃♈	4:49 am	**1:49 am**
☽♊ □ ♆♓	8:15 am	**5:15 am** ☽ v/c
☽ enters ♋	2:58 pm	**11:58 am**
☽♋ ⚻ ♀♒	3:40 pm	**12:40 pm**
☽♋ ⚹ ☉♉		**9:11 pm**
☽♋ △ ♄♓		**9:40 pm**

25 Tue
1st ♋

☽♋ ⚹ ☉♉	12:11 am	
☽♋ △ ♄♓	12:40 am	
☉♉ ⚹ ♄♓	6:48 am	**3:48 am**
☽♋ ⚹ ☿♉	7:47 pm	**4:47 pm**
♀♊ ⚹ ⚷♈	7:50 pm	**4:50 pm**
☽♋ ☌ ♂♋	11:08 pm	**8:08 pm**
☽♋ □ ⚷♈		**9:32 pm**
☽♋ ⚹ ♅♉		**11:45 pm**

26 Wed
1st ♋

OP: After Moon squares Jupiter today until Moon enters Leo today or on Thursday. (Cancer is one of the four signs in which the v/c Moon is a good thing. See page 77.) This short OP is an opportunity to get in touch with loved ones, although the warning from last Friday still applies.

☽♋ □ ⚷♈	12:32 am	
☽♋ ⚹ ♅♉	2:45 am	
☽♋ □ ♃♈	5:09 pm	**2:09 pm**
☽♋ △ ♆♓	7:41 pm	**4:41 pm** ☽ v/c
☽ enters ♌		**11:30 pm**

27 Thu
1st ♋
◐ 2nd Quarter 7 ♌ 21

☽ enters ♌	2:30 am	
☽♌ ☍ ♀♒	3:13 am	**12:13 am**
♂♋ □ ⚷♈	9:34 am	**6:34 am**
☽♌ ⚻ ♄♓	12:54 pm	**9:54 am**
☽♌ □ ☉♉	5:20 pm	**2:20 pm**

April

Fri 28
2nd ♌

☽♌ □ ☿ ♉	5:44 am	**2:44 am**
☽♌ △ ♃ ♈	1:11 pm	**10:11 am**
☽♌ □ ♅ ♉	3:26 pm	**12:26 pm**
☽♌ ✶ ♀ ♊	7:42 pm	**4:42 pm**

OP: After Moon squares Uranus today until v/c Moon on Saturday. This OP is a great opportunity for creativity and love; same warning as for last Friday.

Sat 29
2nd ♌

☽♌ △ ♃ ♈	6:53 am	**3:53 am**	☽ v/c
☽♌ ⚻ ♆ ♓	8:20 am	**5:20 am**	
☽ enters ♍	2:59 pm	**11:59 am**	
☽♍ ⚻ ♀ ♒	3:43 pm	**12:43 pm**	
♂♋ ✶ ♅ ♉	4:05 pm	**1:05 pm**	
☽♍ ☍ ♄ ♓		**10:41 pm**	

Sun 30
2nd ♍

☽♍ ☍ ♄ ♓	1:41 am	
☽♍ △ ☉ ♉	10:59 am	**7:59 am**
☽♍ △ ☿ ♉	3:05 pm	**12:05 pm**
☽♍ ⚻ ♃ ♈		**10:26 pm**

Eastern Daylight Time (EDT) plain / **Pacific Daylight Time (PDT) bold**

MARCH

S	M	T	W	T	F	S
			1	2	3	4
5	6	7	8	9	10	11
12	13	14	15	16	17	18
19	20	21	22	23	24	25
26	27	28	29	30	31	

APRIL

S	M	T	W	T	F	S
						1
2	3	4	5	6	7	8
9	10	11	12	13	14	15
16	17	18	19	20	21	22
23	24	25	26	27	28	29
30						

MAY

S	M	T	W	T	F	S
	1	2	3	4	5	6
7	8	9	10	11	12	13
14	15	16	17	18	19	20
21	22	23	24	25	26	27
28	29	30	31			

May

1 Mon
2nd ♍
BELTANE
PLUTO RETROGRADE

☽♍ ⚻ ♅♈	1:26 am	
☽♍ △ ♅♉	3:38 am	**12:38 am**
☽♍ ⚹ ♂♋	5:08 am	**2:08 am**
♀℞	1:09 pm	**10:09 am**
☽♍ □ ♀♊	1:31 pm	**10:31 am**
☉♉ ☌ ☿♉	7:28 pm	**4:28 pm**
☽♍ ⚻ ♃♈	7:30 pm	**4:30 pm**
☽♍ ☍ ♆♓	7:53 pm	**4:53 pm** ☽ v/c
☽ enters ♎		**11:09 pm**
☽♎ △ ♀♒		**11:51 pm**

2 Tue
2nd ♍

☽ enters ♎	2:09 am	
☽♎ △ ♀♒	2:51 am	
☽♎ ⚻ ♄♓	12:46 pm	**9:46 am**
☽♎ ⚻ ☿♉	10:26 pm	**7:26 pm**
☽♎ ⚻ ☉♉		**11:09 pm**

3 Wed
2nd ♎

☽♎ ⚻ ☉♉	2:09 am	
☽♎ ☍ ♅♈	11:20 am	**8:20 am**
☽♎ ⚻ ♅♉	1:26 pm	**10:26 am**
☽♎ □ ♂♋	5:10 pm	**2:10 pm**

4 Thu
2nd ♎

OP: After Moon trines Venus until v/c Moon. The Moon lies between two benefics during this short and lovely OP. Night owls should use this time for communication and promotion.

☽♎ △ ♀♊	3:54 am	**12:54 am**
☽♎ ⚻ ♆♓	4:43 am	**1:43 am**
☽♎ ☍ ♃♈	5:17 am	**2:17 am** ☽ v/c
☽ enters ♏	10:32 am	**7:32 am**
☽♏ □ ♀♒	11:12 am	**8:12 am**
♀♊ □ ♆♓	1:40 pm	**10:40 am**
☽♏ △ ♄♓	8:53 pm	**5:53 pm**
♀♊ ⚹ ♃♈		**9:03 pm**

MAY

♀Ⅱ ⚹ ♃♈	12:03 am	
☽♏ ☍ ☿♉	3:15 am	**12:15 am**
☽♏ ☍ ☉♉	1:34 pm	**10:34 am**
☽♏ ⚻ ⚷♈	6:12 pm	**3:12 pm**
☽♏ ☍ ♅♉	8:13 pm	**5:13 pm**
☽♏ △ ♂♋		**10:51 pm**

Fri 5
2nd ♏
Lunar Eclipse | ○ Full Moon 14 ♏ 58
Cinco de Mayo
OP: After Moon trines Mars today or on Saturday until v/c Moon on Saturday. After the eclipse, this emotional time can be a positive opportunity to sort out deep feelings.

☽♏ △ ♂♋	1:51 am	
☽♏ △ ♆♓	10:38 am	**7:38 am** ☽ v/c
☽♏ ⚻ ♃♈	11:59 am	**8:59 am**
☽♏ ⚻ ♀Ⅱ	2:28 pm	**11:28 am**
☽ enters ♐	4:04 pm	**1:04 pm**
☽♐ ⚹ ♀♒	4:41 pm	**1:41 pm**
☽♐ □ ♄♓		**11:12 pm**

Sat 6
3rd ♏

☽♐ □ ♄♓	2:12 am	
☽♐ ⚻ ☿♉	5:58 am	**2:58 am**
♀ enters ♋	10:25 am	**7:25 am**
♀♋ ⚻ ♀♒	6:10 pm	**3:10 pm**
☽♐ ⚻ ☉♉	9:50 pm	**6:50 pm**
☽♐ △ ⚷♈	10:36 pm	**7:36 pm**
☽♐ ⚻ ♅♉		**9:34 pm**

Sun 7
3rd ♐

Eastern Daylight Time (EDT) plain / **Pacific Daylight Time (PDT) bold**

APRIL							MAY							JUNE						
S	M	T	W	T	F	S	S	M	T	W	T	F	S	S	M	T	W	T	F	S
						1		1	2	3	4	5	6					1	2	3
2	3	4	5	6	7	8	7	8	9	10	11	12	13	4	5	6	7	8	9	10
9	10	11	12	13	14	15	14	15	16	17	18	19	20	11	12	13	14	15	16	17
16	17	18	19	20	21	22	21	22	23	24	25	26	27	18	19	20	21	22	23	24
23	24	25	26	27	28	29	28	29	30	31				25	26	27	28	29	30	
30																				

May

8 Mon
3rd ♐

OP: After Moon squares Neptune until Moon enters Capricorn. (Sagittarius is one of the four signs in which the v/c Moon is a good thing. See page 77.) Utilize these Monday hours for creative work. Since Mercury remains retrograde, use this time to review and edit unfinished projects.

☽♐ ⚻ ♅♉   12:34 am
☽♐ ⚻ ♂♋   7:55 am **4:55 am**
☽♐ □ ♆♓   2:22 pm **11:22 am**
☽♐ △ ♃♈   4:28 pm **1:28 pm** ☽ v/c
☽ enters ♑ 7:33 pm **4:33 pm**
☽♑ ☍ ♀♋ 10:20 pm **7:20 pm**

9 Tue
3rd ♑

☽♑ ✶ ♄♓   5:39 am **2:39 am**
☽♑ △ ☿♉   7:28 am **4:28 am**
☉♉ ☌ ♅♉   3:56 pm **12:56 pm**
☽♑ □ ⚷♈   **10:35 pm**

10 Wed
3rd ♑

☽♑ □ ⚷♈   1:35 am
☽♑ △ ♅♉   3:32 am **12:32 am**
☽♑ △ ☉♉   4:20 am **1:20 am**
☽♑ ☍ ♂♋   12:38 pm **9:38 am**
☽♑ ✶ ♆♓   5:03 pm **2:03 pm**
☽♑ □ ♃♈   7:52 pm **4:52 pm** ☽ v/c
☽ enters ♒ 10:05 pm **7:05 pm**
☽♒ ☌ ♀♒ 10:40 pm **7:40 pm**

11 Thu
3rd ♒

☽♒ ⚻ ♀♋   5:01 am **2:01 am**
☽♒ □ ☿♉   8:45 am **5:45 am**

Mercury Note: Mercury goes direct on Sunday, May 14, but remains in its Storm, moving slowly, until May 24.

Fri 12

3rd ♒

◑ 4th Quarter 21 ♒ 37

☽♒ ⚹ ⚷♈	4:14 am	**1:14 am**	
☿♉ ⚹ ♄♓	4:42 am	**1:42 am**	
☽♒ □ ♅♉	6:12 am	**3:12 am**	
☽♒ □ ☉♉	10:28 am	**7:28 am**	
☽♒ ⚻ ♂♋	5:13 pm	**2:13 pm**	
☿♉ ⚹ ♀♋	10:44 pm	**7:44 pm**	
☽♒ ⚹ ♃♈	11:15 pm	**8:15 pm**	☽ v/c
☽ enters ♓		**9:39 pm**	
♀♋ △ ♄♓		**11:57 pm**	

OP: After Moon squares the Sun until v/c Moon. Excellent OP for group activities or whatever interests you, aided by the easy aspect between Mercury and Venus.

Sat 13

4th ♒

☽ enters ♓	12:39 am	
♀♋ △ ♄♓	2:57 am	
☽♓ ⚹ ☿♉	10:44 am	**7:44 am**
☽♓ ☌ ♄♓	11:12 am	**8:12 am**
☽♓ △ ♀♋	11:51 am	**8:51 am**

OP: After Moon conjoins Saturn today until Moon enters Aries on Monday. An excellent time for the arts and healing.

Sun 14

4th ♓

Mother's Day

Mercury direct

☽♓ ⚹ ♅♉	9:22 am	**6:22 am**	
☽♓ ⚹ ☉♉	5:17 pm	**2:17 pm**	
☽♓ △ ♂♋	10:30 pm	**7:30 pm**	
☽♓ ☌ ♆♓	10:56 pm	**7:56 pm**	☽ v/c
☿ D	11:17 pm	**8:17 pm**	

Eastern Daylight Time (EDT) plain / **Pacific Daylight Time (PDT) bold**

APRIL

S	M	T	W	T	F	S
						1
2	3	4	5	6	7	8
9	10	11	12	13	14	15
16	17	18	19	20	21	22
23	24	25	26	27	28	29
30						

MAY

S	M	T	W	T	F	S
	1	2	3	4	5	6
7	8	9	10	11	12	13
14	15	16	17	18	19	20
21	22	23	24	25	26	27
28	29	30	31			

JUNE

S	M	T	W	T	F	S
				1	2	3
4	5	6	7	8	9	10
11	12	13	14	15	16	17
18	19	20	21	22	23	24
25	26	27	28	29	30	

May

15 Mon
4th ♓

☽ enters ♈ 3:56 am **12:56 am**
☽♈ ⚹ ♇♒ 4:29 am **1:29 am**
♂♋ △ ♆♓ 9:44 am **6:44 am**
☽♈ □ ♀♋ 7:42 pm **4:42 pm**

16 Tue
4th ♈

☽♈ ☌ ⚷♈ 11:29 am **8:29 am**
♃ enters ♉ 1:20 pm **10:20 am**

17 Wed
4th ♈

☽♈ □ ♂♋ 5:10 am **2:10 am** ☽ v/c
☽ enters ♉ 8:28 am **5:28 am**
☽♉ ☌ ♃♉ 8:47 am **5:47 am**
☽♉ □ ♇♒ 9:00 am **6:00 am**
☽♉ ☌ ☿♉ 7:27 pm **4:27 pm**
☽♉ ⚹ ♄♓ 7:57 pm **4:57 pm**
♃♉ □ ♇♒ 9:11 pm **6:11 pm**

18 Thu
4th ♉

☉♉ ⚹ ♆♓ 5:00 am **2:00 am**
☽♉ ⚹ ♀♋ 5:18 am **2:18 am**
☽♉ ☌ ♅♉ 7:28 pm **4:28 pm**
☿♉ ⚹ ♄♓ **11:40 pm**

126

☿♉ ⚹ ♄♓	2:40 am	
☽♉ ⚹ ♆♓	9:39 am	**6:39 am**
☽♉ ☌ ☉♉	11:53 am	**8:53 am**
☽♉ ⚹ ♂♋	1:51 pm	**10:51 am** ☽ v/c
☽ enters ♊	2:48 pm	**11:48 am**
☽♊ △ ♇♒	3:20 pm	**12:20 pm**
☽♊ □ ♄♓		**11:58 pm**

Fri 19

4th ♉

● New Moon 28 ♉ 25

OP: This Cazimi Moon is usable ½ hour before and ½ hour after the Sun-Moon conjunction. If you have something important to begin around now that's part of a larger project started before April 15, this is a great time to do it.

☽♊ □ ♄♓	2:58 am	
♂ enters ♌	11:31 am	**8:31 am**
♂♌ ☍ ♇♒	11:12 pm	**8:12 pm**
☽♊ ⚹ ⚷♈		**10:10 pm**

Sat 20

1st ♊

☽♊ ⚹ ⚷♈	1:10 am	
☉ enters ♊	3:09 am	**12:09 am**
☉♊ △ ♇♒	9:58 am	**6:58 am**
☽♊ □ ♆♓	6:12 pm	**3:12 pm** ☽ v/c
☽ enters ♋	11:28 pm	**8:28 pm**
☽♋ ⚻ ♇♒		**9:00 pm**
☽♋ ⚹ ♃♉		**10:54 pm**
☉♊ ⚹ ♂♌		**10:57 pm**

Sun 21

1st ♊

Sun enters Gemini

OP: After Moon enters Cancer today until Moon enters Leo on Wednesday. This rare entire-sign OP is suitable for virtually anything, including investments. However, with the stressful aspects of Mars, Jupiter, and Pluto, it is important to find a balance between desire and self-control.

Eastern Daylight Time (EDT) plain / **Pacific Daylight Time (PDT) bold**

APRIL

S	M	T	W	T	F	S
						1
2	3	4	5	6	7	8
9	10	11	12	13	14	15
16	17	18	19	20	21	22
23	24	25	26	27	28	29
30						

MAY

S	M	T	W	T	F	S
	1	2	3	4	5	6
7	8	9	10	11	12	13
14	15	16	17	18	19	20
21	22	23	24	25	26	27
28	29	30	31			

JUNE

S	M	T	W	T	F	S
				1	2	3
4	5	6	7	8	9	10
11	12	13	14	15	16	17
18	19	20	21	22	23	24
25	26	27	28	29	30	

May

Mercury Note: Mercury finally leaves its Storm on Thursday. Look over your notes on any ideas that occurred to you while Mercury was retrograde or slow. How do they look now?

22 Mon
1st ♋
Victoria Day (Canada)

☽♋ ⚻ ♀♒ 12:00 am
☽♋ ⚹ ♃♉ 1:54 am
☉♊ ⚹ ♂♌ 1:57 am
☽♋ △ ♄♓ 12:24 pm **9:24 am**
☽♋ ⚹ ☿♉ 3:07 pm **12:07 pm**
♂♌ □ ♃♉ **10:13 pm**

23 Tue
1st ♋

♂♌ □ ♃♉ 1:13 am
☽♋ ☌ ♀♋ 8:45 am **5:45 am**
☽♋ □ ⚷♈ 11:36 am **8:36 am**
☽♋ ⚹ ♅♉ 2:07 pm **11:07 am**

24 Wed
1st ♋

☽♋ △ ♆♓ 5:12 am **2:12 am** ☽ v/c
☽ enters ♌ 10:35 am **7:35 am**
☽♌ ☍ ♀♒ 11:04 am **8:04 am**
☽♌ □ ♃♉ 2:13 pm **11:13 am**
☽♌ ☌ ♂♌ 3:21 pm **12:21 pm**
☽♌ ⚹ ☉♊ 5:31 pm **2:31 pm**
♀♋ □ ⚷♈ 7:39 pm **4:39 pm**
☽♌ ⚻ ♄♓ **9:09 pm**

25 Thu
1st ♌
Shavuot begins at sundown

☽♌ ⚻ ♄♓ 12:09 am
☽♌ □ ☿♉ 6:11 am **3:11 am**
☽♌ △ ⚷♈ **9:00 pm**
☽♌ □ ♅♉ **11:38 pm** ☽ v/c

FRI 26
1st ♌

☽♌ △ ⚷♈	12:00 am		
☽♌ □ ♅♉	2:38 am		☽ v/c
♀♋ ⚹ ♅♉	3:37 am	**12:37 am**	
☽♌ ⚻ ♆♓	5:45 pm	**2:45 pm**	
☽ enters ♍	11:05 pm	**8:05 pm**	
☽♍ ⚻ ♇♒	11:31 pm	**8:31 pm**	

SAT 27
1st ♍
◐ 2nd Quarter 6 ♍ 06

☽♍ △ ♃♉	3:53 am	**12:53 am**
☽♍ □ ☉♊	11:22 am	**8:22 am**
☽♍ ☍ ♄♓	12:53 pm	**9:53 am**
☽♍ △ ☿♉	11:07 pm	**8:07 pm**

SUN 28
2nd ♍

☉♊ □ ♄♓	6:46 am	**3:46 am**
☽♍ ⚻ ⚷♈	12:33 pm	**9:33 am**
☽♍ △ ♅♉	3:12 pm	**12:12 pm**
☽♍ ⚹ ♀♋	8:19 pm	**5:19 pm**

Eastern Daylight Time (EDT) plain / **Pacific Daylight Time (PDT) bold**

APRIL

S	M	T	W	T	F	S
						1
2	3	4	5	6	7	8
9	10	11	12	13	14	15
16	17	18	19	20	21	22
23	24	25	26	27	28	29
30						

MAY

S	M	T	W	T	F	S
	1	2	3	4	5	6
7	8	9	10	11	12	13
14	15	16	17	18	19	20
21	22	23	24	25	26	27
28	29	30	31			

JUNE

S	M	T	W	T	F	S
				1	2	3
4	5	6	7	8	9	10
11	12	13	14	15	16	17
18	19	20	21	22	23	24
25	26	27	28	29	30	

May • June

29 Mon
2nd ♍

MEMORIAL DAY
OP: After Moon enters Libra today until v/c Moon on Wednesday. Another long OP that's even better than the last one; it relies on the mutual reception between the Moon and Venus, which makes it a fine time for strong connections and relationships.

☽♍ ☍ ♆♓　5:46 am　**2:46 am** ☽ v/c
☽ enters ♎　10:51 am　**7:51 am**
☽♎ △ ♀≈　11:13 am　**8:13 am**
☽♎ ⚻ ♃♉　4:33 pm　**1:33 pm**
☽♎ ⚹ ♂♌　9:21 pm　**6:21 pm**
☽♎ ⚻ ♄♓　　　　**9:18 pm**

30 Tue
2nd ♎

☽♎ ⚻ ♄♓　12:18 am
☽♎ △ ☉♊　3:39 am　**12:39 am**
☽♎ ⚻ ☿♉　2:50 pm　**11:50 am**
☽♎ ☍ ⚷♈　10:54 pm　**7:54 pm**
☽♎ ⚻ ♅♉　　　　**10:29 pm**

31 Wed
2nd ♎

☽♎ ⚻ ♅♉　1:29 am
☽♎ □ ♀♋　10:53 am　**7:53 am** ☽ v/c
☽♎ ⚻ ♆♓　3:02 pm　**12:02 pm**
☽ enters ♏　7:45 pm　**4:45 pm**
☽♏ □ ♀≈　8:02 pm　**5:02 pm**
☽♏ ☍ ♃♉　　　　**11:04 pm**

1 Thu
2nd ♏

☽♏ ☍ ♃♉　2:04 am
☽♏ □ ♂♌　8:11 am　**5:11 am**
☽♏ △ ♄♓　8:30 am　**5:30 am**
♂♌ ⚻ ♄♓　3:31 pm　**12:31 pm**
☽♏ ⚻ ☉♊　3:50 pm　**12:50 pm**
☽♏ ☍ ☿♉　　　　**11:53 pm**

June

Fri 2
2nd ♏

☽♏ ☌ ☿ ♉	2:53 am	
☽♏ ⚻ ♂ ♈	5:42 am	**2:42 am**
☽♏ ☌ ♅ ♉	8:10 am	**5:10 am**
♀♋ △ ♆ ♓	6:42 pm	**3:42 pm**
☽♏ △ ♆ ♓	8:42 pm	**5:42 pm**
☽♏ △ ♀ ♋	8:51 pm	**5:51 pm** ☽ v/c
☽ enters ♐		10:03 pm
☽♐ ⚹ ♇ ♒		10:16 pm

OP: After Moon opposes Uranus until v/c Moon. Wait two hours after the opposition and you'll get a powerful OP. This time is good for just about anything, from deep romance to hard work.

Sat 3
2nd ♏
○ Full Moon 13 ♐ 18

☽ enters ♐	1:03 am	
☽♐ ⚹ ♇ ♒	1:16 am	
☽♐ ⚻ ♃ ♉	7:48 am	**4:48 am**
☽♐ □ ♄ ♓	1:07 pm	**10:07 am**
☽♐ △ ♂ ♌	2:59 pm	**11:59 am**
☽♐ ☌ ☉ ♊	11:42 pm	**8:42 pm**

Sun 4
3rd ♐

☽♐ △ ♂ ♈	9:12 am	**6:12 am**
☽♐ ⚻ ☿ ♉	11:12 am	**8:12 am**
☽♐ ⚻ ♅ ♉	11:35 am	**8:35 am**
☿ ♉ ☌ ♅ ♉	3:49 pm	**12:49 pm**
☽♐ □ ♆ ♓	11:24 pm	**8:24 pm** ☽ v/c

Eastern Daylight Time (EDT) plain / **Pacific Daylight Time (PDT) bold**

MAY							JUNE							JULY						
S	M	T	W	T	F	S	S	M	T	W	T	F	S	S	M	T	W	T	F	S
	1	2	3	4	5	6					1	2	3							1
7	8	9	10	11	12	13	4	5	6	7	8	9	10	2	3	4	5	6	7	8
14	15	16	17	18	19	20	11	12	13	14	15	16	17	9	10	11	12	13	14	15
21	22	23	24	25	26	27	18	19	20	21	22	23	24	16	17	18	19	20	21	22
28	29	30	31				25	26	27	28	29	30		23	24	25	26	27	28	29
														30	31					

June

5 Mon
3rd ♐

OP: After Moon enters Capricorn today until v/c Moon on Tuesday or Wednesday. Long OP where you have Monday and Tuesday to be productive.

☽♐ ⚻ ♀♋	3:05 am	**12:05 am**
☽ enters ♑	3:31 am	**12:31 am**
♀ enters ♌	9:46 am	**6:46 am**
☽♑ △ ♃ ♉	10:44 am	**7:44 am**
♀♌ ☍ ♀≈	12:05 pm	**9:05 am**
☽♑ ✶ ♄ ♓	3:12 pm	**12:12 pm**
☽♑ ⚻ ♂♌	7:00 pm	**4:00 pm**

6 Tue
3rd ♑

☽♑ ⚻ ☉♊	4:51 am	**1:51 am**
☽♑ □ ☊ ♈	10:46 am	**7:46 am**
☽♑ △ ♅ ♉	1:10 pm	**10:10 am**
☽♑ △ ☿ ♉	5:34 pm	**2:34 pm**
☽♑ ✶ ♆ ♓		**9:40 pm** ☽ v/c

7 Wed
3rd ♑

☽♑ ✶ ♆ ♓	12:40 am	☽ v/c
☽ enters ≈	4:42 am	**1:42 am**
☽≈ ☌ ♀≈	4:48 am	**1:48 am**
☽≈ ☍ ♀♌	7:39 am	**4:39 am**
☽≈ □ ♃ ♉	12:35 pm	**9:35 am**
☽≈ ☍ ♂♌	10:11 pm	**7:11 pm**

8 Thu
3rd ≈

☽≈ △ ☉♊	9:29 am	**6:29 am**
☽≈ ✶ ☊ ♈	12:08 pm	**9:08 am**
☽≈ □ ♅ ♉	2:37 pm	**11:37 am**
☽≈ □ ☿ ♉		**9:24 pm** ☽ v/c

June

Fri 9
3rd ≈

☽≈ □ ☿♉	12:24 am	☽ v/c
☽ enters ♓	6:14 am **3:14 am**	
☽♓ ⊼ ♀♌	12:41 pm **9:41 am**	
☽♓ ⚹ ♃♉	3:02 pm **12:02 pm**	
☿♉ ⚹ ♆♓	5:14 pm **2:14 pm**	
☽♓ ☌ ♄♓	6:16 pm **3:16 pm**	
☽♓ ⊼ ♂♌	**11:20 pm**	

Sat 10
3rd ♓
☾ 4th Quarter 19 ♓ 40

☽♓ ⊼ ♂♌	2:20 am
☉♊ ⚹ ⚷♈	3:07 am **12:07 am**
☽♓ □ ☉♊	3:31 am **12:31 am**
☽♓ ⚹ ♅♉	5:21 am **2:21 am**

Sun 11
4th ♓

☽♓ ☌ ♆♓	5:09 am **2:09 am**	
♀ enters ♑	5:47 am **2:47 am**	
♅♉ △ ♀♑	6:26 am **3:26 am**	
☿ enters ♊	6:27 am **3:27 am**	
☽♓ ⚹ ♀♑	9:20 am **6:20 am** ☽ v/c	
☽ enters ♈	9:20 am **6:20 am**	
☽♈ ⚹ ☿♊	9:43 am **6:43 am**	
♀♌ □ ♃♉	11:40 am **8:40 am**	
☽♈ △ ♀♌	7:40 pm **4:40 pm**	

OP: After Moon conjoins Neptune until Moon enters Aries. (Pisces is one of the four signs in which the v/c Moon is a good thing. See page 77.) This is a good time to help others and deepen your connections.

Eastern Daylight Time (EDT) plain / **Pacific Daylight Time (PDT) bold**

MAY						
S	M	T	W	T	F	S
	1	2	3	4	5	6
7	8	9	10	11	12	13
14	15	16	17	18	19	20
21	22	23	24	25	26	27
28	29	30	31			

JUNE						
S	M	T	W	T	F	S
				1	2	3
4	5	6	7	8	9	10
11	12	13	14	15	16	17
18	19	20	21	22	23	24
25	26	27	28	29	30	

JULY						
S	M	T	W	T	F	S
						1
2	3	4	5	6	7	8
9	10	11	12	13	14	15
16	17	18	19	20	21	22
23	24	25	26	27	28	29
30	31					

June

12 Mon
4th ♈

☽♈ △ ♂♌	8:35 am	**5:35 am**
☽♈ ☌ ⚷♈	7:15 pm	**4:15 pm**
☽♈ ⚹ ☉♊	11:59 pm	**8:59 pm**

13 Tue
4th ♈

♀♌ ⚻ ♄♓	5:59 am	**2:59 am**
☽♈ □ ♇♑	2:27 pm	**11:27 am** ☽ v/c
☽ enters ♉	2:31 pm	**11:31 am**
☽♉ ☌ ♃♉		**10:40 pm**

14 Wed
4th ♉
Flag Day

☽♉ ☌ ♃♉	1:40 am	
☽♉ ⚹ ♄♓	3:36 am	**12:36 am**
☽♉ □ ♀♌	5:08 am	**2:08 am**
☽♉ □ ♂♌	5:15 pm	**2:15 pm**

15 Thu
4th ♉

OP: After Moon sextiles Neptune until Moon enters Gemini. (See "Translating Darkness" on page 80.) This interesting OP during the Last Quarter Moon can be used to finish up existing projects and to address practical matters.

☽♉ ☌ ♅♉	4:55 am	**1:55 am**
☿♊ □ ♄♓	12:09 pm	**9:09 am**
☽♉ ⚹ ♆♓	5:19 pm	**2:19 pm**
☽♉ △ ♇♑	9:36 pm	**6:36 pm** ☽ v/c
☽ enters ♊	9:46 pm	**6:46 pm**

June

Fri 16
4th ♊

☽♊ □ ♄♓ 11:20 am **8:20 am**
☽♊ ☌ ☿♊ 3:12 pm **12:12 pm**
☽♊ ✶ ♀♌ 4:57 pm **1:57 pm**

Sat 17
4th ♊
● New Moon 26 ♊ 43 (Pacific)
SATURN RETROGRADE

☽♊ ✶ ♂♌   4:14 am **1:14 am**
☽♊ ✶ ♅♈ 10:33 am **7:33 am**
☿♊ ✶ ♀♌ 11:29 am **8:29 am**
♄℞   1:27 pm **10:27 am**
☽♊ ☌ ☉♊   9:37 pm
☽♊ □ ♆♓   11:24 pm ☽ v/c

Sun 18
4th ♊
● New Moon 26 ♊ 43 (Eastern)
FATHER'S DAY

☽♊ ☌ ☉♊ 12:37 am
☽♊ □ ♆♓   2:24 am   ☽ v/c
☽♊ ⚻ ♇♑   6:43 am **3:43 am**
☽ enters ♋ 6:58 am **3:58 am**
☽♋ ✶ ♃♉   8:45 pm **5:45 pm**
☽♋ △ ♄♓   9:00 pm **6:00 pm**
☉♊ □ ♆♓ 11:54 pm **8:54 pm**

Eastern Daylight Time (EDT) plain / **Pacific Daylight Time (PDT) bold**

MAY							JUNE							JULY						
S	M	T	W	T	F	S	S	M	T	W	T	F	S	S	M	T	W	T	F	S
	1	2	3	4	5	6					1	2	3							1
7	8	9	10	11	12	13	4	5	6	7	8	9	10	2	3	4	5	6	7	8
14	15	16	17	18	19	20	11	12	13	14	15	16	17	9	10	11	12	13	14	15
21	22	23	24	25	26	27	18	19	20	21	22	23	24	16	17	18	19	20	21	22
28	29	30	31				25	26	27	28	29	30		23	24	25	26	27	28	29
														30	31					

June

19 Mon
1st ♋
Juneteenth

♃♉ ⚹ ♄♓	11:53 am	**8:53 am**
☽♋ □ ⚷♈	9:09 pm	**6:09 pm**
☽♋ ⚹ ♅♉		**9:33 pm**

20 Tue
1st ♋

☽♋ ⚹ ♅♉	12:33 am	
☽♋ △ ♆♓	1:24 pm	**10:24 am**
☽♋ ☍ ♇♑	5:43 pm	**2:43 pm** ☽ v/c
☽ enters ♌	6:04 pm	**3:04 pm**

21 Wed
1st ♌
Summer Solstice
Litha
Sun enters Cancer

☉♊ ⚻ ♇♑	6:20 am	**3:20 am**
☽♌ ⚻ ♄♓	8:30 am	**5:30 am**
☽♌ □ ♃♉	9:15 am	**6:15 am**
☉ enters ♋	10:58 am	**7:58 am**
☿♊ ⚹ ♂♌	11:23 am	**8:23 am**
☿♊ ⚹ ⚷♈	9:42 pm	**6:42 pm**
☽♌ ☌ ♀♌	11:08 pm	**8:08 pm**

22 Thu
1st ♌

☽♌ ☌ ♂♌	8:41 am	**5:41 am**
☽♌ △ ⚷♈	9:25 am	**6:25 am**
☽♌ ⚹ ☿♊	11:51 am	**8:51 am**
☽♌ □ ♅♉	1:01 pm	**10:01 am** ☽ v/c
♂♌ △ ⚷♈	11:52 pm	**8:52 pm**
☽♌ ⚻ ♆♓		**10:52 pm**

FRI 23
1st ♌

☽♌ ⚻ ♆♓	1:52 am	
☽♌ ⚻ ♇♑	6:08 am	**3:08 am**
☽ enters ♍	6:35 am	**3:35 am**
☽♍ ⚹ ☉♋	10:24 am	**7:24 am**
☽♍ ☍ ♄♓	9:07 pm	**6:07 pm**
☽♍ △ ♃♉	10:53 pm	**7:53 pm**

SAT 24
1st ♍

☽♍ ⚻ ⚷♈	10:13 pm	**7:13 pm**
☽♍ △ ♅♉		**10:53 pm**

SUN 25
1st ♍

☽♍ △ ♅♉	1:53 am	
☽♍ □ ☿♊	1:25 pm	**10:25 am**
☽♍ ☍ ♆♓	2:20 pm	**11:20 am**
☽♍ △ ♇♑	6:24 pm	**3:24 pm** ☽ v/c
☿♊ □ ♆♓	6:36 pm	**3:36 pm**
☽ enters ♎	6:57 pm	**3:57 pm**

OP: After Moon opposes Neptune until v/c Moon. Wait two hours after the opposition, then focus on what's important and use this opportunity for productivity.

Eastern Daylight Time (EDT) plain / **Pacific Daylight Time (PDT) bold**

MAY

S	M	T	W	T	F	S
	1	2	3	4	5	6
7	8	9	10	11	12	13
14	15	16	17	18	19	20
21	22	23	24	25	26	27
28	29	30	31			

JUNE

S	M	T	W	T	F	S
				1	2	3
4	5	6	7	8	9	10
11	12	13	14	15	16	17
18	19	20	21	22	23	24
25	26	27	28	29	30	

JULY

S	M	T	W	T	F	S
						1
2	3	4	5	6	7	8
9	10	11	12	13	14	15
16	17	18	19	20	21	22
23	24	25	26	27	28	29
30	31					

June

26 Mon
1st ♎
◐ 2nd Quarter 4 ♎ 29

☽♎□☉♋	3:50 am	**12:50 am**
♂♌□♅♉	5:23 am	**2:23 am**
☽♎⊼♄♓	9:04 am	**6:04 am**
☽♎⊼♃♉	11:44 am	**8:44 am**
☿♊⊼♀♑	5:07 pm	**2:07 pm**
☿ enters ♋	8:24 pm	**5:24 pm**

27 Tue
2nd ♎

☽♎⚹♀♌	6:56 am	**3:56 am**
☽♎☍⚷♈	9:22 am	**6:22 am**
☽♎⊼♅♉	12:58 pm	**9:58 am**
☽♎⚹♂♌	2:26 pm	**11:26 am**
☽♎⊼♆♓		**9:35 pm**

28 Wed
2nd ♎

☽♎⊼♆♓	12:35 am	
☽♎□♀♑	4:19 am	**1:19 am** ☽ v/c
☽ enters ♏	4:55 am	**1:55 am**
☽♏△☿♋	11:32 am	**8:32 am**
☽♏△☉♋	5:49 pm	**2:49 pm**
☽♏△♄♓	6:07 pm	**3:07 pm**
☽♏☍♃♉	9:29 pm	**6:29 pm**
☉♋△♄♓	9:43 pm	**6:43 pm**

29 Thu
2nd ♏

♀♌△⚷♈	4:41 am	**1:41 am**
☽♏⊼⚷♈	4:56 pm	**1:56 pm**
☽♏□♀♌	5:32 pm	**2:32 pm**
☽♏☍♅♉	8:22 pm	**5:22 pm**
☽♏□♂♌		**9:05 pm**
☿♋△♄♓		**11:24 pm**

June • July

Fri 30
2nd ♏

NEPTUNE RETROGRADE

☽♏ □ ♂♌	12:05 am	
☿♋ △ ♄♓	2:24 am	
☽♏ △ ♆♓	6:58 am	3:58 am
☽♏ ⚹ ♀♑	10:20 am	7:20 am ☽ v/c
☽ enters ♐	10:59 am	7:59 am
♆℞	5:07 pm	2:07 pm
☽♐ □ ♄♓	11:08 pm	8:08 pm
☉♋ ☌ ☿♋		10:06 pm
☽♐ ⚻ ☉♋		11:48 pm
☽♐ ⚻ ☿♋		11:58 pm

OP: After Moon squares Mars on Thursday or today until v/c Moon today. Wait two hours after the square, and the early morning is still available for getting things done the way you want.

Sat 1
2nd ♐

CANADA DAY

☉♋ ☌ ☿♋	1:06 am	
☽♐ ⚻ ☉♋	2:48 am	
☽♐ ⚻ ☿♋	2:58 am	
☽♐ ⚻ ♃♉	3:00 am	12:00 am
☿♋ ⚹ ♃♉	3:10 am	12:10 am
☉♋ ⚹ ♃♉	6:26 am	3:26 am
☽♐ △ ⚷♈	8:30 pm	5:30 pm
☽♐ △ ♀♌	11:21 pm	8:21 pm
☽♐ ⚻ ♅♉	11:48 pm	8:48 pm

Sun 2
2nd ♐

☽♐ △ ♂♌	5:19 am	2:19 am
☽♐ □ ♆♓	9:33 am	6:33 am ☽ v/c
♀♌ □ ♅♉	10:34 am	7:34 am
☽ enters ♑	1:20 pm	10:20 am
☽♑ ⚹ ♄♓		9:43 pm

Eastern Daylight Time (EDT) plain / **Pacific Daylight Time (PDT) bold**

MAY							JUNE							JULY						
S	M	T	W	T	F	S	S	M	T	W	T	F	S	S	M	T	W	T	F	S
	1	2	3	4	5	6					1	2	3							1
7	8	9	10	11	12	13	4	5	6	7	8	9	10	2	3	4	5	6	7	8
14	15	16	17	18	19	20	11	12	13	14	15	16	17	9	10	11	12	13	14	15
21	22	23	24	25	26	27	18	19	20	21	22	23	24	16	17	18	19	20	21	22
28	29	30	31				25	26	27	28	29	30		23	24	25	26	27	28	29
														30	31					

July

3 Mon
2nd ♑
○ Full Moon 11 ♑ 19

☽♑ ⚹ ♄♓	12:43 am	
☽♑ △ ♃♉	5:02 am	**2:02 am**
☽♑ ☍ ☉♋	7:39 am	**4:39 am**
☽♑ ☍ ☿♋	12:50 pm	**9:50 am**
☽♑ □ ⚷♈	9:14 pm	**6:14 pm**
☽♑ △ ♅♉		**9:30 pm**
☽♑ ⚻ ♀♌		**10:55 pm**

4 Tue
3rd ♑
INDEPENDENCE DAY

☽♑ △ ♅♉	12:30 am	
☽♑ ⚻ ♀♌	1:55 am	
☽♑ ⚻ ♂♌	7:43 am	**4:43 am**
☽♑ ⚹ ♆♓	9:49 am	**6:49 am**
☽♑ ☌ ♀♑	12:45 pm	**9:45 am** ☽ v/c
☽ enters ♒	1:30 pm	**10:30 am**

5 Wed
3rd ♒

☽♒ □ ♃♉	5:28 am	**2:28 am**
☽♒ ⚻ ☉♋	10:46 am	**7:46 am**
☽♒ ⚻ ☿♋	8:36 pm	**5:36 pm**
☽♒ ⚹ ⚷♈	9:09 pm	**6:09 pm**
☿♋ □ ⚷♈		**9:28 pm**
☽♒ □ ♅♉		**9:30 pm**

6 Thu
3rd ♒

☿♋ □ ⚷♈	12:28 am	
☽♒ □ ♅♉	12:30 am	
☽♒ ☍ ♀♌	3:38 am	**12:38 am**
☽♒ ☍ ♂♌	9:42 am	**6:42 am** ☽ v/c
♂♌ ⚻ ♆♓	11:48 am	**8:48 am**
☽ enters ♓	1:33 pm	**10:33 am**
☽♓ ☌ ♄♓		**9:47 pm**
♀♋ ⚹ ♅♉		**9:55 pm**

July

Fri 7
3rd ♓

☽♓ ☌ ♄♓ 12:47 am
☿♋ ⚹ ♅♉ 12:55 am
☽♓ ⚹ ♃♉ 6:28 am **3:28 am**
☽♓ △ ☉♋ 2:48 pm **11:48 am**
☽♓ ⚹ ♅♉ **10:48 pm**

OP: After Moon conjoins Saturn on Thursday or today until Moon enters Aries on Saturday. This long OP is a positive opportunity for the arts, meditation, having fun, and helping others.

Sat 8
3rd ♓

☽♓ ⚹ ♅♉ 1:48 am
☽♓ △ ☿♋ 5:56 am **2:56 am**
☽♓ ⚻ ♀♌ 6:42 am **3:42 am**
☽♓ ☌ ♆♓ 11:22 am **8:22 am**
☽♓ ⚻ ♂♌ 1:30 pm **10:30 am**
☽♓ ⚹ ♀♑ 2:22 pm **11:22 am** ☽ v/c
☽ enters ♈ 3:19 pm **12:19 pm**

Sun 9
3rd ♈
◐ 4th Quarter 17 ♈ 36

♂♌ ⚻ ♀♑ 8:54 am **5:54 am**
☿♋ △ ♆♓ 7:57 pm **4:57 pm**
☽♈ □ ☉♋ 9:48 pm **6:48 pm**
☽♈ ☌ ⚸♈ **10:51 pm**

Eastern Daylight Time (EDT) plain / **Pacific Daylight Time (PDT) bold**

		JUNE							JULY							AUGUST				
S	M	T	W	T	F	S	S	M	T	W	T	F	S	S	M	T	W	T	F	S
				1	2	3							1			1	2	3	4	5
4	5	6	7	8	9	10	2	3	4	5	6	7	8	6	7	8	9	10	11	12
11	12	13	14	15	16	17	9	10	11	12	13	14	15	13	14	15	16	17	18	19
18	19	20	21	22	23	24	16	17	18	19	20	21	22	20	21	22	23	24	25	26
25	26	27	28	29	30		23	24	25	26	27	28	29	27	28	29	30	31		
							30	31												

July

10 Mon
4th ♈

☽♈ ☌ ⚷♈	1:51 am	
♂ enters ♍	7:40 am	**4:40 am**
☽♈ △ ♀♌	12:34 pm	**9:34 am**
☿♋ ☍ ♀♑	4:48 pm	**1:48 pm**
☽♈ □ ♀♑	6:50 pm	**3:50 pm**
☽♈ □ ☿♋	7:11 pm	**4:11 pm** ☽ v/c
☽ enters ♉	7:55 pm	**4:55 pm**
☽♉ △ ♂♍	8:31 pm	**5:31 pm**
☿ enters ♌		**9:11 pm**

11 Tue
4th ♉

☿ enters ♌	12:11 am	
☽♉ ✶ ♄♓	8:11 am	**5:11 am**
☽♉ ☌ ♃♉	4:04 pm	**1:04 pm**

12 Wed
4th ♉

OP: After Moon squares Venus today until Moon enters Gemini on Thursday. The Last Quarter Moon provides the perfect chance for a productive evening of finishing ongoing projects.

☉♋ □ ⚷♈	8:06 am	**5:06 am**
☽♉ ✶ ☉♋	8:30 am	**5:30 am**
☽♉ ☌ ♅♉	12:42 pm	**9:42 am**
☽♉ □ ♀♌	9:24 pm	**6:24 pm**
☽♉ ✶ ♆♓	10:59 pm	**7:59 pm**
☽♉ △ ♀♑		**11:11 pm** ☽ v/c

13 Thu
4th ♉

☽♉ △ ♀♑	2:11 am	☽ v/c
☽ enters ♊	3:26 am	**12:26 am**
☽♊ □ ♂♍	6:51 am	**3:51 am**
☽♊ ✶ ☿♌	12:40 pm	**9:40 am**
☽♊ □ ♄♓	4:06 pm	**1:06 pm**

July

Fri 14
4th ♊

☿♌ ⚻ ♄♓ 11:17 am **8:17 am**
☽♊ ⚹ ♂♈ 5:37 pm **2:37 pm**
☉♋ ⚹ ♅♉ 7:02 pm **4:02 pm**

Sat 15
4th ♊

☽♊ ⚹ ♀♌ 8:27 am **5:27 am**
☽♊ □ ♆♓ 8:35 am **5:35 am** ☽ v/c
☽♊ ⚻ ♀♑ 11:49 am **8:49 am**
☽ enters ♋ 1:13 pm **10:13 am**
♀♌ ⚻ ♆♓ 2:42 pm **11:42 am**
☽♋ ⚹ ♂♍ 7:48 pm **4:48 pm**
☽♋ △ ♄♓ **11:06 pm**

Sun 16
4th ♋

☽♋ △ ♄♓ 2:06 am
☽♋ ⚹ ♃♉ 12:23 pm **9:23 am**

Eastern Daylight Time (EDT) plain / **Pacific Daylight Time (PDT) bold**

JUNE								JULY								AUGUST					
S	M	T	W	T	F	S	S	M	T	W	T	F	S	S	M	T	W	T	F	S
				1	2	3							1			1	2	3	4	5
4	5	6	7	8	9	10	2	3	4	5	6	7	8	6	7	8	9	10	11	12
11	12	13	14	15	16	17	9	10	11	12	13	14	15	13	14	15	16	17	18	19
18	19	20	21	22	23	24	16	17	18	19	20	21	22	20	21	22	23	24	25	26
25	26	27	28	29	30		23	24	25	26	27	28	29	27	28	29	30	31		
							30	31												

July

17 Mon
4th ♋
● New Moon 24 ♋ 56

OP: This Cazimi Moon is usable ½ hour before and ½ hour after the Sun-Moon conjunction. If you have something important to start around now, this is a great time to do it.

☽♋ □ ♅♈	4:35 am	**1:35 am**
☿♋ □ ♃♉	8:49 am	**5:49 am**
☽♋ ✶ ♅♉	9:21 am	**6:21 am**
☽♋ ☌ ☉♋	2:32 pm	**11:32 am**
☽♋ △ ♆♓	7:52 pm	**4:52 pm**
☽♋ ☍ ♇♑	11:06 pm	**8:06 pm** ☽ v/c
☽ enters ♌		**9:39 pm**

18 Tue
1st ♋
Islamic New Year begins at sundown

☽ enters ♌	12:39 am	
☽♌ ⚻ ♄♓	1:36 pm	**10:36 am**
☽♌ □ ♃♉		**10:02 pm**

19 Wed
1st ♌

OP: After Moon squares Uranus today until v/c Moon on Thursday. This OP is a great time for self-improvement, investments, or anything that will help support you later.

☽♌ □ ♃♉	1:02 am	
☽♌ ☌ ☿♌	7:23 am	**4:23 am**
☽♌ △ ♅♈	4:52 pm	**1:52 pm**
☽♌ □ ♅♉	9:51 pm	**6:51 pm**

20 Thu
1st ♌

☽♌ ⚻ ♆♓	8:19 am	**5:19 am**
☉♋ △ ♆♓	9:07 am	**6:07 am**
☽♌ ☌ ♀♌	10:08 am	**7:08 am** ☽ v/c
☽♌ ⚻ ♇♑	11:31 am	**8:31 am**
☽ enters ♍	1:13 pm	**10:13 am**
♂♍ ☍ ♄♓	4:39 pm	**1:39 pm**
☽♍ ☍ ♄♓		**11:03 pm**
☽♍ ☌ ♂♍		**11:36 pm**

July

Fri 21
1st ♍

☽♍ ☍ ♄♓ 2:03 am
☽♍ ☌ ♂♍ 2:36 am
☽♍ △ ♃♉ 2:30 pm **11:30 am**
☉⊗ ☍ ♀♑ 11:53 pm **8:53 pm**
☿♌ △ ⚷♈ **11:57 pm**

Sat 22
1st ♍
VENUS RETROGRADE
SUN ENTERS LEO

☿♌ △ ⚷♈ 2:57 am
☽♍ ⚹ ⚷♈ 5:41 am **2:41 am**
☽♍ △ ♅♉ 10:48 am **7:48 am**
☽♍ ☍ ♆♓ 9:00 pm **6:00 pm**
♀℞ 9:33 pm **6:33 pm**
☉ enters ♌ 9:50 pm **6:50 pm**
☽♍ △ ♀♑ **9:06 pm** ☽ v/c
☽ enters ♎ **10:54 pm**
☽♎ ⚹ ☉♌ **11:15 pm**

Sun 23
1st ♍
CHIRON RETROGRADE

☽♍ △ ♀♑ 12:06 am ☽ v/c
☽ enters ♎ 1:54 am
☽♎ ⚹ ☉♌ 2:15 am
⚷℞ 8:42 am **5:42 am**
☽♎ ⚼ ♄♓ 2:18 pm **11:18 am**
☿♌ □ ♅♉ 5:39 pm **2:39 pm**

Eastern Daylight Time (EDT) plain / **Pacific Daylight Time (PDT) bold**

		JUNE							JULY							AUGUST				
S	M	T	W	T	F	S	S	M	T	W	T	F	S	S	M	T	W	T	F	S
				1	2	3							1			1	2	3	4	5
4	5	6	7	8	9	10	2	3	4	5	6	7	8	6	7	8	9	10	11	12
11	12	13	14	15	16	17	9	10	11	12	13	14	15	13	14	15	16	17	18	19
18	19	20	21	22	23	24	16	17	18	19	20	21	22	20	21	22	23	24	25	26
25	26	27	28	29	30		23	24	25	26	27	28	29	27	28	29	30	31		
							30	31												

July

24 Mon
1st ♎

☽ ☌ ♃ ♉	3:24 am	**12:24 am**
☽ ☍ ⚷ ♈	5:30 pm	**2:30 pm**
☽ ☌ ♅ ♉	10:35 pm	**7:35 pm**
☽ ⚹ ☿ ♌		**11:39 pm**

25 Tue
1st ♎
● 2nd Quarter 2 ♏ 43

☽ ⚹ ☿ ♌	2:39 am	
☽ ☌ ♆ ♓	8:10 am	**5:10 am**
☽ ⚹ ♀ ♌	10:00 am	**7:00 am**
☽ □ ♇ ♑	11:05 am	**8:05 am** ☽ v/c
☽ enters ♏	12:55 pm	**9:55 am**
☽♏ □ ☉♌	6:07 pm	**3:07 pm**
☽♏ △ ♄ ♓		**9:27 pm**

26 Wed
2nd ♏

☽♏ △ ♄ ♓	12:27 am	
☽♏ ⚹ ♂ ♍	7:31 am	**4:31 am**
☽♏ ☍ ♃ ♉	1:38 pm	**10:38 am**
☿♌ ☌ ♆ ♓		**9:00 pm**
☽♏ ☌ ⚷ ♈		**11:18 pm**

27 Thu
2nd ♏

OP: After Moon squares Venus until v/c Moon. This short OP is good for anything from the arts to getting in touch with others.

☿♌ ☌ ♆ ♓	12:00 am	
☽♏ ☌ ⚷ ♈	2:18 am	
☽♏ ☍ ♅ ♉	7:10 am	**4:10 am**
☿♌ ☌ ♀ ♌	11:16 am	**8:16 am**
☽♏ △ ♆ ♓	3:56 pm	**12:56 pm**
☽♏ □ ♀ ♌	5:06 pm	**2:06 pm**
☽♏ □ ☿ ♌	5:53 pm	**2:53 pm**
☽♏ ⚹ ♇ ♑	6:36 pm	**3:36 pm** ☽ v/c
☽ enters ♐	8:24 pm	**5:24 pm**
☿♌ ☌ ♇ ♑		**9:24 pm**

July

Fri 28
2nd ♐

☿♌ ⚻ ♇♑	12:24 am	
☽♐ △ ☉♌	5:22 am	**2:22 am**
☽♐ □ ♄♓	6:52 am	**3:52 am**
☽♐ □ ♂♍	4:09 pm	**1:09 pm**
☿ enters ♍	5:31 pm	**2:31 pm**
☽♐ ⚻ ♃♉	7:44 pm	**4:44 pm**
☉♌ ⚻ ♄♓		**10:38 pm**

Sat 29
2nd ♐

☉♌ ⚻ ♄♓	1:38 am	
☽♐ △ ⚷♈	6:58 am	**3:58 am**
☽♐ ⚻ ♅♉	11:35 am	**8:35 am**
☽♐ □ ♆♓	7:32 pm	**4:32 pm**
☽♐ △ ♀♌	7:51 pm	**4:51 pm** ☽ v/c
☽ enters ♑	11:44 pm	**8:44 pm**
☽♑ △ ☿♍		**11:55 pm**

OP: After Moon squares Neptune until Moon enters Capricorn. The Sagittarius Moon loves to play, but it is versatile and useful for other interests as well.

OP: Two back-to-back OPs: The second OP starts when the Moon enters Capricorn today until v/c Moon on Tuesday. This long OP is great for productivity and leadership, especially if you are familiar with strong Pluto energy.

Sun 30
2nd ♑

☽♑ △ ☿♍	2:55 am	
☽♑ ✶ ♄♓	9:15 am	**6:15 am**
☽♑ ⚻ ☉♌	11:35 am	**8:35 am**
♀♌ ⚻ ♆♓	12:25 pm	**9:25 am**
☽♑ △ ♂♍	8:18 pm	**5:18 pm**
☽♑ △ ♃♉	9:51 pm	**6:51 pm**

Eastern Daylight Time (EDT) plain / **Pacific Daylight Time (PDT) bold**

JUNE						
S	M	T	W	T	F	S
				1	2	3
4	5	6	7	8	9	10
11	12	13	14	15	16	17
18	19	20	21	22	23	24
25	26	27	28	29	30	

JULY						
S	M	T	W	T	F	S
						1
2	3	4	5	6	7	8
9	10	11	12	13	14	15
16	17	18	19	20	21	22
23	24	25	26	27	28	29
30	31					

AUGUST						
S	M	T	W	T	F	S
		1	2	3	4	5
6	7	8	9	10	11	12
13	14	15	16	17	18	19
20	21	22	23	24	25	26
27	28	29	30	31		

July • August

31 Mon
2nd ♑

☽♑ □ ⚷♈	8:01 am	**5:01 am**	
☽♑ △ ♅♉	12:29 pm	**9:29 am**	
☽♑ ⚻ ♀♌	7:17 pm	**4:17 pm**	
☽♑ ⚹ ♆♓	7:55 pm	**4:55 pm**	
☽♑ ☌ ♀♑	10:13 pm	**7:13 pm**	☽ v/c
☽ enters ♒	11:58 pm	**8:58 pm**	

1 Tue
2nd ♒
○ Full Moon 9 ♒ 16
Lammas

☽♒ ⚻ ☿♍	7:37 am	**4:37 am**
☽♒ ☍ ☉♌	2:32 pm	**11:32 am**
♂♍ △ ♃♉	4:45 pm	**1:45 pm**
☽♒ □ ♃♉	9:38 pm	**6:38 pm**
☽♒ ⚻ ♂♍	9:48 pm	**6:48 pm**
☿♍ ☍ ♄♓	10:18 pm	**7:18 pm**

2 Wed
3rd ♒

☽♒ ⚹ ⚷♈	7:14 am	**4:14 am**	
☽♒ □ ♅♉	11:44 am	**8:44 am**	
☽♒ ☍ ♀♌	5:15 pm	**2:15 pm**	☽ v/c
☽ enters ♓	11:05 pm	**8:05 pm**	

3 Thu
3rd ♓

☽♓ ☌ ♄♓	7:53 am	**4:53 am**
☽♓ ☍ ☿♍	11:03 am	**8:03 am**
☽♓ ⚻ ☉♌	4:59 pm	**1:59 pm**
☽♓ ⚹ ♃♉	9:20 pm	**6:20 pm**
☽♓ ☍ ♂♍	11:15 pm	**8:15 pm**

AUGUST

☽♓ ⚹ ♅♉	11:35 am	**8:35 am**	
☽♓ ⚻ ♀♌	3:49 pm	**12:49 pm**	
☽♓ ☌ ♆♓	7:00 pm	**4:00 pm**	
☽♓ ⚹ ♇♑	9:21 pm	**6:21 pm**	☽ v/c
☽ enters ♈	11:19 pm	**8:19 pm**	

Fri 4
3rd ♓

OP: After Moon conjoins Neptune until Moon enters Aries. This relaxing Friday afternoon can provide solid insights and is also good for meditating and helping others.

☽♈ ⚻ ☿♍	4:14 pm	**1:14 pm**
☽♈ △ ☉♌	9:40 pm	**6:40 pm**

Sat 5
3rd ♈

☽♈ ⚻ ♂♍	3:03 am	**12:03 am**
☽♈ ☌ ⚷♈	8:47 am	**5:47 am**
☽♈ △ ♀♌	4:35 pm	**1:35 pm**
☉♌ □ ♃♉	8:03 pm	**5:03 pm**
☽♈ □ ♇♑		**9:13 pm** ☽ v/c
☽ enters ♉		**11:25 pm**

Sun 6
3rd ♈

Eastern Daylight Time (EDT) plain / **Pacific Daylight Time (PDT) bold**

		JULY								AUGUST							SEPTEMBER				
S	M	T	W	T	F	S	S	M	T	W	T	F	S	S	M	T	W	T	F	S
						1			1	2	3	4	5						1	2
2	3	4	5	6	7	8	6	7	8	9	10	11	12	3	4	5	6	7	8	9
9	10	11	12	13	14	15	13	14	15	16	17	18	19	10	11	12	13	14	15	16
16	17	18	19	20	21	22	20	21	22	23	24	25	26	17	18	19	20	21	22	23
23	24	25	26	27	28	29	27	28	29	30	31			24	25	26	27	28	29	30
30	31																			

August

7 Mon
3rd ♈

☽♈ □ ♀♑ 12:13 am　　　　　　☽ v/c
☽ enters ♉ 2:25 am
☽♉ ⚹ ♄♓ 11:46 am　**8:46 am**
☽♉ △ ☿♍　　　　　　　　**10:10 pm**

8 Tue
3rd ♉
◐ 4th Quarter 15 ♉ 39
OP: After Moon squares Venus today until Moon enters Gemini on Wednesday. Use this Last Quarter Moon OP for clearing up emotional or relationships issues, helped by Venus retrograde.

☽♉ △ ☿♍ 1:10 am
☽♉ ☌ ♃♉ 4:11 am　**1:11 am**
☽♉ □ ☉♌ 6:28 am　**3:28 am**
☽♉ △ ♂♍ 10:46 am　**7:46 am**
☽♉ ☌ ♅♉ 7:50 pm　**4:50 pm**
☽♉ □ ♀♌ 8:21 pm　**5:21 pm**

9 Wed
4th ♉

☽♉ ⚹ ♆♓ 4:00 am　**1:00 am**
☽♉ △ ♀♑ 6:39 am　**3:39 am** ☽ v/c
♀♌ □ ♅♉ 7:08 am　**4:08 am**
☽ enters ♊ 9:05 am　**6:05 am**
☽♊ □ ♄♓ 6:45 pm　**3:45 pm**
☿♍ △ ♃♉ 8:47 pm　**5:47 pm**

10 Thu
4th ♊

☽♊ □ ☿♍ 2:02 pm **11:02 am**
☽♊ ⚹ ☉♌ 7:37 pm　**4:37 pm**
☽♊ □ ♂♍ 10:28 pm　**7:28 pm**
☽♊ ⚹ ⚷♈ 10:58 pm　**7:58 pm**
☽♊ ⚹ ♀♌　　　　　　　**11:52 pm**

150

August

Fri 11
4th ♊

☽♊ ⚹ ♀♌ 2:52 am
♂♍ ⊼ ⚷♈ 8:11 am **5:11 am**
☽♊ □ ♆♓ 1:27 pm **10:27 am** ☽ v/c
☽♊ ⊼ ♀♑ 4:13 pm **1:13 pm**
☽ enters ♋ 6:52 pm **3:52 pm**

Sat 12
4th ♋

☽♋ △ ♄♓ 4:37 am **1:37 am**
☉♌ △ ⚷♈ 2:13 pm **11:13 am**
☽♋ ⚹ ♃♉ **9:06 pm**

Sun 13
4th ♋

☽♋ ⚹ ♃♉ 12:06 am
☽♋ ⚹ ☿♍ 5:26 am **2:26 am**
☉♌ ☌ ♀♌ 7:16 am **4:16 am**
☽♋ □ ⚷♈ 10:06 am **7:06 am**
☽♋ ⚹ ♂♍ 12:56 pm **9:56 am**
☽♋ ⚹ ♅♉ 4:30 pm **1:30 pm**
☽♋ △ ♆♓ **9:57 pm**

Eastern Daylight Time (EDT) plain / **Pacific Daylight Time (PDT) bold**

		JULY							AUGUST							SEPTEMBER				
S	M	T	W	T	F	S	S	M	T	W	T	F	S	S	M	T	W	T	F	S
						1			1	2	3	4	5						1	2
2	3	4	5	6	7	8	6	7	8	9	10	11	12	3	4	5	6	7	8	9
9	10	11	12	13	14	15	13	14	15	16	17	18	19	10	11	12	13	14	15	16
16	17	18	19	20	21	22	20	21	22	23	24	25	26	17	18	19	20	21	22	23
23	24	25	26	27	28	29	27	28	29	30	31			24	25	26	27	28	29	30
30	31																			

August

Mercury Note: Mercury enters its Storm (moving less than 40 minutes of arc per day) on Tuesday, as it slows down before going retrograde. The Storm acts like the retrograde. Not favorable to start new projects—just follow through with the items that are already on your plate. Write down new ideas with date and time they occurred.

14 Mon
4th ♋

☽♋ △ ♆♓ 12:57 am
☽♋ ☍ ♀♑ 3:46 am **12:46 am** ☽ v/c
☽ enters ♌ 6:36 am **3:36 am**
♀♌ △ ⚷♈ 10:55 am **7:55 am**
☽♌ ⚻ ♄♓ 4:12 pm **1:12 pm**

15 Tue
4th ♌

☽♌ □ ♃♉ 12:44 pm **9:44 am**
☽♌ ☌ ♀♌ 8:44 pm **5:44 pm**
☽♌ △ ⚷♈ 10:25 pm **7:25 pm**
☉♌ □ ♅♉ 10:35 pm **7:35 pm**

16 Wed
4th ♌
● New Moon 23 ♌ 17

☽♌ □ ♅♉ 5:04 am **2:04 am**
☽♌ ☌ ☉♌ 5:38 am **2:38 am** ☽ v/c
♂♍ △ ♅♉ 9:53 am **6:53 am**
☽♌ ⚻ ♆♓ 1:26 pm **10:26 am**
☿♍ ⚻ ⚷♈ 2:02 pm **11:02 am**
☽♌ ⚻ ♀♑ 4:17 pm **1:17 pm**
☽ enters ♍ 7:14 pm **4:14 pm**

17 Thu
1st ♍

☽♍ ☍ ♄♓ 4:32 am **1:32 am**
☽♍ △ ♃♉   **10:48 pm**

August

Fri 18
1st ♍

☽♍ △ ♃ ♉   1:48 am
☽♍ ⚻ ⚷ ♈ 11:04 am **8:04 am**
☽♍ ☌ ☿ ♍   1:09 pm **10:09 am**
☽♍ △ ♅ ♉   5:51 pm **2:51 pm**
☽♍ ☌ ♂ ♍   8:57 pm **5:57 pm**
☽♍ ☍ ♆ ♓   **11:01 pm**

OP: After Moon opposes Neptune today or on Saturday until v/c Moon on Saturday. Night owls who want to be productive can use this time to do so.

Sat 19
1st ♍

☽♍ ☍ ♆ ♓   2:01 am

☽♍ △ ♀ ♑   4:51 am **1:51 am** ☽ v/c
☽ enters ♎   7:53 am **4:53 am**
☽♎ ⚻ ♄ ♓   4:43 pm **1:43 pm**

Sun 20
1st ♎

☉♌ ⚻ ♆ ♓   3:40 am **12:40 am**
☽♎ ⚻ ♃ ♉   2:19 pm **11:19 am**
☽♎ ✶ ♀ ♌   4:07 pm **1:07 pm**
☽♎ ☍ ⚷ ♈ 11:01 pm **8:01 pm**

Eastern Daylight Time (EDT) plain / **Pacific Daylight Time (PDT) bold**

		JULY							AUGUST							SEPTEMBER				
S	M	T	W	T	F	S	S	M	T	W	T	F	S	S	M	T	W	T	F	S
						1			1	2	3	4	5						1	2
2	3	4	5	6	7	8	6	7	8	9	10	11	12	3	4	5	6	7	8	9
9	10	11	12	13	14	15	13	14	15	16	17	18	19	10	11	12	13	14	15	16
16	17	18	19	20	21	22	20	21	22	23	24	25	26	17	18	19	20	21	22	23
23	24	25	26	27	28	29	27	28	29	30	31			24	25	26	27	28	29	30
30	31																			

August

Mercury Note: Mercury goes retrograde on Wednesday, August 23, and remains so until September 15, after which it will still be in its Storm until September 19. Projects initiated during this entire period may not work out as planned. It's best to use this time for reviews, editing, escrows, and so forth.

21 Mon
1st ♎

☽ ♎ ⊼ ♅ ♉	5:47 am	**2:47 am**
☽ ♎ ⊼ ♆ ♓	1:34 pm	**10:34 am**
☉ ♌ ⊼ ♀ ♑	2:07 pm	**11:07 am**
☽ ♎ □ ♀ ♑	4:19 pm	**1:19 pm**
☽ ♎ ⚹ ☉ ♌	4:31 pm	**1:31 pm** ☽ v/c
☽ enters ♏	7:22 pm	**4:22 pm**

22 Tue
1st ♏

☽ ♏ △ ♄ ♓	3:33 am	**12:33 am**
♀ ♌ □ ♃ ♉	8:16 am	**5:16 am**
♂ ♍ ☌ ♆ ♓	4:34 pm	**1:34 pm**
☽ ♏ □ ♀ ♌		**9:10 pm**
☽ ♏ ☍ ♃ ♉		**9:48 pm**

23 Wed
1st ♏
Sun enters Virgo
Mercury retrograde
OP: After Moon opposes Uranus until v/c Moon today or Thursday. A good opportunity to take charge and change a situation.

☽ ♏ □ ♀ ♌	12:10 am	
☽ ♏ ☍ ♃ ♉	12:48 am	
☉ enters ♍	5:01 am	**2:01 am**
☽ ♏ ⊼ ☊ ♈	8:46 am	**5:46 am**
☽ ♏ ⚹ ☿ ♍	1:03 pm	**10:03 am**
☽ ♏ ☍ ♅ ♉	3:19 pm	**12:19 pm**
☿ ℞	3:59 pm	**12:59 pm**
☽ ♏ △ ♆ ♓	10:33 pm	**7:33 pm**
☽ ♏ ⚹ ♂ ♍		**9:09 pm**
☽ ♏ ⚹ ♀ ♑		**10:10 pm** ☽ v/c

24 Thu
1st ♏
☽ 2nd Quarter 1 ♐ 00

☽ ♏ ⚹ ♂ ♍	12:09 am	
☽ ♏ ⚹ ♀ ♑	1:10 am	☽ v/c
☽ enters ♐	4:07 am	**1:07 am**
☽ ♐ □ ☉ ♍	5:57 am	**2:57 am**
☽ ♐ □ ♄ ♓	11:29 am	**8:29 am**
♂ ♍ △ ♀ ♑	8:23 pm	**5:23 pm**

August

☽♐ △ ♀♌	5:27 am	**2:27 am**	
☽♐ ☍ ♃♉	7:49 am	**4:49 am**	
☽♐ △ ♅♈	2:59 pm	**11:59 am**	
☽♐ □ ☿♍	6:43 pm	**3:43 pm**	
☽♐ ☍ ♅♉	9:12 pm	**6:12 pm**	

Fri 25
2nd ♐

☽♐ □ ♆♓	3:49 am	**12:49 am**	
☽♐ □ ♂♍	7:56 am	**4:56 am**	☽ v/c
☽ enters ♑	9:05 am	**6:05 am**	
☽♑ △ ☉♍	2:39 pm	**11:39 am**	
☽♑ ⚹ ♄♓	3:39 pm	**12:39 pm**	

Sat 26
2nd ♐

☉♍ ☍ ♄♓	4:28 am	**1:28 am**
☽♑ ☍ ♀♌	7:28 am	**4:28 am**
♂ enters ♎	9:20 am	**6:20 am**
☽♑ △ ♃♉	10:58 am	**7:58 am**
☽♑ □ ♅♈	5:27 pm	**2:27 pm**
☽♑ △ ☿♍	8:00 pm	**5:00 pm**
☽♑ △ ♅♉	11:22 pm	**8:22 pm**

Sun 27
2nd ♑

Eastern Daylight Time (EDT) plain / **Pacific Daylight Time (PDT) bold**

JULY

S	M	T	W	T	F	S
						1
2	3	4	5	6	7	8
9	10	11	12	13	14	15
16	17	18	19	20	21	22
23	24	25	26	27	28	29
30	31					

AUGUST

S	M	T	W	T	F	S
		1	2	3	4	5
6	7	8	9	10	11	12
13	14	15	16	17	18	19
20	21	22	23	24	25	26
27	28	29	30	31		

SEPTEMBER

S	M	T	W	T	F	S
					1	2
3	4	5	6	7	8	9
10	11	12	13	14	15	16
17	18	19	20	21	22	23
24	25	26	27	28	29	30

August

28 Mon
2nd ♑
URANUS RETROGRADE

☽♑ ✶ ♆♓	5:29 am	**2:29 am**	
☽♑ ☌ ♀♑	7:49 am	**4:49 am**	☽ v/c
☽ enters ♒	10:32 am	**7:32 am**	
☽♒ △ ♂♎	11:39 am	**8:39 am**	
☽♒ ⚻ ☉♍	7:08 pm	**4:08 pm**	
♅℞	10:39 pm	**7:39 pm**	

29 Tue
2nd ♒

☽♒ ☍ ♀♌	6:56 am	**3:56 am**
☽♒ □ ♃♉	11:11 am	**8:11 am**
☽♒ ✶ ⚷♈	5:16 pm	**2:16 pm**
☽♒ ⚻ ☿♍	6:18 pm	**3:18 pm**
☽♒ □ ♅♉	11:04 pm	**8:04 pm** ☽ v/c

30 Wed
2nd ♒
○ Full Moon 7 ♓ 25

☽ enters ♓	9:56 am	**6:56 am**
☽♓ ⚻ ♂♎	1:07 pm	**10:07 am**
☽♓ ☌ ♄♓	3:33 pm	**12:33 pm**
☿♍ ⚻ ⚷♈	7:56 pm	**4:56 pm**
☽♓ ☍ ☉♍	9:36 pm	**6:36 pm**

31 Thu
3rd ♓
OP: After Moon opposes Mercury today until today Moon enters Aries on Friday. This OP is favorable for the arts, meditation, and helping others.

☽♓ ⚻ ♀♌	5:33 am	**2:33 am**
☽♓ ✶ ♃♉	10:25 am	**7:25 am**
☽♓ ☍ ☿♍	3:29 pm	**12:29 pm**
☽♓ ✶ ♅♉	10:20 pm	**7:20 pm**

☽♓ ☌ ♆♓	4:13 am	**1:13 am**	
☽♓ ⚹ ♇♑	6:36 am	**3:36 am**	☽ v/c
☽ enters ♈	9:25 am	**6:25 am**	
☽♈ ☍ ♂♎	2:50 pm	**11:50 am**	
♂♎ ⚻ ♄♓	5:01 pm	**2:01 pm**	
☽♈ ⚻ ☉♍		**9:46 pm**	

FRI 1
3rd ♓

☽♈ ⚻ ☉♍	12:46 am		
☽♈ △ ♀♌	5:19 am	**2:19 am**	
☽♈ ⚻ ☿♍	1:25 pm	**10:25 am**	
☽♈ ☌ ⚷♈	4:53 pm	**1:53 pm**	

SAT 2
3rd ♈

☽♈ □ ♇♑	7:57 am	**4:57 am**	☽ v/c
☽ enters ♉	11:00 am	**8:00 am**	
☽♉ ⚹ ♄♓	4:36 pm	**1:36 pm**	
☽♉ ⚻ ♂♎	7:10 pm	**4:10 pm**	
♀D	9:20 pm	**6:20 pm**	

SUN 3
3rd ♈
VENUS DIRECT

Eastern Daylight Time (EDT) plain / **Pacific Daylight Time (PDT) bold**

JULY

S	M	T	W	T	F	S
						1
2	3	4	5	6	7	8
9	10	11	12	13	14	15
16	17	18	19	20	21	22
23	24	25	26	27	28	29
30	31					

AUGUST

S	M	T	W	T	F	S
		1	2	3	4	5
6	7	8	9	10	11	12
13	14	15	16	17	18	19
20	21	22	23	24	25	26
27	28	29	30	31		

SEPTEMBER

S	M	T	W	T	F	S
					1	2
3	4	5	6	7	8	9
10	11	12	13	14	15	16
17	18	19	20	21	22	23
24	25	26	27	28	29	30

September

4 Mon
3rd ♉
Labor Day (US)
Labour Day (Canada)
Jupiter retrograde
OP: After the Moon squares Venus today until Moon enters Gemini on Tuesday. This OP is ideal for constructive and innovative projects, but Mercury retrograde and the waning Moon make it preferable to keep up with work started before mid-August.

☿♍ △ ♃♉	6:29 am	**3:29 am**
☽♉ △ ☉♍	7:12 am	**4:12 am**
☽♉ □ ♀♌	8:08 am	**5:08 am**
♃℞	10:10 am	**7:10 am**
☽♉ △ ☿♍	1:35 pm	**10:35 am**
☽♉ ☌ ♃♉	2:06 pm	**11:06 am**

5 Tue
3rd ♉

☽♉ ☌ ♅♉	3:28 am	**12:28 am**
☽♉ ⚹ ♆♓	9:59 am	**6:59 am**
☽♉ △ ♀♑	12:46 pm	**9:46 am** ☽ v/c
☽ enters ♊	4:07 pm	**1:07 pm**
☽♊ □ ♄♓	9:50 pm	**6:50 pm**

6 Wed
3rd ♊
● 4th Quarter 14 ♊ 04

☽♊ △ ♂♎	3:45 am	**12:45 am**
☉♍ ☌ ☿♍	7:09 am	**4:09 am**
☽♊ ⚹ ♀♌	3:06 pm	**12:06 pm**
☽♊ □ ☿♍	4:46 pm	**1:46 pm**
☽♊ □ ☉♍	6:21 pm	**3:21 pm**

7 Thu
4th ♊

☽♊ ⚹ ☋♈	3:57 am	**12:57 am**
☽♊ □ ♆♓	6:22 pm	**3:22 pm** ☽ v/c
☽♊ ⚻ ♀♑	9:22 pm	**6:22 pm**
☽ enters ♋		**10:00 pm**

September

☽ enters ♋ 1:00 am
☽♋ △ ♄♓ 6:43 am **3:43 am**
☉♍ △ ♃♉ 7:13 am **4:13 am**
☽♋ □ ♂♎ 4:34 pm **1:34 pm**
☽♋ ✶ ☿♍ 10:57 pm **7:57 pm**

Fri 8
4th ♊

☽♋ ✶ ♃♉ 7:38 am **4:38 am**
☽♋ ✶ ☉♍ 9:49 am **6:49 am**
☽♋ □ ⚷♈ 2:34 pm **11:34 am**
☽♋ ✶ ♅♉ 10:34 pm **7:34 pm**

Sat 9
4th ♋

☽♋ △ ♆♓ 5:36 am **2:36 am**
☽♋ ☍ ♀♑ 8:47 am **5:47 am** ☽ v/c
☽ enters ♌ 12:36 pm **9:36 am**
☽♌ ⚻ ♄♓ 6:09 pm **3:09 pm**

Sun 10
4th ♋

Eastern Daylight Time (EDT) plain / **Pacific Daylight Time (PDT) bold**

		AUGUST							SEPTEMBER							OCTOBER				
S	M	T	W	T	F	S	S	M	T	W	T	F	S	S	M	T	W	T	F	S
		1	2	3	4	5						1	2	1	2	3	4	5	6	7
6	7	8	9	10	11	12	3	4	5	6	7	8	9	8	9	10	11	12	13	14
13	14	15	16	17	18	19	10	11	12	13	14	15	16	15	16	17	18	19	20	21
20	21	22	23	24	25	26	17	18	19	20	21	22	23	22	23	24	25	26	27	28
27	28	29	30	31			24	25	26	27	28	29	30	29	30	31				

September

11 Mon
4th ☊

☽☊ ⚹ ♂♎	8:06 am	**5:06 am**
☽☊ ☌ ♀☊	3:32 pm	**12:32 pm**
☉♍ ⚻ ♅♈	6:40 pm	**3:40 pm**
☽☊ □ ♃♉	7:54 pm	**4:54 pm**
☽☊ △ ♅♈		**11:51 pm**

12 Tue
4th ☊

☽☊ △ ♅♈	2:51 am	
☽☊ □ ♅♉	11:06 am	**8:06 am** ☽ v/c
☽☊ ⚻ ♆♓	6:07 pm	**3:07 pm**
☽☊ ⚻ ♇♑	9:24 pm	**6:24 pm**
☽ enters ♍		**10:18 pm**

13 Wed
4th ☊

☽ enters ♍	1:18 am	
☽♍ ☍ ♄♓	6:31 am	**3:31 am**
☽♍ ☌ ☿♍	6:04 pm	**3:04 pm**

14 Thu
4th ♍
● New Moon 21 ♍ 59
OP: This Cazimi Moon is usable ½ hour before and ½ hour after the Sun-Moon conjunction. If you have something important to begin around now that's part of a larger project started before August 15, this is a great time to do it.

☽♍ △ ♃♉	8:27 am	**5:27 am**
☽♍ ⚻ ♅♈	3:19 pm	**12:19 pm**
☽♍ ☌ ☉♍	9:40 pm	**6:40 pm**
☽♍ △ ♅♉	11:38 pm	**8:38 pm**

September

Mercury Note: Mercury goes direct on Friday, September 15, but remains in its Storm, moving slowly, until September 19.

☽♍ ☍ ♆♓	6:30 am	**3:30 am**
☽♍ △ ♀♑	9:49 am	**6:49 am** ☽ v/c
☽ enters ♎	1:44 pm	**10:44 am**
☿ D	4:21 pm	**1:21 pm**
☽♎ ⊼ ♄♓	6:32 pm	**3:32 pm**
☉♍ △ ♅♉	9:24 pm	**6:24 pm**

Fri 15
1st ♍
Rosh Hashanah begins at sundown
Mercury direct

☽♎ ☌ ♂♎	3:53 pm	**12:53 pm**
☽♎ ⚹ ♀♌	7:57 pm	**4:57 pm**
☽♎ ⊼ ♃♉	8:12 pm	**5:12 pm**
♀♌ □ ♃♉		**11:10 pm**
☽♎ ☍ ☷♈		**11:55 pm**

Sat 16
1st ♎

♀♌ □ ♃♉	2:10 am	
☽♎ ☍ ☷♈	2:55 am	
☽♎ ⊼ ♅♉	11:09 am	**8:09 am**
☽♎ ⊼ ♆♓	5:47 pm	**2:47 pm**
☽♎ □ ♀♑	9:06 pm	**6:06 pm** ☽ v/c
☽ enters ♏		**9:58 pm**

Sun 17
1st ♎

Eastern Daylight Time (EDT) plain / Pacific Daylight Time (PDT) bold

AUGUST

S	M	T	W	T	F	S
		1	2	3	4	5
6	7	8	9	10	11	12
13	14	15	16	17	18	19
20	21	22	23	24	25	26
27	28	29	30	31		

SEPTEMBER

S	M	T	W	T	F	S
					1	2
3	4	5	6	7	8	9
10	11	12	13	14	15	16
17	18	19	20	21	22	23
24	25	26	27	28	29	30

OCTOBER

S	M	T	W	T	F	S
1	2	3	4	5	6	7
8	9	10	11	12	13	14
15	16	17	18	19	20	21
22	23	24	25	26	27	28
29	30	31				

September

Mercury Note: Mercury finally leaves its Storm on Wednesday. Look over your notes on any ideas that occurred to you while Mercury was retrograde or slow. How do they look now?

18 Mon
1st ♎

☽ enters ♏ 12:58 am
☽♏ △ ♄ ♓ 5:19 am **2:19 am**
☽♏ ⚹ ☿ ♍ 5:52 pm **2:52 pm**

19 Tue
1st ♏

☽♏ ☍ ♃ ♉ 6:16 am **3:16 am**
☉♍ ☍ ♆ ♓ 7:17 am **4:17 am**
☽♏ □ ♀ ♌ 8:29 am **5:29 am**
☽♏ ⚻ ⚷ ♈ 12:45 pm **9:45 am**
♂♎ ⚻ ♃ ♉ 6:48 pm **3:48 pm**
☽♏ ☍ ♅ ♉ 8:46 pm **5:46 pm**

20 Wed
1st ♏

☽♏ △ ♆ ♓ 3:06 am **12:06 am**
☽♏ ⚹ ☉♍ 4:47 am **1:47 am**
☽♏ ⚹ ♇ ♑ 6:21 am **3:21 am** ☽ v/c
☽ enters ♐ 10:06 am **7:06 am**
☽♐ □ ♄ ♓ 1:58 pm **10:58 am**
☉♍ △ ♇ ♑ **10:21 pm**

21 Thu
1st ♐
UN International Day of Peace

☉♍ △ ♇ ♑ 1:21 am
☽♐ □ ☿ ♍ 5:13 am **2:13 am**
☽♐ ⚻ ♃ ♉ 1:47 pm **10:47 am**
☽♐ ⚹ ♂ ♎ 4:12 pm **1:12 pm**
☽♐ △ ♀ ♌ 6:25 pm **3:25 pm**
☽♐ △ ⚷ ♈ 7:59 pm **4:59 pm**

September

Fri 22
1st ♐
☽ ✗ ⊼ ♅ ♉   3:40 am **12:40 am**
☽ ✗ □ ♆ ♓   9:37 am **6:37 am**
☽ ✗ □ ☉ ♍   3:32 pm **12:32 pm** ☽ v/c
☽ enters ♑   4:20 pm **1:20 pm**
☽ ♑ ✶ ♄ ♓   7:44 pm **4:44 pm**
☉ enters ♎   **11:50 pm**

● 2nd Quarter 29 ♐ 32
Fall Equinox (Pacific)
Mabon (Pacific)
Sun enters Libra (Pacific)

Sat 23
2nd ♑
☉ enters ♎   2:50 am
♀♌ △ ⚷ ♈   4:17 am **1:17 am**
☽♑ △ ☿ ♍   2:24 pm **11:24 am**
☽♑ △ ♃ ♉   6:12 pm **3:12 pm**
☽♑ □ ♂ ♎   11:17 pm **8:17 pm**
☽♑ □ ⚷ ♈   **9:07 pm**
☽♑ ⊼ ♀ ♌   **10:04 pm**

Fall Equinox (Eastern)
Mabon (Eastern)
Sun enters Libra (Eastern)

OP: After Moon squares Mars today until v/c Moon on Sunday. As Mercury picks up speed, this is a fantastic time to take the initiative.

Sun 24
2nd ♑
☽♑ □ ⚷ ♈   12:07 am
☽♑ ⊼ ♀ ♌   1:04 am
☽♑ △ ♅ ♉   7:27 am **4:27 am**
☽♑ ✶ ♆ ♓   1:03 pm **10:03 am**
☽♑ ☌ ♇ ♑   4:05 pm **1:05 pm** ☽ v/c
♂♎ ☍ ⚷ ♈   4:06 pm **1:06 pm**
☽ enters ♒   7:29 pm **4:29 pm**
☽♒ △ ☉♎   10:26 pm **7:26 pm**
☉♎ ⊼ ♄ ♓   11:10 pm **8:10 pm**

Yom Kippur begins at sundown

Eastern Daylight Time (EDT) plain / **Pacific Daylight Time (PDT) bold**

AUGUST
S	M	T	W	T	F	S
		1	2	3	4	5
6	7	8	9	10	11	12
13	14	15	16	17	18	19
20	21	22	23	24	25	26
27	28	29	30	31		

SEPTEMBER
S	M	T	W	T	F	S
					1	2
3	4	5	6	7	8	9
10	11	12	13	14	15	16
17	18	19	20	21	22	23
24	25	26	27	28	29	30

OCTOBER
S	M	T	W	T	F	S
1	2	3	4	5	6	7
8	9	10	11	12	13	14
15	16	17	18	19	20	21
22	23	24	25	26	27	28
29	30	31				

SEPTEMBER

25 Mon
2nd ♒

☿♍ △ ♃♉   8:10 am **5:10 am**
☽♒ □ ♃♉   7:49 pm **4:49 pm**
☽♒ ⊼ ☿♍   9:02 pm **6:02 pm**
☽♒ ✶ ⚷♈   **10:33 pm**

26 Tue
2nd ♒

☽♒ ✶ ⚷♈   1:33 am
☽♒ △ ♂♎   3:13 am **12:13 am**
☽♒ ☍ ♀♌   4:47 am **1:47 am**
☽♒ □ ♅♉   8:38 am **5:38 am** ☽ v/c
☽ enters ♓ 8:18 pm **5:18 pm**
☽♓ ☌ ♄♓ 11:01 pm **8:01 pm**
☽♓ ⊼ ☉♎   **11:33 pm**

27 Wed
2nd ♓

☽♓ ⊼ ☉♎   2:33 am
☿♍ ⊼ ⚷♈   6:30 pm **3:30 pm**
☽♓ ✶ ♃♉   7:46 pm **4:46 pm**
☽♓ ☍ ☿♍   **11:18 pm**

28 Thu
2nd ♓

OP: After Moon conjoins Neptune until Moon enters Aries. This dynamic OP is good for anything, but especially for the arts and healing.

☽♓ ☍ ☿♍   2:18 am
☽♓ ⊼ ♂♎   5:30 am **2:30 am**
☽♓ ⊼ ♀♌   7:06 am **4:06 am**
☽♓ ✶ ♅♉   8:35 am **5:35 am**
☽♓ ☌ ♆♓   1:54 pm **10:54 am**
☽♓ ✶ ♀♑   4:58 pm **1:58 pm** ☽ v/c
☽ enters ♈ 8:17 pm **5:17 pm**

September • October

☽♈ ☍ ☉♎ 5:58 am **2:58 am** ♀♌ □ ♅♉ 1:53 pm **10:53 am** ☽♈ ☌ ⚸♈ **10:45 pm**	**Fri 29** 2nd ♈ ○ Full Moon 6 ♈ 00 Sukkot begins at sundown

☽♈ ☌ ⚸♈ 1:45 am ☽♈ ☍ ♂♎ 8:20 am **5:20 am** ☽♈ ⚻ ☿♍ 8:36 am **5:36 am** ☽♈ △ ♀♌ 10:08 am **7:08 am** ☿♍ △ ♅♉ 12:55 pm **9:55 am** ☽♈ □ ♆♑ 5:50 pm **2:50 pm** ☽ v/c ☽ enters ♉ 9:18 am **6:18 pm** ☽♉ ⚹ ♄♓ 11:45 pm **8:45 pm** ♂♎ ⚻ ♅♉ **9:38 pm**	**Sat 30** 3rd ♈

♂♎ ⚻ ♅♉ 12:38 am ☽♉ ⚻ ☉♎ 11:05 am **8:05 am** ☽♉ ☌ ♃♉ 9:37 pm **6:37 pm**	**Sun 1** 3rd ♉

Eastern Daylight Time (EDT) plain / **Pacific Daylight Time (PDT) bold**

AUGUST	SEPTEMBER	OCTOBER
S M T W T F S	S M T W T F S	S M T W T F S
1 2 3 4 5	1 2	1 2 3 4 5 6 7
6 7 8 9 10 11 12	3 4 5 6 7 8 9	8 9 10 11 12 13 14
13 14 15 16 17 18 19	10 11 12 13 14 15 16	15 16 17 18 19 20 21
20 21 22 23 24 25 26	17 18 19 20 21 22 23	22 23 24 25 26 27 28
27 28 29 30 31	24 25 26 27 28 29 30	29 30 31

October

2 Mon

3rd ♉

OP: After Moon squares Venus today until Moon enters Gemini today or on Tuesday. (Taurus is one of the four signs in which the v/c Moon is a good thing. See page 77.) Trade, communication, and anything that interests you are very favorable at this time.

☿♍ ☍ ♆♓	11:34 am	**8:34 am**	
☽♉ ☌ ♅♉	11:57 am	**8:57 am**	
☽♉ ⚻ ♂♎	1:50 pm	**10:50 am**	
☽♉ □ ♀♌	4:07 pm	**1:07 pm**	
☽♉ ⚹ ♆♓	5:47 pm	**2:47 pm**	
☽♉ △ ☿♍	6:41 pm	**3:41 pm**	
☽♉ △ ♇♑	9:20 pm	**6:20 pm**	☽ v/c
☽ enters ♊		**10:03 pm**	

3 Tue

3rd ♉

☽ enters ♊	1:03 am		
☽♊ □ ♄♓	3:29 am	**12:29 am**	
☿♍ △ ♇♑	3:20 pm	**12:20 pm**	
☽♊ △ ☉♎	8:03 pm	**5:03 pm**	
♀♌ ⚻ ♆♓	8:21 pm	**5:21 pm**	

4 Wed

3rd ♊

OP: After Moon squares Neptune today or on Thursday until v/c Moon today or on Thursday. This is another good time for connecting with others, especially if you like late-night conversations.

☽♊ ⚹ ⚷♈	9:51 am	**6:51 am**	
☿ enters ♎	8:09 pm	**5:09 pm**	
☽♊ △ ♂♎	11:33 pm	**8:33 pm**	
☽♊ □ ♆♓		**9:37 pm**	
☽♊ ⚹ ♀♌		**11:34 pm**	☽ v/c

5 Thu

3rd ♊

☽♊ □ ♆♓	12:37 am		
☽♊ ⚹ ♀♌	2:34 am		☽ v/c
☽♊ ⚻ ♇♑	4:31 am	**1:31 am**	
☽ enters ♋	8:32 am	**5:32 am**	
☽♋ □ ☿♎	10:33 am	**7:33 am**	
☽♋ △ ♄♓	10:55 am	**7:55 am**	
☿♎ ⚻ ♄♓	1:03 pm	**10:03 am**	
♂♎ ⚻ ♆♓	7:09 pm	**4:09 pm**	

October

Fri 6

♀☊ ⚻ ♀♑ 8:50 am **5:50 am**
☽♋ □ ☉♎ 9:48 am **6:48 am**
☽♋ ✶ ♃♉ 11:30 am **8:30 am**
☽♋ □ ⚷♈ 7:17 pm **4:17 pm**

3rd ♋
● 4th Quarter 13 ♋ 03
SUKKOT ENDS

Sat 7

☽♋ ✶ ♅♉ 4:22 am **1:22 am**
☉♎ ⚻ ♃♉ 5:04 am **2:04 am**
☽♋ △ ♆♓ 10:58 am **7:58 am**
☽♋ □ ♂♎ 1:25 pm **10:25 am**
☽♋ ☍ ♀♑ 3:12 pm **12:12 pm** ☽ v/c
☽ enters ♌ 7:24 pm **4:24 pm**
☽♌ ⚻ ♄♓ 9:41 pm **6:41 pm**

4th ♋

Sun 8

☽♌ ✶ ☿♎ 7:47 am **4:47 am**
♂♎ □ ♀♑ 9:05 pm **6:05 pm**
♀ enters ♍ 9:11 pm **6:11 pm**
☽♌ □ ♃♉ 10:55 pm **7:55 pm**

4th ♌

Eastern Daylight Time (EDT) plain / **Pacific Daylight Time (PDT) bold**

SEPTEMBER	OCTOBER	NOVEMBER
S M T W T F S	S M T W T F S	S M T W T F S
1 2	1 2 3 4 5 6 7	1 2 3 4
3 4 5 6 7 8 9	8 9 10 11 12 13 14	5 6 7 8 9 10 11
10 11 12 13 14 15 16	15 16 17 18 19 20 21	12 13 14 15 16 17 18
17 18 19 20 21 22 23	22 23 24 25 26 27 28	19 20 21 22 23 24 25
24 25 26 27 28 29 30	29 30 31	26 27 28 29 30

October

9 Mon
4th ♌
Indigenous Peoples' Day
Thanksgiving Day (Canada)

☽♌ ✶ ☉♎   3:07 am **12:07 am**
☽♌ △ ⚷♈   7:13 am **4:13 am**
☽♌ □ ♅♉   4:36 pm **1:36 pm**
☽♌ ⚻ ♆♓   11:21 pm **8:21 pm**
♀♍ ☍ ♄♓   **11:11 pm**

10 Tue
4th ♌
Pluto direct

♀♍ ☍ ♄♓   2:11 am
☽♌ ⚻ ♀♑   3:45 am **12:45 am**
☽♌ ✶ ♂♎   5:37 am **2:37 am** ☽ v/c
☽ enters ♍ 8:02 am **5:02 am**
☽♍ ☍ ♄♓   10:06 am **7:06 am**
☽♍ ☌ ♀♍   10:46 am **7:46 am**
♀D   9:10 pm **6:10 pm**
☉♎ ☍ ⚷♈   **11:21 pm**

11 Wed
4th ♍

☉♎ ☍ ⚷♈   2:21 am
☽♍ △ ♃♉   11:06 am **8:06 am**
☽♍ ⚻ ⚷♈   7:40 pm **4:40 pm**
♂ enters ♏   **9:04 pm**

12 Thu
4th ♍
OP: After Moon opposes Neptune until v/c Moon. During the Balsamic Moon, use this productive time to finish up projects.

♂ enters ♏ 12:04 am
☽♍ △ ♅♉   5:01 am **2:01 am**
☿♎ ⚻ ♃♉   8:32 am **5:32 am**
☽♍ ☍ ♆♓   11:42 am **8:42 am**

☽♍ △ ♀♑   4:10 pm **1:10 pm** ☽ v/c
☽ enters ♎ 8:22 pm **5:22 pm**
☽♎ ⚻ ♄♓   10:13 pm **7:13 pm**

Fri 13
4th ♎

♂♏ △ ♄♓ 8:29 am **5:29 am**
☽♎ ⊼ ♃♉ 10:16 pm **7:16 pm**

Sat 14
4th ♎
Solar Eclipse | ● New Moon 21 ♎ 08

☽♎ ☌ ☿♎ 4:58 am **1:58 am**
☽♎ ☍ ⚷♈ 6:55 am **3:55 am**
☽♎ ☌ ☉♎ 1:55 pm **10:55 am**
☽♎ ⊼ ♅♉ 4:03 pm **1:03 pm**
☿♎ ☍ ⚷♈ 6:31 pm **3:31 pm**
☽♎ ⊼ ♆♓ 10:34 pm **7:34 pm**

Sun 15
1st ♎

☽♎ □ ♇♑ 3:01 am **12:01 am** ☽ v/c
☽ enters ♏ 7:04 am **4:04 am**
☽♏ △ ♄♓ 8:41 am **5:41 am**
☽♏ ☌ ♂♏ 11:35 am **8:35 am**
☉♎ ⊼ ♅♉ 3:44 pm **12:44 pm**
☽♏ ⚹ ♀♍ 6:51 pm **3:51 pm**

Eastern Daylight Time (EDT) plain / **Pacific Daylight Time (PDT) bold**

SEPTEMBER

S	M	T	W	T	F	S
					1	2
3	4	5	6	7	8	9
10	11	12	13	14	15	16
17	18	19	20	21	22	23
24	25	26	27	28	29	30

OCTOBER

S	M	T	W	T	F	S
1	2	3	4	5	6	7
8	9	10	11	12	13	14
15	16	17	18	19	20	21
22	23	24	25	26	27	28
29	30	31				

NOVEMBER

S	M	T	W	T	F	S
			1	2	3	4
5	6	7	8	9	10	11
12	13	14	15	16	17	18
19	20	21	22	23	24	25
26	27	28	29	30		

October

16 Mon
1st ♏

☽♏ ☌ ♃ ♉	7:31 am	**4:31 am**
☽♏ ⚻ ♇ ♈	4:11 pm	**1:11 pm**
☽♏ ☌ ♅ ♉		**10:01 pm**

17 Tue
1st ♏

OP: After Moon trines Neptune until v/c Moon. (See "Translating Darkness" on page 80.) Get up early to catch this opportunity to work on ambitious projects.

☽♏ ☌ ♅ ♉	1:01 am	
☽♏ △ ♆ ♓	7:20 am	**4:20 am**
☿♎ ⚻ ♅ ♉	10:48 am	**7:48 am**
☽♏ ⚹ ♀ ♑	11:44 am	**8:44 am** ☽ v/c
☽ enters ♐	3:36 pm	**12:36 pm**
☽♐ □ ♄ ♓	5:02 pm	**2:02 pm**

18 Wed
1st ♐

☽♐ □ ♀ ♍	7:15 am	**4:15 am**
☽♐ ⚻ ♃ ♉	2:35 pm	**11:35 am**
☽♐ △ ♇ ♈	11:14 pm	**8:14 pm**
☉♎ ⚻ ♆ ♓	11:40 pm	**8:40 pm**

19 Thu
1st ♐

OP: After Moon squares Neptune until Moon enters Capricorn. Wait two hours after the square, and you will still have time for fun, adventures, and socializing.

☽♐ ⚻ ♅ ♉	7:45 am	**4:45 am**
☿♎ ⚻ ♆ ♓	10:12 am	**7:12 am**
☽♐ □ ♆ ♓	1:53 pm	**10:53 am**
☽♐ ⚹ ☿ ♎	2:25 pm	**11:25 am**
☽♐ ⚹ ☉ ♎	3:02 pm	**12:02 pm** ☽ v/c
☽ enters ♑	9:55 pm	**6:55 pm**
☽♑ ⚹ ♄ ♓	11:10 pm	**8:10 pm**
☉♎ ☌ ☿ ♎		**10:38 pm**

October

☉♎ ☌ ☿♎	1:38 am	
☽♑ ⚹ ♂♏	7:54 am	**4:54 am**
☽♑ △ ♀♍	4:59 pm	**1:59 pm**
☽♑ △ ♃♉	7:30 pm	**4:30 pm**
☿♎ □ ♀♑	8:51 pm	**5:51 pm**

Fri 20
1st ♑

☽♑ □ ♇♈	4:07 am	**1:07 am**
☉♎ □ ♀♑	10:09 am	**7:09 am**
☽♑ △ ♅♉	12:21 am	**9:21 am**
☽♑ ⚹ ♆♓	6:17 pm	**3:17 pm**
☽♑ ☌ ♀♑	10:33 pm	**7:33 pm**
☽♑ □ ☉♎	11:29 pm	**8:29 pm**
♀♍ △ ♃♉		**9:32 pm**
☽♑ □ ☿♎		**11:00 pm** ☽ v/c
☽ enters ♒		**11:06 pm**
☿ enters ♏		**11:49 pm**

Sat 21
1st ♑
◐ 2nd Quarter 28 ♑ 28

♀♍ △ ♃♉	12:32 am	
☽♑ □ ☿♎	2:00 am	☽ v/c
☽ enters ♒	2:06 am	
☿ enters ♏	2:49 am	
☿♏ △ ♄♓	12:12 pm	**9:12 am**
☽♒ □ ♂♏	2:21 pm	**11:21 am**
☽♒ □ ♃♉	10:27 pm	**7:27 pm**
☽♒ ⊼ ♀♍		**9:17 pm**

Sun 22
2nd ♑

Eastern Daylight Time (EDT) plain / **Pacific Daylight Time (PDT) bold**

	SEPTEMBER								OCTOBER								NOVEMBER				
S	M	T	W	T	F	S	S	M	T	W	T	F	S	S	M	T	W	T	F	S
					1	2	1	2	3	4	5	6	7				1	2	3	4
3	4	5	6	7	8	9	8	9	10	11	12	13	14	5	6	7	8	9	10	11
10	11	12	13	14	15	16	15	16	17	18	19	20	21	12	13	14	15	16	17	18
17	18	19	20	21	22	23	22	23	24	25	26	27	28	19	20	21	22	23	24	25
24	25	26	27	28	29	30	29	30	31					26	27	28	29	30		

October

23 Mon
2nd ≈
Sun enters Scorpio

☽≈ ☌ ♀♍ 12:17 am
☽≈ ⚹ ♂♈ 7:05 am **4:05 am**
☉ enters ♏ 12:21 pm **9:21 am**
☽≈ □ ♅♉ 3:04 pm **12:04 pm** ☽ v/c

24 Tue
2nd ≈

☉♏ △ ♄ ♓ 3:14 am **12:14 am**
☽ enters ♓ 4:33 am **1:33 am**
☽♓ ☌ ♄♓ 5:34 am **2:34 am**
☽♓ △ ☉♏ 5:45 am **2:45 am**
☽♓ △ ☿♏ 10:57 am **7:57 am**
☽♓ △ ♂♏ 6:58 pm **3:58 pm**
☽♓ ⚹ ♃♉ 11:57 pm **8:57 pm**

25 Wed
2nd ♓
OP: After Moon opposes Venus today until Moon enters Aries on Thursday. While this is a promising OP for creative insights and mind expansion, keep it flexible since we are currently between eclipses.

☽♓ ☍ ♀♍ 5:52 am **2:52 am**
☽♓ ⚹ ♅♉ 4:35 am **1:35 pm**
☽♓ ☌ ♆♓ 10:22 pm **7:22 pm**
☽♓ ⚹ ♇♑ **11:39 pm** ☽ v/c

26 Thu
2nd ♓

☽♓ ⚹ ♇♑ 2:39 am ☽ v/c
☽ enters ♈ 6:02 am **3:02 am**
☽♈ ☍ ☉♏ 10:50 am **7:50 am**
☽♈ ☍ ☿♏ 6:36 pm **3:36 pm**
♀♍ ☍ ♂♈ 9:10 pm **6:10 pm**
☽♈ ☍ ♂♏ 10:49 pm **7:49 pm**

Fri 27
2nd ♈

☽♈ ☌ ⚷♈ 10:00 am **7:00 am**
☽♈ ⚻ ♀♍ 11:00 am **8:00 am**

Sat 28
2nd ♈

Lunar Eclipse | ○ Full Moon 5 ♉ 09

☽♈ □ ♇♑ 4:20 am **1:20 am** ☽ v/c
☽ enters ♉ 7:44 am **4:44 am**
☽♉ ⚹ ♄♓ 8:40 am **5:40 am**
♂♏ ☍ ♃♉ 12:03 pm **9:03 am**
☽♉ ☍ ☉♏ 4:24 pm **1:24 pm**
☿♏ ☍ ♃♉ 11:44 pm **8:44 pm**
☽♉ ☌ ♃♉ **11:37 pm**

Sun 29
3rd ♉

☽♉ ☌ ♃♉ 2:37 am
☽♉ ☍ ☿♏ 3:00 am **12:00 am**
☽♉ ☍ ♂♏ 3:30 am **12:30 am**
☿♏ ☌ ♂♏ 10:22 am **7:22 am**
☽♉ △ ♀♍ 5:33 pm **2:33 pm**
☽♉ ☌ ♅♉ 8:36 pm **5:36 pm**
☽♉ ⚹ ♆♓ **11:51 pm**

OP: After Moon opposes Mars today until Moon enters Gemini on Monday. Wait two hours after the opposition, get organized, and take advantage of this productive OP to get a lot done.

Eastern Daylight Time (EDT) plain / **Pacific Daylight Time (PDT) bold**

SEPTEMBER

S	M	T	W	T	F	S
					1	2
3	4	5	6	7	8	9
10	11	12	13	14	15	16
17	18	19	20	21	22	23
24	25	26	27	28	29	30

OCTOBER

S	M	T	W	T	F	S
1	2	3	4	5	6	7
8	9	10	11	12	13	14
15	16	17	18	19	20	21
22	23	24	25	26	27	28
29	30	31				

NOVEMBER

S	M	T	W	T	F	S
			1	2	3	4
5	6	7	8	9	10	11
12	13	14	15	16	17	18
19	20	21	22	23	24	25
26	27	28	29	30		

October • November

30 Mon
3rd ♉

☽ ♉ ⚹ ♆ ♓	2:51 am	
☽ ♉ △ ♀ ♑	7:36 am	**4:36 am** ☽ v/c
☽ enters ♊	11:08 am	**8:08 am**
☽ ♊ □ ♄ ♓	12:04 pm	**9:04 am**
☽ ♊ ☍ ☉ ♏		**9:22 pm**

31 Tue
3rd ♊
Halloween
Samhain

☽ ♊ ☍ ☉ ♏	12:22 am	
♀ ♍ △ ♅ ♉	8:51 am	**5:51 am**
☽ ♊ ☍ ♂ ♏	10:48 am	**7:48 am**
☽ ♊ ☍ ☿ ♏	2:31 pm	**11:31 am**
☽ ♊ ⚹ ⚷ ♈	5:06 pm	**2:06 pm**

1 Wed
3rd ♊
All Saints' Day

☽ ♊ □ ♀ ♍	3:26 am	**12:26 am**
☽ ♊ □ ♆ ♓	8:36 am	**5:36 am** ☽ v/c
☿ ♏ ☍ ⚷ ♈	11:45 am	**8:45 am**
☽ ♊ ☍ ♀ ♑	1:47 pm	**10:47 am**
☽ enters ♋	5:30 pm	**2:30 pm**
☽ ♋ △ ♄ ♓	6:29 pm	**3:29 pm**

2 Thu
3rd ♋

☽ ♋ △ ☉ ♏	12:23 pm	**9:23 am**
☽ ♋ ⚹ ♃ ♉	1:31 pm	**10:31 am**
☽ ♋ △ ♂ ♏	10:01 pm	**7:01 pm**
☉ ♏ ☍ ♃ ♉		**10:02 pm**
☽ ♋ □ ⚷ ♈		**10:15 pm**

November

Fri 3
3rd ♋

☉♏ ☍ ♃♉	1:02 am	
☽♋ □ ⚷♈	1:15 am	
☽♋ △ ☿♏	6:49 am	**3:49 am**
☽♋ ✶ ♅♉	10:36 am	**7:36 am**
☽♋ ✶ ♀♍	5:49 pm	**2:49 pm**
☽♋ △ ♆♓	5:50 pm	**2:50 pm**
♀♍ ☍ ♆♓	6:06 pm	**3:06 pm**
☽♋ ☍ ♇♑	11:28 pm	**8:28 pm** ☽ v/c

Sat 4
3rd ♋
SATURN DIRECT

♄ D	3:03 am	**12:03 am**
☽ enters ♌	3:21 am	**12:21 am**
☽♌ ⚻ ♄♓	4:22 am	**1:22 am**
☿♏ ☍ ♅♉	12:07 pm	**9:07 am**
☽♌ □ ♃♉	11:46 pm	**8:46 pm**

Sun 5
3rd ♌
◐ 4th Quarter 12 ♌ 40
DAYLIGHT SAVING TIME ENDS AT 2:00 A.M.

☽♌ □ ☉♏	3:37 am	**1:37 am**
♂♏ ⚻ ⚷♈	3:44 am	**1:44 am**
☽♌ △ ⚷♈	11:29 am	**8:29 am**
☽♌ □ ♂♏	12:00 pm	**9:00 am**
☽♌ □ ♅♉	9:11 pm	**6:11 pm**
☽♌ □ ☿♏		**11:25 pm** ☽ v/c

Eastern Daylight Time (EDT) becomes Eastern Standard Time (EST) November 5 (plain)
Pacific Daylight Time (PDT) becomes Pacific Standard Time (PST) November 5 (bold)

OCTOBER							NOVEMBER							DECEMBER						
S	M	T	W	T	F	S	S	M	T	W	T	F	S	S	M	T	W	T	F	S
1	2	3	4	5	6	7				1	2	3	4						1	2
8	9	10	11	12	13	14	5	6	7	8	9	10	11	3	4	5	6	7	8	9
15	16	17	18	19	20	21	12	13	14	15	16	17	18	10	11	12	13	14	15	16
22	23	24	25	26	27	28	19	20	21	22	23	24	25	17	18	19	20	21	22	23
29	30	31					26	27	28	29	30			24	25	26	27	28	29	30
														31						

November

6 Mon
4th ♌

☽♌ □ ☿♏	2:25 am	☽ v/c
☽♌ ⊼ ♆♓	4:48 am	**1:48 am**
♀♍ △ ♇♑	9:38 am	**6:38 am**
☽♌ ⊼ ♇♑	10:44 am	**7:44 am**
☽ enters ♍	2:39 pm	**11:39 am**
☽♍ ☍ ♄♓	3:42 pm	**12:42 pm**
☿♏ △ ♆♓	8:37 pm	**5:37 pm**

7 Tue
4th ♍
Election Day (general)

☽♍ △ ♃♉	10:43 am	**7:43 am**
☽♍ ⚹ ☉♏	9:54 pm	**6:54 pm**
☽♍ ⊼ ♅♈		**9:00 pm**

8 Wed
4th ♍

OP: After Moon opposes Neptune until v/c Moon. You can apply this energy to hard work while keeping your emotions steady.

☽♍ ⊼ ♅♈	12:00 am	
☽♍ ⚹ ♂♏	4:29 am	**1:29 am**
♀ enters ♎	4:30 am	**1:30 am**
☽♍ △ ♅♉	9:40 am	**6:40 am**
♀♎ ⊼ ♄♓	4:13 pm	**1:13 pm**
☽♍ ☍ ♆♓	5:20 pm	**2:20 pm**
☿♏ ⚹ ♇♑	7:17 pm	**4:17 pm**
☉♏ ⊼ ♅♈	10:01 pm	**7:01 pm**
☽♍ △ ♇♑	11:20 pm	**8:20 pm**
☽♍ ⚹ ☿♏	11:55 pm	**8:55 pm** ☽ v/c

9 Thu
4th ♍

☽ enters ♎	3:08 am	**12:08 am**
☽♎ ⊼ ♄♓	4:12 am	**1:12 am**
☽♎ ☌ ♀♎	5:23 am	**2:23 am**
☽♎ ⊼ ♃♉	10:05 pm	**7:05 pm**
☿ enters ♐		**10:25 pm**

Fri 10
4th ♎

☿ enters ♐ 1:25 am
☿♐ □ ♄♓ 10:07 am **7:07 am**
☽♎ ☍ ⚷♈ 11:25 am **8:25 am**
☽♎ ⚻ ♅♉ 8:43 pm **5:43 pm**

Sat 11
4th ♎
Veterans Day
Remembrance Day (Canada)

☽♎ ⚻ ♆♓ 4:13 am **1:13 am**
☽♎ □ ♇♑ 10:05 am **7:05 am** ☽ v/c
☽ enters ♏ 1:39 pm **10:39 am**
☽♏ △ ♄♓ 2:43 pm **11:43 am**
♂♏ ☍ ♅♉ 4:11 pm **1:11 pm**

Sun 12
4th ♏

☽♏ ☍ ♃♉ 7:09 am **4:09 am**
☽♏ ⚻ ⚷♈ 8:16 pm **5:16 pm**

Eastern Standard Time (EST) plain / **Pacific Standard Time (PST) bold**

OCTOBER

S	M	T	W	T	F	S
1	2	3	4	5	6	7
8	9	10	11	12	13	14
15	16	17	18	19	20	21
22	23	24	25	26	27	28
29	30	31				

NOVEMBER

S	M	T	W	T	F	S
			1	2	3	4
5	6	7	8	9	10	11
12	13	14	15	16	17	18
19	20	21	22	23	24	25
26	27	28	29	30		

DECEMBER

S	M	T	W	T	F	S
					1	2
3	4	5	6	7	8	9
10	11	12	13	14	15	16
17	18	19	20	21	22	23
24	25	26	27	28	29	30
31						

November

13 Mon
4th ♏
● New Moon 20 ♏ 44

☽♏ ☌ ☉♏	4:27 am	**1:27 am**
☽♏ ☍ ♅♉	5:05 am	**2:05 am**
☽♏ ☌ ♂♏	7:18 am	**4:18 am**
☽♏ △ ♆♓	12:20 pm	**9:20 am**
☉♏ ☍ ♅♉	12:21 pm	**9:21 am**
☽♏ ✶ ♀♑	6:03 pm	**3:03 pm** ☽ v/c
☽ enters ♐	9:23 pm	**6:23 pm**
☽♐ □ ♄♓	10:28 pm	**7:28 pm**

14 Tue
1st ♐

☽♐ ☌ ☿♐	9:04 am	**6:04 am**
☽♐ ✶ ♀♎	9:44 am	**6:44 am**
☽♐ ⚻ ♃♉	1:32 pm	**10:32 am**
☽♐ △ ⚷♈		**11:27 pm**

15 Wed
1st ♐

☽♐ △ ⚷♈	2:27 am	
☿♐ ✶ ♀♎	7:48 am	**4:48 am**
☽♐ ⚻ ♅♉	10:52 am	**7:52 am**
☽♐ □ ♆♓	5:57 pm	**2:57 pm** ☽ v/c
☿♐ ⚻ ♃♉	10:35 pm	**7:35 pm**
☽ enters ♑		**11:41 pm**
♀♎ ⚻ ♃♉		**11:48 pm**

16 Thu
1st ♐

☽ enters ♑	2:41 am	
♀♎ ⚻ ♃♉	2:48 am	
☽♑ ✶ ♄♓	3:49 am	**12:49 am**
☽♑ △ ♃♉	5:48 pm	**2:48 pm**
☽♑ □ ♀♎	7:16 pm	**4:16 pm**

Fri 17
1st ♑

♂♏△♆♓ 3:36 am **12:36 am**
☽♑□⚷♈ 6:41 am **3:41 am**
☉♏△♆♓ 9:52 am **6:52 am**
☽♑△♅♉ 2:51 pm **11:51 am**
☽♑⚹♆♓ 9:52 pm **6:52 pm**
☽♑⚹☉♏ 10:49 pm **7:49 pm**
☽♑⚹♂♏ 10:51 pm **7:51 pm**
☉♏☌♂♏ **9:42 pm**

Sat 18
1st ♑

☉♏☌♂♏ 12:42 am
☽♑☌♇♑ 3:27 am **12:27 am** ☽ v/c
☽ enters ♒ 6:28 am **3:28 am**
☽♒□♃♉ 8:50 pm **5:50 pm**

Sun 19
1st ♒

☽♒△♀♎ 3:12 am **12:12 am**
☽♒⚹☿♐ 5:39 am **2:39 am**
☽♒⚹⚷♈ 9:51 am **6:51 am**
☽♒□♅♉ 5:53 pm **2:53 pm**

Eastern Standard Time (EST) plain / **Pacific Standard Time (PST) bold**

OCTOBER

S	M	T	W	T	F	S
1	2	3	4	5	6	7
8	9	10	11	12	13	14
15	16	17	18	19	20	21
22	23	24	25	26	27	28
29	30	31				

NOVEMBER

S	M	T	W	T	F	S
			1	2	3	4
5	6	7	8	9	10	11
12	13	14	15	16	17	18
19	20	21	22	23	24	25
26	27	28	29	30		

DECEMBER

S	M	T	W	T	F	S
					1	2
3	4	5	6	7	8	9
10	11	12	13	14	15	16
17	18	19	20	21	22	23
24	25	26	27	28	29	30
31						

November

20 Mon
1st ≈
☽ 2nd Quarter 27 ≈ 51

☽≈ □ ♂♏	4:38 am	**1:38 am**
☽≈ □ ☉♏	5:50 am	**2:50 am** ☽ v/c
☽ enters ♓	9:29 am	**6:29 am**
☽♓ ☌ ♄♓	10:45 am	**7:45 am**
☉♏ ⚹ ♀♑	4:26 pm	**1:26 pm**
☿♐ △ ⚷♈	10:08 pm	**7:08 pm**
☽♓ ⚹ ♃♉	11:20 pm	**8:20 pm**

21 Tue
2nd ♓

OP: After Moon squares Mercury today until Moon enters Aries on Wednesday. This is a great time to hone your intuition and for inspiration and artistic activities.

☽♓ ⚻ ♀♎	10:32 am	**7:32 am**
☽♓ □ ☿♐	2:16 pm	**11:16 am**
♂♏ ⚹ ♀♑	8:18 pm	**5:18 pm**
☽♓ ⚹ ♅♉	8:35 pm	**5:35 pm**

22 Wed
2nd ♓
Sun enters Sagittarius

☽♓ ☌ ♆♓	3:45 am	**12:45 am**
☉ enters ♐	9:03 am	**6:03 am**
☽♓ ⚹ ♀♑	9:29 am	**6:29 am**
☽♓ △ ♂♏	10:10 am	**7:10 am** ☽ v/c
♀♎ ☍ ⚷♈	11:45 am	**8:45 am**
☽ enters ♈	12:19 pm	**9:19 am**
☽♈ △ ☉♐	12:35 pm	**9:35 am**

23 Thu
2nd ♈
Thanksgiving Day (US)

☉♐ □ ♄♓	4:47 am	**1:47 am**
☽♈ ☌ ⚷♈	3:26 pm	**12:26 pm**
☽♈ ☍ ♀♎	5:57 pm	**2:57 pm**
☽♈ △ ☿♐	10:52 pm	**7:52 pm**

Fri 24
2nd ♈

☿♐ ⚻ ♅♉	4:27 am	**1:27 am**	
♂ enters ♐	5:15 am	**2:15 am**	
☽♈ □ ♇♑	12:40 pm	**9:40 am**	☽ v/c
☽ enters ♉	3:29 pm	**12:29 pm**	
☽♉ ⚻ ♂♐	4:02 pm	**1:02 pm**	
☽♉ ⚹ ♄♓	5:00 pm	**2:00 pm**	
☽♉ ⚻ ☉♐	7:43 pm	**4:43 pm**	

Sat 25
2nd ♉

☽♉ ☌ ♃♉	4:43 am	**1:43 am**	
♂♐ □ ♄♓	11:57 am	**8:57 am**	
☽♉ ⚻ ♀♎		**11:19 pm**	

Sun 26
2nd ♉

☽♉ ⚻ ♀♎	2:19 am		
☽♉ ☌ ♅♉	3:03 am	**12:03 am**	
☽♉ ⚻ ☿♐	8:21 am	**5:21 am**	
☽♉ ⚹ ♆♓	10:42 am	**7:42 am**	
♀♎ ⚻ ♅♉	10:49 am	**7:49 am**	
☽♉ △ ♇♑	4:52 pm	**1:52 pm**	☽ v/c
☽ enters ♊	7:40 pm	**4:40 pm**	
☽♊ □ ♄♓	9:22 pm	**6:22 pm**	
☽♊ ☍ ♂♐	11:08 pm	**8:08 pm**	

OP: After Moon conjoins Uranus until Moon enters Gemini. You can use this Sunday for anything, from romance to creativity to serious work.

Eastern Standard Time (EST) plain / **Pacific Standard Time (PST) bold**

OCTOBER

S	M	T	W	T	F	S
1	2	3	4	5	6	7
8	9	10	11	12	13	14
15	16	17	18	19	20	21
22	23	24	25	26	27	28
29	30	31				

NOVEMBER

S	M	T	W	T	F	S
			1	2	3	4
5	6	7	8	9	10	11
12	13	14	15	16	17	18
19	20	21	22	23	24	25
26	27	28	29	30		

DECEMBER

S	M	T	W	T	F	S
					1	2
3	4	5	6	7	8	9
10	11	12	13	14	15	16
17	18	19	20	21	22	23
24	25	26	27	28	29	30
31						

NOVEMBER

27 Mon
2nd ♊
○ Full Moon 4 ♊ 51

☽♊ ☍ ☉♐ 4:16 am **1:16 am**
☿♐ □ ♆♓ 8:27 am **5:27 am**
☽♊ ⚹ ⚷♈ 11:58 am **8:58 pm**

28 Tue
3rd ♊

☽♊ △ ♀♎ 12:54 pm **9:54 am**
☽♊ □ ♆♓ 4:30 pm **1:30 pm**
☽♊ ☍ ☿♐ 8:03 pm **5:03 pm** ☽ v/c
☽♊ ⚻ ♀♑ 11:03 pm **8:03 pm**
☽ enters ♋   **10:54 pm**

29 Wed
3rd ♊

☽ enters ♋ 1:54 am
☽♋ △ ♄♓ 3:51 am **12:51 am**
☽♋ ⚻ ♂♐ 8:43 am **5:43 am**
☉♐ ⚻ ♃♉ 12:38 pm **9:38 am**
☽♋ ⚹ ♃♉ 3:21 pm **12:21 pm**
☽♋ ⚻ ☉♐ 3:37 pm **12:37 pm**

30 Thu
3rd ♋

♀♎ ⚻ ♆♓ 5:13 am **2:13 am**
☽♋ □ ⚷♈ 7:32 am **4:32 am**
☽♋ ⚹ ♅♉ 4:20 pm **1:20 pm**
☽♋ △ ♆♓   **10:05 pm**

182

December

Fri 1
3rd ♋

☽♋ △ ♆ ♓	1:05 am	
☽♋ □ ♀ ♎	3:09 am	**12:09 am**
☽♋ ☍ ♀ ♑	8:07 am	**5:07 am** ☽ v/c
☿ enters ♑	9:31 am	**6:31 am**
☽ enters ♌	11:00 am	**8:00 am**
☽♌ ⚻ ☿ ♑	11:10 am	**8:10 am**
☽♌ ⚻ ♄ ♓	1:17 pm	**10:17 am**
☽♌ △ ♂ ♐	9:48 pm	**6:48 pm**
☽♌ □ ♃ ♉		**9:44 pm**

Sat 2
3rd ♌

☽♌ □ ♃ ♉	12:44 am	
☽♌ △ ☉ ♐	6:45 am	**3:45 am**
♀♑ ⚹ ♄ ♓	10:27 am	**7:27 am**
☽♌ △ ⚷ ♈	6:06 pm	**3:06 pm**

Sun 3
3rd ♌

☽♌ □ ♅ ♉	3:13 am	**12:13 am**
♀♎ □ ♀ ♑	8:29 am	**5:29 am**
☽♌ ⚻ ♆ ♓	12:31 pm	**9:31 am**
♂♐ ⚻ ♃ ♉	6:20 pm	**3:20 pm**
☽♌ ⚻ ♀ ♑	7:57 pm	**4:57 pm**
☽♌ ⚹ ♀ ♎	9:11 pm	**6:11 pm** ☽ v/c
☽ enters ♍	10:50 pm	**7:50 pm**
☽♍ ☍ ♄ ♓		**10:26 pm**

OP: After Moon squares Uranus until v/c Moon. After the square, wait two hours for stability. Then you can use this OP for self-improvement, relationship-building, or whatever interests you.

Eastern Standard Time (EST) plain / **Pacific Standard Time (PST) bold**

OCTOBER
S	M	T	W	T	F	S
1	2	3	4	5	6	7
8	9	10	11	12	13	14
15	16	17	18	19	20	21
22	23	24	25	26	27	28
29	30	31				

NOVEMBER
S	M	T	W	T	F	S
			1	2	3	4
5	6	7	8	9	10	11
12	13	14	15	16	17	18
19	20	21	22	23	24	25
26	27	28	29	30		

DECEMBER
S	M	T	W	T	F	S
					1	2
3	4	5	6	7	8	9
10	11	12	13	14	15	16
17	18	19	20	21	22	23
24	25	26	27	28	29	30
31						

December

4 Mon
3rd ♍
☽ 4th Quarter 12 ♍ 49 (Pacific)

☽♍ ☌ ♄ ♓ 1:26 am
☽♍ △ ☿ ♑ 5:12 am **2:12 am**
☽♍ △ ♃ ♉ 12:33 pm **9:33 am**
♀ enters ♏ 1:51 pm **10:51 am**
☽♍ ☐ ♂ ♐ 1:52 pm **10:52 am**
☽♍ ☐ ☉ ♐ **9:49 pm**

5 Tue
3rd ♍
☽ 4th Quarter 12 ♍ 49 (Eastern)

☽♍ ☐ ☉ ♐ 12:49 am
☽♍ ⊼ ♅ ♈ 6:37 am **3:37 am**
☽♍ △ ♇ ♑ 3:45 pm **12:45 pm**
♀♏ △ ♄ ♓ 5:51 pm **2:51 pm**
☽♍ ☌ ♆ ♓ **10:17 pm**

6 Wed
4th ♍
NEPTUNE DIRECT
OP: After Moon opposes Neptune on Tuesday or today until v/c Moon today. Early birds can use this time for high productivity.

☽♍ ☌ ♆ ♓ 1:17 am
♆D 8:20 am **5:20 am**
☽♍ △ ♀ ♑ 8:50 am **5:50 am** ☽ v/c
☽ enters ♎ 11:35 am **8:35 am**
☽♎ ⊼ ♄ ♓ 2:26 pm **11:26 am**
☽♎ ☐ ☿ ♑ 11:00 pm **8:00 pm**
☽♎ ⊼ ♃ ♉ **9:42 pm**

7 Thu
4th ♎
HANUKKAH BEGINS AT SUNDOWN

☽♎ ⊼ ♃ ♉ 12:42 am
☽♎ ⚹ ♂ ♐ 6:16 am **3:16 am**
☽♎ ⚹ ☉ ♐ 6:37 pm **3:37 pm**
☽♎ ☌ ♅ ♈ 6:40 pm **3:40 pm**
☉♐ △ ♅ ♈ 7:12 pm **4:12 pm**
☿♑ △ ♃ ♉ 11:09 pm **8:09 pm**

December

Mercury Note: Mercury enters its Storm (moving less than 40 minutes of arc per day) on Saturday, as it slows down before going retrograde. The Storm acts like the retrograde. Not favorable to start new projects—just follow through with the items that are already on your plate. Write down new ideas with date and time they occurred.

Fri 8
4th ♎

☽♎ ⚻ ♅♉ 3:24 am **12:24 am**
☽♎ ⚻ ♆♓ 12:45 pm **9:45 am**
☽♎ □ ♇♑ 8:05 pm **5:05 pm** ☽ v/c
☽ enters ♏ 10:35 pm **7:35 pm**
☽♏ △ ♄♓ **10:33 pm**

Sat 9
4th ♏

☽♏ △ ♄♓ 1:33 am
☽♏ ☌ ♀♏ 9:24 am **6:24 am**
☽♏ ☍ ♃♉ 10:41 am **7:41 am**
☽♏ ⚹ ☿♑ 12:46 pm **9:46 am**
♀♏ ☍ ♃♉ 10:35 pm **7:35 pm**

Sun 10
4th ♏

☽♏ ⚻ ⚷♈ 3:55 am **12:55 am**
☽♏ ☍ ♅♉ 12:03 pm **9:03 am**
☽♏ △ ♆♓ 8:58 pm **5:58 pm**

OP: After Moon opposes Uranus today until v/c Moon on Monday. This Sunday OP during the Balsamic Moon should be used for clearing up emotions and deep thinking.

Eastern Standard Time (EST) plain / **Pacific Standard Time (PST) bold**

NOVEMBER

S	M	T	W	T	F	S
			1	2	3	4
5	6	7	8	9	10	11
12	13	14	15	16	17	18
19	20	21	22	23	24	25
26	27	28	29	30		

DECEMBER

S	M	T	W	T	F	S
					1	2
3	4	5	6	7	8	9
10	11	12	13	14	15	16
17	18	19	20	21	22	23
24	25	26	27	28	29	30
31						

JANUARY 2024

S	M	T	W	T	F	S
	1	2	3	4	5	6
7	8	9	10	11	12	13
14	15	16	17	18	19	20
21	22	23	24	25	26	27
28	29	30	31			

December

Mercury Note: Mercury goes retrograde on Tuesday, December 12 (PST), or Wednesday, December 13 (EST), and remains so until January 1, after which it will still be in its Storm until January 7. Projects initiated during this entire period may not work out as planned. It's best to use this time for reviews, editing, escrows, and so forth.

11 Mon
4th ♏

☽♏ ⚹ ♀♑	3:57 am **12:57 am** ☽ v/c
☽ enters ♐	6:11 am **3:11 am**
☽♐ □ ♄♓	9:13 am **6:13 am**
☿♑ ⚹ ♀♏	2:17 pm **11:17 am**
☽♐ ⚻ ♃♉	5:15 pm **2:15 pm**
☉♐ ⚻ ♅♉	10:21 pm

12 Tue
4th ♐
● New Moon 20 ♐ 40
Mercury retrograde (Pacific)

☉♐ ⚻ ♅♉	1:21 am
☽♐ ☌ ♂♐	5:05 am **2:05 am**
☽♐ △ ⚷♈	9:39 am **6:39 am**
☽♐ ⚻ ♅♉	5:14 pm **2:14 pm**
☽♐ ☌ ☉♐	6:32 pm **3:32 pm**
☽♐ □ ♆♓	10:48 pm ☽ v/c
☿℞	11:09 pm

13 Wed
1st ♐
Mercury retrograde (Eastern)

☽♐ □ ♆♓	1:48 am ☽ v/c
☿℞	2:09 am
☽ enters ♑	10:31 am **7:31 am**
☽♑ ⚹ ♄♓	1:39 pm **10:39 am**
☽♑ △ ♃♉	8:51 pm **5:51 pm**
☽♑ ☌ ☿♑	9:47 pm

14 Thu
1st ♑

☽♑ ☌ ☿♑	12:47 am
☽♑ ⚹ ♀♏	5:55 am **2:55 am**
☽♑ □ ⚷♈	12:45 pm **9:45 am**
☽♑ △ ♅♉	8:00 pm **5:00 pm**

December

Fri 15
1st ♑
Hanukkah ends

☽♑ ⚹ ♆♓ 4:27 am **1:27 am**
☽♑ ☌ ♀♑ 11:04 am **8:04 am** ☽ v/c
☽ enters ♒ 12:56 pm **9:56 am**
♂♐ △ ⚷♈ 5:55 pm **2:55 pm**
☽♒ □ ♃♉ 10:52 pm **7:52 pm**

Sat 16
1st ♒

☽♒ □ ♀♏ 12:33 pm **9:33 am**
☽♒ ⚹ ⚷♈ 2:45 pm **11:45 am**
☽♒ ⚹ ♂♐ 3:52 pm **12:52 pm**
☽♒ □ ♅♉ 9:53 pm **6:53 pm**
☉♐ □ ♆♓ 10:43 pm **7:43 pm**

OP: After Moon squares Uranus today until v/c Moon on Sunday. Very positive OP for reaching out to people and building rapport.

Sun 17
1st ♒

☽♒ ⚹ ☉♐ 7:04 am **4:04 am** ☽ v/c
♀♏ ⚻ ⚷♈ 2:50 pm **11:50 am**
☽ enters ♓ 2:58 pm **11:58 am**
☽♓ ☌ ♄♓ 6:32 pm **3:32 pm**
☽♓ ⚹ ♃♉   **9:49 pm**
☽♓ ⚹ ☿♑   **10:21 pm**

Eastern Standard Time (EST) plain / **Pacific Standard Time (PST) bold**

NOVEMBER							**DECEMBER**							**JANUARY 2024**						
S	M	T	W	T	F	S	S	M	T	W	T	F	S	S	M	T	W	T	F	S
			1	2	3	4						1	2		1	2	3	4	5	6
5	6	7	8	9	10	11	3	4	5	6	7	8	9	7	8	9	10	11	12	13
12	13	14	15	16	17	18	10	11	12	13	14	15	16	14	15	16	17	18	19	20
19	20	21	22	23	24	25	17	18	19	20	21	22	23	21	22	23	24	25	26	27
26	27	28	29	30			24	25	26	27	28	29	30	28	29	30	31			
							31													

December

18 Mon
1st ♓

☽♓ ⚹ ♃♉	12:49 am	
☽♓ ⚹ ☿♑	1:21 am	
♃♉ △ ♃♉	9:28 am	**6:28 am**
☽♓ △ ♀♏	7:30 pm	**4:30 pm**
☽♓ □ ♂♐	8:58 pm	**5:58 pm**
☽♓ ⚹ ♅♉		**9:14 pm**

19 Tue
1st ♓
◐ 2nd Quarter 27 ♓ 35
OP: After Moon squares the Sun until Moon enters Aries. A good time for anything, especially the arts and healing.

☽♓ ⚹ ♅♉	12:14 am	
☽♓ ☌ ♆♓	9:07 am	**6:07 am**
☽♓ □ ☉♐	1:39 pm	**10:39 am**
☽♓ ⚹ ♀♑	4:03 pm	**1:03 pm** ☽ v/c
☽ enters ♈	5:47 pm	**2:47 pm**
☽♈ □ ☿♑		**9:42 pm**

20 Wed
2nd ♈

☽♈ □ ☿♑	12:42 am	
☽♈ ☌ ⚷♈	8:27 pm	**5:27 pm**
♀♏ ☍ ♅♉		**11:04 pm**

21 Thu
2nd ♈
WINTER SOLSTICE
YULE
SUN ENTERS CAPRICORN
OP: After Moon squares Pluto until v/c Moon. Use this extra boost of energy in positive ways for optimal results!

♀♏ ☍ ♅♉	2:04 am	
☽♈ △ ♂♐	3:23 am	**12:23 am**
☽♈ ⚻ ♀♏	3:54 am	**12:54 am**
♃♑ ⚹ ♄♓	7:33 am	**4:33 am**
♂♐ ⚻ ♅♉	9:44 am	**6:44 am**
☽♈ □ ♀♑	8:11 pm	**5:11 pm**
☽♈ △ ☉♐	9:47 pm	**6:47 pm** ☽ v/c
☽ enters ♉	9:50 pm	**6:50 pm**
☉ enters ♑	10:27 pm	**7:27 pm**
☽♉ △ ☿♑		**9:21 pm**
☽♉ ⚹ ♄♓		**11:08 pm**

December

Fri 22
2nd ♉

☽♉ △ ☿♑ 12:21 am
☽♉ ⚹ ♄♓ 2:08 am
☽♉ ☌ ♃♉ 7:53 am **4:53 am**
☉♑ ☌ ☿♑ 1:54 pm **10:54 am**
☿ enters ♐ **10:18 pm**

Sat 23
2nd ♉

☿ enters ♐ 1:18 am
☽♉ ☌ ♅♉ 8:33 am **5:33 am**
☽♉ ⚻ ♂♐ 11:22 am **8:22 am**
☽♉ ☍ ♀♏ 2:04 pm **11:04 am**
☽♉ ⚹ ♆♓ 6:12 pm **3:12 pm**
☽♉ ⚻ ☿♐ **9:50 pm**
☽♉ △ ♇♑ **10:40 pm** ☽ v/c

OP: After Moon opposes Venus today until Moon enters Gemini on Sunday. Take advantage of this perfect time before the holidays for anything from the arts to practical matters or for connecting with others.

Sun 24
2nd ♉
Christmas Eve

☽♉ ⚻ ☿♐ 12:50 am
☽♉ △ ♇♑ 1:40 am ☽ v/c
☽ enters ♊ 3:15 am **12:15 am**
☽♊ ⚻ ☉♑ 7:38 am **4:38 am**
☽♊ □ ♄♓ 7:58 am **4:58 am**
☉♑ ⚹ ♄♓ 12:28 pm **9:28 am**

Eastern Standard Time (EST) plain / **Pacific Standard Time (PST) bold**

	NOVEMBER							DECEMBER							JANUARY 2024					
S	M	T	W	T	F	S	S	M	T	W	T	F	S	S	M	T	W	T	F	S
			1	2	3	4						1	2		1	2	3	4	5	6
5	6	7	8	9	10	11	3	4	5	6	7	8	9	7	8	9	10	11	12	13
12	13	14	15	16	17	18	10	11	12	13	14	15	16	14	15	16	17	18	19	20
19	20	21	22	23	24	25	17	18	19	20	21	22	23	21	22	23	24	25	26	27
26	27	28	29	30			24	25	26	27	28	29	30	28	29	30	31			
							31													

December

25 Mon
2nd ♊
Christmas Day

☽♊ ✶ ⚷♈	7:21 am	**4:21 am**
♀♏ △ ♆♓	12:15 pm	**9:15 am**
☽♊ ☍ ♂♐	9:08 pm	**6:08 pm**
☽♊ □ ♆♓		**9:57 pm**
☽♊ ⚻ ♀♏		**11:15 pm**
☽♊ ☍ ☿♐		**11:55 pm** ☽ v/c

26 Tue
2nd ♊
○ Full Moon 4 ♋ 58
Kwanzaa begins
Boxing Day (Canada & UK)
Chiron direct

☽♊ □ ♆♓	12:57 am	
☽♊ ⚻ ♀♏	2:15 am	
☽♊ ☍ ☿♐	2:55 am	☽ v/c
☽♊ ⚻ ♀♑	8:45 am	**5:45 am**
☽ enters ♋	10:15 am	**7:15 am**
☽♋ △ ♄♓	3:30 pm	**12:30 pm**
☽♋ ☍ ☉♑	7:33 pm	**4:33 pm**
☽♋ ✶ ♃♉	8:45 pm	**5:45 pm**
⚷ D	10:10 pm	**7:10 pm**
☿♐ □ ♆♓		**11:43 pm**

27 Wed
3rd ♋

☿♐ □ ♆♓	2:43 am	
☉♑ △ ♃♉	10:28 am	**7:28 am**
☽♋ □ ⚷♈	3:23 pm	**12:23 pm**
☿♐ ☌ ♂♐	7:31 pm	**4:31 pm**
☽♋ ✶ ♅♉	11:04 pm	**8:04 pm**

28 Thu
3rd ♋

☽♋ ⚻ ☿♐	7:40 am	**4:40 am**
☽♋ ⚻ ♂♐	9:17 am	**6:17 am**
☽♋ △ ♆♓	9:45 am	**6:45 am**
☽♋ △ ♀♏	5:12 pm	**2:12 pm**
♂♐ □ ♆♓	5:16 pm	**2:16 pm**
☽♋ ☍ ♀♑	5:57 pm	**2:57 pm** ☽ v/c
☽ enters ♌	7:23 pm	**4:23 pm**
♀♏ ✶ ♀♑		**10:01 pm**
☽♌ ⚻ ♄♓		**10:15 pm**

December

Fri 29
3rd ♌

♀♏ ⚹ ♀♑ 1:01 am
☽♌ ⚻ ♄♓ 1:15 am
☽♌ □ ♃♉ 6:18 am **3:18 am**
☽♌ ⚻ ☉♑ 10:19 am **7:19 am**
♀ enters ♐ 3:24 pm **12:24 pm**
☽♌ △ ⚷♈ **10:46 pm**

Sat 30
3rd ♌

JUPITER DIRECT

☽♌ △ ⚷♈ 1:46 am
☽♌ □ ♅♉ 9:39 am **6:39 am**
☽♌ △ ☿♐ 4:00 pm **1:00 pm**
☽♌ ⚻ ♆♓ 8:57 pm **5:57 pm**
♃ D 9:40 pm **6:40 pm**
☽♌ △ ♂♐ **9:18 pm** ☽ v/c

OP: After Moon squares Uranus today until v/c Moon today or on Sunday. Despite Mercury being retrograde, this OP is excellent for creativity and celebrating a happy new year.

Sun 31
3rd ♌
NEW YEAR'S EVE

☽♌ △ ♂♐ 12:18 am ☽ v/c
☽♌ ⚻ ♀♑ 5:34 am **2:34 am**
☽ enters ♍ 6:53 am **3:53 am**
☽♍ □ ♀♐ 11:23 am **8:23 am**
☽♍ ☍ ♄♓ 1:24 pm **10:24 am**
☽♍ △ ♃♉ 6:10 pm **3:10 pm**

Eastern Standard Time (EST) plain / **Pacific Standard Time (PST) bold**

NOVEMBER

S	M	T	W	T	F	S
			1	2	3	4
5	6	7	8	9	10	11
12	13	14	15	16	17	18
19	20	21	22	23	24	25
26	27	28	29	30		

DECEMBER

S	M	T	W	T	F	S
					1	2
3	4	5	6	7	8	9
10	11	12	13	14	15	16
17	18	19	20	21	22	23
24	25	26	27	28	29	30
31						

JANUARY 2024

S	M	T	W	T	F	S
	1	2	3	4	5	6
7	8	9	10	11	12	13
14	15	16	17	18	19	20
21	22	23	24	25	26	27
28	29	30	31			

World Time Zones
Compared to Eastern Standard Time

(R)   EST
(S)   CST/Subtract 1 hour
(Q)   Add 1 hour
(P)   Add 2 hours
(O)   Add 3 hours
(Z)   Add 5 hours
(T)   MST/Subtract 2 hours
(U)   PST/Subtract 3 hours
(U*) Subtract 3.5 hours
(V)   Subtract 4 hours
(V*) Subtract 4.5 hours
(W) Subtract 5 hours
(X)   Subtract 6 hours
(Y)   Subtract 7 hours
(A)   Add 6 hours
(B)   Add 7 hours
(C)   Add 8 hours
(C*) Add 8.5 hours

(D)   Add 9 hours
(D*) Add 9.5 hours
(E)   Add 10 hours
(E*) Add 10.5 hours
(F)   Add 11 hours
(F*) Add 11.5 hours
(G)   Add 12 hours
(H)   Add 13 hours
(I)   Add 14 hours
(I*) Add 14.5 hours
(K)   Add 15 hours
(K*) Add 15.5 hours
(L)   Add 16 hours
(L*) Add 16.5 hours
(M)   Add 17 hours
(M*) Add 18 hours
(P*) Add 2.5 hours

Eastern Standard Time = Universal Time (Greenwich Mean Time) + or − the value from the table.

World Map of Time Zones

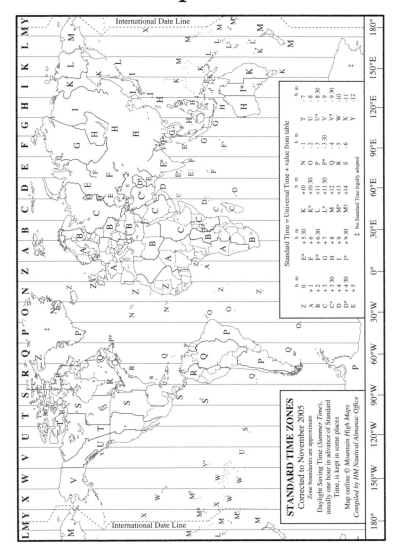

2023 Ephemeris Tables
January 2023

DATE	SID. TIME	SUN	MOON	NODE	MERCURY	VENUS	MARS	JUPITER	SATURN	URANUS	NEPTUNE	PLUTO	CERES	PALLAS	JUNO	VESTA	CHIRON
1 Su	6 41 33	10♑17 02	3♉39	11♉45 Rx	23♑42 Rx	27♐23	9♊04 Rx	1♈12	22♒25	15♉09 Rx	22♓52	27♑39	3♎09	20♋49 Rx	24♓34	14♓01	11♈58
2 M	6 45 30	11 18 11	16 14	11 45	23 06	28 38	8 55	1 19	22 31	15 08	22 53	27 41	3 22	20 30	25 00	14 25	11 59
3 T	6 49 26	12 19 19	28 36	11 44	22 18	29 53	8 46	1 26	22 37	15 07	22 54	27 43	3 34	20 10	25 25	14 48	11 59
4 W	6 53 23	13 20 27	10♊48	11 39	21 20	1♒08	8 39	1 34	22 43	15 06	22 55	27 45	3 46	19 50	25 51	15 12	12 00
5 Th	6 57 19	14 21 35	22 53	11 33	20 13	2 23	8 32	1 42	22 49	15 05	22 56	27 47	3 58	19 30	26 17	15 36	12 00
6 F	7 1 16	15 22 43	4♋52	11 23	18 59	3 39	8 26	1 50	22 56	15 04	22 57	27 49	4 09	19 10	26 43	16 00	12 01
7 Sa	7 5 13	16 23 51	16 47	11 11	17 40	4 54	8 21	1 58	23 02	15 03	22 59	27 51	4 20	18 50	27 10	16 24	12 02
8 Su	7 9 9	17 24 59	28 41	10 58	16 20	6 09	8 17	2 06	23 08	15 02	23 00	27 53	4 31	18 29	27 37	16 48	12 03
9 M	7 13 6	18 26 06	10♌33	10 44	15 00	7 24	8 14	2 14	23 15	15 01	23 01	27 55	4 41	18 09	28 03	17 12	12 04
10 T	7 17 2	19 27 14	22 26	10 32	13 42	8 39	8 11	2 23	23 21	15 01	23 02	27 57	4 51	17 49	28 30	17 37	12 05
11 W	7 20 59	20 28 21	4♍21	10 21	12 31	9 54	8 09	2 32	23 28	15 00	23 03	27 59	5 01	17 29	28 58	18 01	12 06
12 Th	7 24 55	21 29 29	16 21	10 13	11 26	11 09	8 08 D	2 40	23 34	15 00	23 05	28 01	5 10	17 09	29 25	18 26	12 07
13 F	7 28 52	22 30 36	28 30	10 08	10 30	12 24	8 08	2 49	23 41	14 59	23 06	28 03	5 19	16 49	29 53	18 50	12 08
14 Sa	7 32 48	23 31 43	10♎51	10 05	9 42	13 39	8 08	2 58	23 47	14 59	23 07	28 05	5 28	16 29	0♈20	19 15	12 09
15 Su	7 36 45	24 32 50	23 29	10 04 D	9 05	14 54	8 09	3 08	23 54	14 58	23 09	28 07	5 36	16 10	0 48	19 40	12 10
16 M	7 40 42	25 33 57	6♏28	10 05 Rx	8 37	16 09	8 11	3 17	24 00	14 58	23 10	28 09	5 44	15 51	1 16	20 05	12 11
17 T	7 44 38	26 35 04	19 53	10 04	8 19	17 24	8 14	3 26	24 07	14 57	23 11	28 11	5 52	15 32	1 44	20 29	12 13
18 W	7 48 35	27 36 10	3♐47	10 02	8 09 D	18 39	8 18	3 36	24 14	14 57	23 13	28 12	5 59	15 13	2 13	20 54	12 14
19 Th	7 52 31	28 37 17	18 10	9 58	8 09	19 54	8 22	3 46	24 21	14 57	23 14	28 14	6 06	14 55	2 41	21 20	12 15
20 F	7 56 28	29 38 23	3♑00	9 51	8 17	21 08	8 27	3 56	24 27	14 57	23 16	28 16	6 12	14 38	3 10	21 45	12 17
21 Sa	8 0 24	0♒29 29	18 11	9 41	8 32	22 23	8 32	4 06	24 34	14 57	23 17	28 18	6 18	14 20	3 39	22 10	12 18
22 Su	8 4 21	1 40 34	3♒32	9 30	8 54	23 38	8 39	4 16	24 41	14 57	23 19	28 20	6 23	14 04	4 08	22 35	12 20
23 M	8 8 17	2 41 38	18 53	9 18	9 22	24 53	8 46	4 26	24 48	14 56	23 21	28 22	6 29	13 47	4 37	23 01	12 22
24 T	8 12 14	3 42 42	4♓00	9 07	9 56	26 08	8 53	4 36	24 55	14 56	23 22	28 24	6 33	13 32	5 06	23 26	12 23
25 W	8 16 11	4 43 44	18 46	8 59	10 35	27 23	9 02	4 47	25 02	14 57	23 24	28 26	6 38	13 16	5 36	23 52	12 25
26 Th	8 20 7	5 44 46	3♈03	8 53	11 19	28 37	9 10	4 57	25 09	14 57	23 25	28 28	6 42	13 02	6 05	24 17	12 27
27 F	8 24 4	6 45 46	16 51	8 51	12 07	29 52	9 20	5 08	25 16	14 57	23 27	28 30	6 45	12 48	6 35	24 43	12 28
28 Sa	8 28 0	7 46 46	0♉10	8 50	12 58	1♓07	9 30	5 19	25 23	14 57	23 29	28 32	6 48	12 34	7 05	25 08	12 30
29 Su	8 31 57	8 47 44	13 03	8 50	13 54	2 21	9 41	5 30	25 30	14 57	23 31	28 34	6 51	12 22	7 35	25 34	12 32
30 M	8 35 53	9 48 41	25 35	8 49	14 52	3 36	9 52	5 41	25 37	14 58	23 32	28 36	6 53	12 09	8 05	26 00	12 34
31 T	8 39 50	10 49 37	7♊51	8 47	15 53	4 51	10 04	5 52	25 44	14 58	23 34	28 38	6 55	11 58	8 36	26 26	12 36

Tables are calculated for midnight Greenwich Mean Time

February 2023

DATE	SID.TIME	SUN	MOON	NODE	MERCURY	VENUS	MARS	JUPITER	SATURN	URANUS	NEPTUNE	PLUTO	CERES	PALLAS	JUNO	VESTA	CHIRON
1 W	8 43 46	11≈50 31	19Ⅱ56	8♉42R	16♑57	6✹05	10Ⅱ17	6♈03	25≈51	14♉59	23✹36	28♑40	6♎57	11♋47R	9♈06	26✹52	12♈38
2 Th	8 47 43	12 51 25	1♋54	8 35	18 03	7 20	10 30	6 15	25 58	14 59	23 38	28 42	6 58	11 37	9 37	27 18	12 40
3 F	8 51 40	13 52 17	13 47	8 24	19 12	8 34	10 43	6 26	26 05	15 00	23 40	28 44	6 58R	11 28	10 07	27 44	12 42
4 Sa	8 55 36	14 53 08	25 39	8 11	20 22	9 49	10 57	6 38	26 13	15 00	23 41	28 46	6 58	11 19	10 38	28 10	12 45
5 Su	8 59 33	15 53 58	7♌31	7 56	21 35	11 03	11 12	6 49	26 20	15 01	23 43	28 48	6 58	11 11	11 09	28 36	12 47
6 M	9 3 29	16 54 46	19 25	7 41	22 49	12 18	11 27	7 01	26 27	15 02	23 45	28 49	6 57	11 03	11 40	29 02	12 49
7 T	9 7 26	17 55 34	1♍23	7 27	24 04	13 32	11 43	7 13	26 34	15 02	23 47	28 51	6 56	10 56	12 11	29 28	12 51
8 W	9 11 22	18 56 20	13 25	7 15	25 21	14 46	11 59	7 25	26 41	15 03	23 49	28 53	6 54	10 50	12 42	29 55	12 54
9 Th	9 15 19	19 57 05	25 32	7 06	26 40	16 01	12 15	7 37	26 48	15 04	23 51	28 55	6 52	10 45	13 14	0♈21	12 56
10 F	9 19 15	20 57 49	7♎48	7 00	28 00	17 15	12 32	7 49	26 56	15 05	23 53	28 57	6 50	10 40	13 45	0 47	12 58
11 Sa	9 23 12	21 58 32	20 13	6 56	29 21	18 29	12 49	8 01	27 03	15 06	23 55	28 59	6 47	10 36	14 17	1 14	13 01
12 Su	9 27 9	22 59 14	2♏53	6 55D	0≈43	19 43	13 07	8 13	27 10	15 07	23 57	29 01	6 44	10 33	14 48	1 40	13 03
13 M	9 31 5	23 59 54	15 50	6 55R	2 07	20 58	13 25	8 25	27 17	15 08	23 59	29 02	6 40	10 30	15 20	2 07	13 06
14 T	9 35 2	25 00 34	29 09	6 55	3 32	22 12	13 44	8 38	27 25	15 09	24 01	29 04	6 36	10 28	15 52	2 33	13 08
15 W	9 38 58	26 01 13	12✹51	6 54	4 57	23 26	14 03	8 50	27 32	15 10	24 03	29 06	6 31	10 27	16 24	3 00	13 11
16 Th	9 42 55	27 01 51	27 00	6 51	6 24	24 40	14 22	9 03	27 39	15 12	24 05	29 08	6 26	10 26D	16 56	3 26	13 14
17 F	9 46 51	28 02 27	11♑34	6 45	7 52	25 54	14 42	9 15	27 46	15 13	24 07	29 10	6 20	10 26	17 28	3 53	13 16
18 Sa	9 50 48	29 03 02	26 30	6 37	9 21	27 08	15 02	9 28	27 54	15 14	24 09	29 11	6 14	10 26	18 00	4 20	13 19
19 Su	9 54 45	0✹03 36	11≈39	6 27	10 51	28 22	15 23	9 41	28 01	15 16	24 11	29 13	6 08	10 28	18 33	4 46	13 22
20 M	9 58 41	1 04 09	26 53	6 16	12 22	29 36	15 44	9 54	28 08	15 17	24 14	29 15	6 01	10 29	19 05	5 13	13 24
21 T	10 2 38	2 04 39	11✹59	6 07	13 53	0♈49	16 05	10 07	28 16	15 18	24 16	29 17	5 54	10 32	19 38	5 40	13 27
22 W	10 6 34	3 05 09	26 49	5 59	15 26	2 03	16 27	10 20	28 23	15 20	24 18	29 18	5 46	10 35	20 10	6 07	13 30
23 Th	10 10 31	4 05 36	11♈14	5 54	17 00	3 17	16 49	10 33	28 30	15 21	24 20	29 20	5 38	10 39	20 43	6 34	13 33
24 F	10 14 27	5 06 01	25 11	5 52D	18 35	4 31	17 11	10 46	28 37	15 23	24 22	29 22	5 30	10 43	21 16	7 01	13 36
25 Sa	10 18 24	6 06 25	8♉39	5 51	20 10	5 44	17 33	10 59	28 44	15 25	24 24	29 23	5 21	10 48	21 49	7 27	13 39
26 Su	10 22 20	7 06 47	21 39	5 52	21 47	6 58	17 56	11 12	28 52	15 26	24 27	29 25	5 12	10 53	22 22	7 54	13 42
27 M	10 26 17	8 07 07	4Ⅱ17	5 53R	23 24	8 11	18 19	11 25	28 59	15 28	24 29	29 26	5 02	10 59	22 55	8 21	13 45
28 T	10 30 13	9 07 25	16 35	5 52	25 03	9 25	18 43	11 39	29 06	15 30	24 31	29 28	4 53	11 06	23 28	8 48	13 48

March 2023

DATE	SID. TIME	SUN	MOON	NODE	MERCURY	VENUS	MARS	JUPITER	SATURN	URANUS	NEPTUNE	PLUTO	CERES	PALLAS	JUNO	VESTA	CHIRON
1 Th	10 34 10	10⨯07 41	28Ⅱ40	5♏50R	26≈43	10⨯38	19Ⅱ07	11⨯52	29≈13	15♉32	24⨯33	29♑30	4≏42R	11♋13	24⨉01	9⨉15	13⨉51
2 F	10 38 7	11 07 55	10♋36	5 46	28 23	11 52	19 31	12 06	29 20	15 34	24 35	29 31	4 32	11 20	24 34	9 42	13 54
3 F	10 42 3	12 08 06	22 28	5 39	0⨯05	13 05	19 55	12 19	29 28	15 36	24 38	29 33	4 21	11 29	25 08	10 09	13 57
4 Sa	10 46 0	13 08 16	4♌19	5 31	1 48	14 18	20 19	12 33	29 35	15 38	24 40	29 34	4 10	11 37	25 41	10 36	14 00
5 Su	10 49 56	14 08 24	16 12	5 21	3 31	15 31	20 44	12 46	29 42	15 40	24 42	29 36	3 59	11 46	26 15	11 03	14 03
6 M	10 53 53	15 08 30	28 11	5 11	5 16	16 44	21 09	13 00	29 49	15 42	24 44	29 37	3 47	11 56	26 48	11 31	14 06
7 T	10 57 49	16 08 34	10♍15	5 01	7 02	17 58	21 35	13 14	29 56	15 44	24 47	29 39	3 35	12 06	27 22	11 58	14 10
8 W	11 1 46	17 08 36	22 27	4 53	8 49	19 10	22 00	13 27	0⨉03	15 46	24 49	29 40	3 23	12 17	27 56	12 25	14 13
9 Th	11 5 42	18 08 36	4≏47	4 47	10 37	20 23	22 26	13 41	0 10	15 48	24 51	29 42	3 11	12 28	28 29	12 52	14 16
10 F	11 9 39	19 08 35	17 17	4 43	12 26	21 36	22 52	13 55	0 17	15 50	24 53	29 43	2 58	12 39	29 03	13 19	14 19
11 Sa	11 13 36	20 08 32	29 57	4 42D	14 17	22 49	23 18	14 09	0 24	15 52	24 56	29 45	2 45	12 51	29 37	13 46	14 23
12 Su	11 17 32	21 08 27	12♏50	4 42	16 08	24 02	23 45	14 23	0 31	15 55	24 58	29 46	2 32	13 03	0♉11	14 13	14 26
13 M	11 21 29	22 08 20	25 56	4 43	18 01	25 14	24 11	14 37	0 38	15 57	25 00	29 47	2 19	13 16	0 45	14 41	14 29
14 T	11 25 25	23 08 12	9⨯19	4 44	19 54	26 27	24 38	14 51	0 45	15 59	25 02	29 49	2 06	13 29	1 19	15 08	14 32
15 W	11 29 22	24 08 02	22 59	4 45R	21 49	27 39	25 05	15 05	0 52	16 04	25 05	29 50	1 52	13 42	1 53	15 35	14 36
16 Th	11 33 18	25 07 50	6♑59	4 44	23 45	28 52	25 32	15 19	0 59	16 04	25 07	29 51	1 39	13 56	2 27	16 02	14 39
17 F	11 37 15	26 07 37	21 17	4 42	25 42	0♉04	26 00	15 33	1 06	16 07	25 09	29 52	1 25	14 10	3 02	16 29	14 43
18 Sa	11 41 11	27 07 22	5≈51	4 38	27 40	1 17	26 27	15 47	1 12	16 09	25 12	29 54	1 11	14 25	3 36	16 57	14 46
19 Su	11 45 8	28 07 06	20 36	4 33	29 38	2 29	26 55	16 01	1 19	16 12	25 14	29 55	0 58	14 40	4 10	17 24	14 49
20 M	11 49 5	29 06 47	5⨯27	4 28	1⨉38	3 41	27 23	16 15	1 26	16 14	25 16	29 56	0 44	14 55	4 45	17 51	14 53
21 T	11 53 1	0⨉06 27	20 14	4 23	3 38	4 53	27 51	16 30	1 33	16 17	25 18	29 57	0 30	15 11	5 19	18 19	14 56
22 W	11 56 58	1 06 04	4⨉49	4 18	5 38	6 05	28 20	16 44	1 39	16 20	25 21	29 58	0 16	15 27	5 53	18 46	15 00
23 Th	12 0 54	2 05 40	19 07	4 16	7 39	7 17	28 48	16 58	1 46	16 22	25 23	29 59	0 02	15 43	6 28	19 13	15 03
24 F	12 4 51	3 05 13	3♉02	4 15D	9 40	8 29	29 17	17 12	1 52	16 25	25 25	0≈01	29♍48	16 00	7 03	19 40	15 07
25 Sa	12 8 47	4 04 45	16 32	4 16	11 41	9 41	29 46	17 27	1 59	16 28	25 27	0 02	29 34	16 17	7 37	20 08	15 10
26 Su	12 12 44	5 04 14	29 38	4 17	13 41	10 52	0♋15	17 41	2 05	16 31	25 30	0 03	29 21	16 34	8 12	20 35	15 13
27 M	12 16 40	6 03 41	12Ⅱ20	4 19	15 41	12 04	0 44	17 55	2 12	16 33	25 32	0 04	29 07	16 52	8 46	21 02	15 17
28 T	12 20 37	7 03 06	24 44	4 20	17 40	13 15	1 13	18 10	2 18	16 36	25 34	0 05	28 54	17 09	9 21	21 30	15 20
29 W	12 24 34	8 02 28	6♋52	4 21R	19 38	14 27	1 43	18 24	2 25	16 39	25 36	0 06	28 40	17 27	9 56	21 57	15 24
30 Th	12 28 30	9 01 48	18 51	4 20	21 33	15 38	2 12	18 38	2 31	16 42	25 39	0 07	28 27	17 46	10 31	22 24	15 27
31 F	12 32 27	10 01 06	0♌44	4 19	23 27	16 49	2 42	18 53	2 37	16 45	25 41	0 07	28 14	18 04	11 06	22 52	15 31

Tables are calculated for midnight Greenwich Mean Time

April 2023

DATE	SID. TIME	SUN	MOON	NODE	MERCURY	VENUS	MARS	JUPITER	SATURN	URANUS	NEPTUNE	PLUTO	CERES	PALLAS	JUNO	VESTA	CHIRON
1 Sa	12 36 23	11♈00 21	12♌36	4♉16R	25♈18	18♉01	3♋12	19♈07	2♓44	16♉48	25♓43	0♒08	28♍01R	18♋23	11♉41	23♈19	15♈35
2 Su	12 40 20	11 59 34	24 31	4 13	27 06	19 12	3 42	19 22	2 50	16 51	25 45	0 09	27 48	18 42	12 15	23 46	15 38
3 M	12 44 16	12 58 45	6♍33	4 09	28 51	20 22	4 12	19 36	2 56	16 54	25 48	0 10	27 36	19 02	12 50	24 13	15 42
4 T	12 48 13	13 57 54	18 45	4 06	0♉32	21 33	4 42	19 51	3 02	16 57	25 50	0 11	27 24	19 21	13 25	24 41	15 45
5 W	12 52 9	14 57 00	1♎07	4 03	2 09	22 44	5 13	20 05	3 08	17 00	25 52	0 12	27 12	19 41	14 00	25 08	15 49
6 Th	12 56 6	15 56 05	13 42	4 01	3 41	23 55	5 43	20 20	3 14	17 03	25 54	0 12	27 00	20 01	14 35	25 35	15 52
7 F	13 0 2	16 55 07	26 30	4 00D	5 09	25 05	6 14	20 34	3 20	17 06	25 56	0 13	26 48	20 21	15 10	26 03	15 56
8 Sa	13 3 59	17 54 07	9♏32	4 00	6 32	26 16	6 45	20 48	3 26	17 09	25 58	0 14	26 37	20 42	15 45	26 30	15 59
9 Su	13 7 56	18 53 06	22 46	4 01	7 49	27 26	7 16	21 03	3 32	17 12	26 01	0 14	26 26	21 02	16 21	26 57	16 03
10 M	13 11 52	19 52 02	6♐14	4 02	9 01	28 36	7 47	21 17	3 37	17 15	26 03	0 15	26 16	21 23	16 56	27 24	16 06
11 T	13 15 49	20 50 57	19 53	4 03	10 08	29 46	8 18	21 32	3 43	17 19	26 05	0 16	26 05	21 44	17 31	27 52	16 10
12 W	13 19 45	21 49 51	3♑44	4 04	11 08	0♊56	8 49	21 46	3 49	17 22	26 07	0 16	25 55	22 06	18 06	28 19	16 13
13 Th	13 23 42	22 48 42	17 46	4 04R	12 03	2 06	9 20	22 01	3 54	17 25	26 09	0 17	25 45	22 27	18 41	28 46	16 17
14 F	13 27 38	23 47 32	1♒57	4 04	12 51	3 16	9 52	22 15	4 00	17 28	26 11	0 17	25 36	22 49	19 16	29 13	16 20
15 Sa	13 31 35	24 46 20	16 16	4 04	13 34	4 25	10 23	22 30	4 05	17 32	26 13	0 18	25 27	23 10	19 52	29 41	16 24
16 Su	13 35 32	25 45 07	0♓38	4 03	14 10	5 35	10 55	22 44	4 11	17 35	26 15	0 18	25 18	23 32	20 27	0♉08	16 27
17 M	13 39 28	26 43 51	15 00	4 02	14 40	6 44	11 26	22 59	4 16	17 38	26 17	0 19	25 10	23 54	21 02	0 35	16 31
18 T	13 43 25	27 42 34	29 19	4 01	15 03	7 53	11 58	23 13	4 22	17 41	26 19	0 19	25 02	24 17	21 38	1 02	16 34
19 W	13 47 21	28 41 15	13♈29	4 01	15 21	9 02	12 30	23 28	4 27	17 45	26 21	0 20	24 55	24 39	22 13	1 30	16 38
20 Th	13 51 18	29 39 54	27 25	4 00D	15 32	10 11	13 02	23 42	4 32	17 48	26 23	0 20	24 48	25 02	22 48	1 57	16 41
21 F	13 55 14	0♉38 31	11♉05	4 00	15 37R	11 20	13 34	23 57	4 37	17 51	26 25	0 20	24 41	25 24	23 24	2 24	16 45
22 Sa	13 59 11	1 37 07	24 26	4 01	15 36	12 29	14 06	24 11	4 42	17 55	26 27	0 20	24 34	25 47	23 59	2 51	16 48
23 Su	14 3 7	2 35 40	7♊27	4 01	15 30	13 37	14 39	24 25	4 47	17 58	26 29	0 21	24 29	26 10	24 34	3 18	16 52
24 M	14 7 4	3 34 12	20 10	4 01R	15 18	14 46	15 11	24 40	4 52	18 02	26 31	0 21	24 23	26 33	25 10	3 45	16 55
25 T	14 11 0	4 32 41	2♋35	4 01	15 00	15 54	15 43	24 54	4 57	18 05	26 33	0 21	24 18	26 57	25 45	4 12	16 58
26 W	14 14 57	5 31 08	14 46	4 01	14 39	17 02	16 16	25 08	5 02	18 08	26 35	0 22	24 13	27 20	26 20	4 40	17 02
27 Th	14 18 54	6 29 33	26 46	4 01D	14 13	18 10	16 49	25 23	5 06	18 12	26 37	0 22	24 09	27 43	26 56	5 07	17 05
28 F	14 22 50	7 27 56	8♌41	4 01	13 43	19 18	17 21	25 37	5 11	18 15	26 38	0 22	24 05	28 07	27 31	5 34	17 09
29 Sa	14 26 47	8 26 17	20 34	4 01	13 10	20 26	17 54	25 51	5 15	18 19	26 40	0 22	24 02	28 31	28 07	6 01	17 12
30 Su	14 30 43	9 24 36	2♍30	4 01	12 35	21 33	18 27	26 06	5 20	18 22	26 42	0 22	23 58	28 55	28 42	6 28	17 15

May 2023

DATE	SID. TIME	SUN	MOON	NODE	MERCURY	VENUS	MARS	JUPITER	SATURN	URANUS	NEPTUNE	PLUTO	CERES	PALLAS	JUNO	VESTA	CHIRON
1 M	14 34 40	10♉22 52	14♍34	4♉02	11♉57 ℞	22♊40	19♊00	26♈20	5♓24	18♉26	26♓44	0♒22 ℞	23♍56 ℞	29♎19	29♉17	6♊55	17♈19
2 T	14 38 36	11 21 07	26 49	4 02	11 19	23 48	19 33	26 34	5 29	18 29	26 46	0 22	23 54	29 43	29 53	7 22	17 22
3 W	14 42 33	12 19 19	9♎19	4 03	10 40	24 55	20 06	26 48	5 33	18 32	26 47	0 22	23 52	0♏07	0♊28	7 49	17 25
4 Th	14 46 29	13 17 30	22 06	4 04 ℞	10 02	26 01	20 39	27 02	5 37	18 36	26 49	0 22	23 51	0 31	1 04	8 16	17 28
5 F	14 50 26	14 15 39	5♏12	4 04	9 24	27 08	21 12	27 17	5 41	18 39	26 51	0 22	23 50	0 56	1 39	8 43	17 32
6 Sa	14 54 23	15 13 46	18 35	4 03	8 48	28 14	21 45	27 31	5 45	18 43	26 52	0 22	23 49 D	1 20	2 15	9 09	17 35
7 Su	14 58 19	16 11 52	2♐16	4 03	8 14	29 20	22 19	27 45	5 49	18 46	26 54	0 21	23 49	1 45	2 50	9 36	17 38
8 M	15 2 16	17 09 56	16 10	4 01	7 43	0♋26	22 52	27 59	5 53	18 50	26 56	0 21	23 49	2 09	3 25	10 03	17 41
9 T	15 6 12	18 07 59	0♑16	3 59	7 15	1 32	23 26	28 13	5 57	18 53	26 57	0 21	23 50	2 34	4 01	10 30	17 44
10 W	15 10 9	19 06 00	14 29	3 58	6 50	2 38	23 59	28 27	6 00	18 57	26 59	0 21	23 51	2 59	4 36	10 57	17 48
11 Th	15 14 5	20 04 00	28 45	3 56	6 30	3 43	24 33	28 41	6 04	19 00	27 00	0 21	23 52	3 24	5 12	11 24	17 51
12 F	15 18 2	21 01 58	13♒02	3 55 D	6 13	4 48	25 06	28 55	6 07	19 04	27 02	0 20	23 54	3 49	5 47	11 50	17 54
13 Sa	15 21 59	21 59 55	27 15	3 55	6 01	5 53	25 40	29 09	6 11	19 07	27 03	0 20	23 57	4 14	6 22	12 17	17 57
14 Su	15 25 55	22 57 51	11♓23	3 56	5 54	6 58	26 14	29 23	6 14	19 11	27 05	0 20	23 59	4 39	6 58	12 44	18 00
15 M	15 29 52	23 55 46	25 24	3 57	5 51 D	8 02	26 48	29 36	6 17	19 14	27 06	0 19	24 02	5 04	7 33	13 10	18 03
16 T	15 33 48	24 53 39	9♈16	3 59	5 53	9 06	27 22	29 50	6 21	19 18	27 07	0 19	24 06	5 30	8 08	13 37	18 06
17 W	15 37 45	25 51 31	22 58	4 00 ℞	5 59	10 10	27 56	0♉04	6 24	19 21	27 09	0 19	24 10	5 55	8 44	14 04	18 09
18 Th	15 41 41	26 49 22	6♉28	4 00	6 10	11 14	28 30	0 17	6 27	19 25	27 11	0 18	24 14	6 21	9 19	14 30	18 12
19 F	15 45 38	27 47 12	19 45	3 59	6 25	12 17	29 04	0 31	6 30	19 28	27 12	0 18	24 19	6 46	9 54	14 57	18 15
20 Sa	15 49 34	28 45 00	2♊49	3 57	6 45	13 21	29 38	0 45	6 32	19 31	27 13	0 17	24 24	7 12	10 30	15 24	18 17
21 Su	15 53 31	29 42 47	15 38	3 54	7 09	14 24	0♋12	0 58	6 35	19 35	27 14	0 17	24 29	7 37	11 05	15 50	18 20
22 M	15 57 28	0♊40 33	28 12	3 50	7 38	15 26	0 46	1 12	6 38	19 38	27 16	0 16	24 35	8 03	11 40	16 17	18 23
23 T	16 1 24	1 38 17	10♋33	3 45	8 10	16 28	1 21	1 25	6 40	19 42	27 17	0 16	24 41	8 29	12 16	16 43	18 26
24 W	16 5 21	2 35 59	22 42	3 41	8 47	17 31	1 55	1 39	6 43	19 45	27 18	0 15	24 47	8 55	12 51	17 10	18 29
25 Th	16 9 17	3 33 40	4♌42	3 37	9 27	18 32	2 29	1 52	6 45	19 49	27 19	0 15	24 54	9 21	13 26	17 36	18 31
26 F	16 13 14	4 31 20	16 36	3 34	10 11	19 34	3 04	2 05	6 47	19 52	27 21	0 14	25 01	9 47	14 01	18 02	18 34
27 Sa	16 17 10	5 28 57	28 28	3 33 D	10 59	20 35	3 38	2 18	6 49	19 55	27 22	0 14	25 09	10 13	14 37	18 29	18 37
28 Su	16 21 7	6 26 34	10♍24	3 32	11 50	21 35	4 13	2 32	6 52	19 59	27 23	0 13	25 16	10 39	15 12	18 55	18 39
29 M	16 25 3	7 24 09	22 27	3 33	12 45	22 36	4 48	2 45	6 53	20 02	27 24	0 12	25 25	11 05	15 47	19 21	18 42
30 T	16 29 0	8 21 42	4♎42	3 35	13 43	23 36	5 22	2 58	6 55	20 05	27 25	0 11	25 33	11 31	16 22	19 47	18 44
31 W	16 32 57	9 19 15	17 15	3 36	14 45	24 35	5 57	3 11	6 57	20 09	27 26	0 10	25 42	11 57	16 57	20 14	18 47

Tables are calculated for midnight Greenwich Mean Time

June 2023

DATE	SID.TIME	SUN	MOON	NODE	MERCURY	VENUS	MARS	JUPITER	SATURN	URANUS	NEPTUNE	PLUTO	CERES	PALLAS	JUNO	VESTA	CHIRON
1 Th	16 36 53	10Ⅱ16 45	0♏,08	3♉37R,	15♉49	25♋35	6♋32	3♉24	6♓59	20♉12	27♓27	0≈09R,	25♍51	12♌23	17Ⅱ32	20♉40	18♈49
2 F	16 40 50	11 14 15	13 24	3 37	16 57	26 33	7 07	3 37	7 00	20 15	27 28	0 09	26 00	12 50	18 07	21 06	18 52
3 Sa	16 44 46	12 11 44	27 04	3 35	18 08	27 32	7 41	3 49	7 02	20 19	27 29	0 08	26 10	13 16	18 42	21 32	18 54
4 Su	16 48 43	13 09 11	11♐07	3 31	19 21	28 30	8 16	4 02	7 03	20 22	27 30	0 07	26 20	13 42	19 18	21 58	18 57
5 M	16 52 39	14 06 38	25 27	3 26	20 38	29 27	8 51	4 15	7 05	20 25	27 30	0 06	26 30	14 09	19 53	22 24	18 59
6 T	16 56 36	15 04 03	10♑01	3 20	21 58	0♌24	9 26	4 28	7 06	20 28	27 31	0 05	26 41	14 35	20 27	22 50	19 01
7 W	17 00 32	16 01 28	24 41	3 14	23 20	1 21	10 01	4 40	7 07	20 32	27 32	0 04	26 52	15 02	21 02	23 16	19 04
8 Th	17 04 29	16 58 52	9≈20	3 08	24 46	2 17	10 36	4 53	7 08	20 35	27 33	0 03	27 03	15 28	21 37	23 42	19 06
9 F	17 08 26	17 56 16	23 52	3 04	26 14	3 13	11 12	5 05	7 09	20 38	27 33	0 02	27 15	15 55	22 12	24 08	19 08
10 Sa	17 12 22	18 53 38	8♓12	3 02D	27 45	4 08	11 47	5 17	7 10	20 41	27 34	0 01	27 26	16 22	22 47	24 33	19 10
11 Su	17 16 19	19 51 01	22 17	3 01	29 18	5 02	12 22	5 30	7 10	20 44	27 35	0 00	27 39	16 48	23 22	24 59	19 12
12 M	17 20 15	20 48 22	6♈07	3 02	0Ⅱ55	5 56	12 57	5 42	7 11	20 47	27 35	29♑59	27 51	17 15	23 57	25 25	19 14
13 T	17 24 12	21 45 44	19 41	3 03	2 34	6 50	13 33	5 54	7 12	20 51	27 36	29 58	28 03	17 42	24 32	25 51	19 16
14 W	17 28 8	22 43 05	3♉02	3 04R,	4 16	7 43	14 08	6 06	7 12	20 54	27 37	29 57	28 16	18 08	25 06	26 16	19 18
15 Th	17 32 5	23 40 25	16 09	3 03	6 01	8 35	14 43	6 18	7 12	20 57	27 37	29 56	28 29	18 35	25 41	26 42	19 20
16 F	17 36 1	24 37 45	29 04	3 00	7 48	9 26	15 19	6 30	7 12	21 00	27 38	29 55	28 43	19 02	26 16	27 07	19 22
17 Sa	17 39 58	25 35 05	11Ⅱ47	2 55	9 38	10 17	15 54	6 41	7 13R,	21 03	27 38	29 54	28 56	19 29	26 50	27 33	19 24
18 Su	17 43 55	26 32 24	24 20	2 47	11 30	11 08	16 30	6 53	7 13	21 06	27 39	29 53	29 10	19 56	27 25	27 58	19 26
19 M	17 47 51	27 29 42	6♋42	2 38	13 25	11 57	17 05	7 05	7 13	21 09	27 39	29 52	29 24	20 22	28 00	28 24	19 27
20 T	17 51 48	28 27 00	18 54	2 28	15 22	12 46	17 41	7 16	7 12	21 12	27 39	29 51	29 38	20 49	28 34	28 49	19 29
21 W	17 55 44	29 24 17	0♌58	2 18	17 22	13 34	18 17	7 28	7 12	21 15	27 40	29 49	29 53	21 16	29 09	29 14	19 31
22 Th	17 59 41	0♋21 34	12 55	2 08	19 24	14 21	18 53	7 39	7 12	21 18	27 40	29 48	0≏08	21 43	29 43	29 40	19 32
23 F	18 3 37	1 18 50	24 47	2 01	21 27	15 08	19 28	7 50	7 11	21 20	27 40	29 47	0 23	22 10	0♋18	0Ⅱ05	19 34
24 Sa	18 7 34	2 16 05	6♍37	1 55	23 33	15 54	20 04	8 02	7 11	21 23	27 40	29 46	0 38	22 37	0 52	0 30	19 35
25 Su	18 11 30	3 13 20	18 31	1 52	25 40	16 39	20 40	8 13	7 10	21 26	27 41	29 45	0 53	23 04	1 26	0 55	19 37
26 M	18 15 27	4 10 34	0≏32	1 51D	27 48	17 22	21 16	8 24	7 09	21 29	27 41	29 43	1 09	23 31	2 01	1 20	19 38
27 T	18 19 24	5 07 47	12 45	1 51	29 58	18 05	21 52	8 34	7 08	21 32	27 41	29 42	1 25	23 58	2 35	1 45	19 40
28 W	18 23 20	6 05 00	25 15	1 51R,	2♋08	18 47	22 28	8 45	7 07	21 34	27 41	29 41	1 41	24 26	3 09	2 10	19 41
29 Th	18 27 17	7 02 13	8♏,08	1 51	4 19	19 28	23 04	8 56	7 06	21 37	27 41	29 40	1 57	24 53	3 44	2 35	19 42
30 F	18 31 13	7 59 25	21 27	1 50	6 30	20 08	23 40	9 06	7 05	21 40	27 41R,	29 38	2 14	25 20	4 18	3 00	19 43

July 2023

DATE	SID.TIME	SUN	MOON	NODE	MERCURY	VENUS	MARS	JUPITER	SATURN	URANUS	NEPTUNE	PLUTO	CERES	PALLAS	JUNO	VESTA	CHIRON
1 Sa	18 35 10	8♋56 36	5♓14	1♎46R	8♋41	20♌47	24♌16	9♉17	7♓04R	21♉42	27♓41R	29♑37R	2♎30	25♌47	4♋52	3♊25	19♈45
2 Su	18 39 6	9 53 48	19 28	1 40	10 52	21 24	24 52	9 27	7 03	21 45	27 41	29 36	2 47	26 14	5 26	3 49	19 46
3 M	18 43 3	10 50 59	4♑06	1 31	13 02	22 00	25 28	9 38	7 01	21 47	27 41	29 34	3 04	26 41	6 00	4 14	19 47
4 T	18 47 0	11 48 10	19 01	1 22	15 11	22 36	26 04	9 48	7 00	21 50	27 41	29 33	3 21	27 09	6 34	4 39	19 48
5 W	18 50 56	12 45 21	4♒05	1 12	17 19	23 09	26 41	9 58	6 58	21 52	27 41	29 32	3 39	27 36	7 08	5 03	19 49
6 Th	18 54 53	13 42 32	19 07	1 03	19 26	23 42	27 17	10 08	6 56	21 55	27 41	29 30	3 56	28 03	7 42	5 28	19 50
7 F	18 58 49	14 39 43	3♓58	0 56	21 32	24 13	27 53	10 17	6 55	21 57	27 41	29 29	4 14	28 30	8 16	5 52	19 51
8 Sa	19 2 46	15 36 55	18 32	0 51	23 36	24 42	28 29	10 27	6 53	22 00	27 40	29 28	4 32	28 58	8 49	6 16	19 51
9 Su	19 6 42	16 34 06	2♈45	0 49	25 39	25 11	29 06	10 37	6 51	22 02	27 40	29 26	4 50	29 25	9 23	6 41	19 52
10 M	19 10 39	17 31 18	16 34	0 48D	27 40	25 37	29 42	10 46	6 49	22 04	27 40	29 25	5 08	29 52	9 57	7 05	19 53
11 T	19 14 35	18 28 31	0♉03	0 48R	29 39	26 02	0♍19	10 56	6 46	22 07	27 39	29 23	5 26	0♍19	10 31	7 29	19 54
12 W	19 18 32	19 25 44	13 11	0 48	1♌37	26 25	0 55	11 05	6 44	22 09	27 39	29 22	5 45	0 47	11 04	7 53	19 54
13 Th	19 22 29	20 22 58	26 04	0 46	3 33	26 47	1 32	11 14	6 42	22 11	27 39	29 21	6 04	1 14	11 38	8 17	19 55
14 F	19 26 25	21 20 12	8♊42	0 41	5 26	27 07	2 08	11 23	6 39	22 13	27 38	29 19	6 22	1 41	12 11	8 41	19 55
15 Sa	19 30 22	22 17 26	21 10	0 34	7 18	27 25	2 45	11 32	6 37	22 15	27 38	29 18	6 41	2 09	12 45	9 05	19 56
16 Su	19 34 18	23 14 41	3♋27	0 24	9 08	27 41	3 22	11 40	6 34	22 17	27 38	29 16	7 01	2 36	13 18	9 28	19 56
17 M	19 38 15	24 11 57	15 37	0 11	10 57	27 55	3 58	11 49	6 32	22 19	27 37	29 15	7 20	3 04	13 52	9 52	19 57
18 T	19 42 11	25 09 13	27 40	29♍58	12 43	28 07	4 35	11 58	6 29	22 21	27 37	29 14	7 39	3 31	14 25	10 16	19 57
19 W	19 46 8	26 06 29	9♌38	29 44	14 27	28 18	5 12	12 06	6 26	22 23	27 36	29 12	7 59	3 58	14 58	10 39	19 57
20 Th	19 50 4	27 03 45	21 31	29 31	16 10	28 26	5 49	12 14	6 23	22 25	27 35	29 11	8 19	4 26	15 32	11 03	19 58
21 F	19 54 1	28 01 02	3♍21	29 20	17 51	28 31	6 26	12 22	6 20	22 27	27 35	29 09	8 39	4 53	16 05	11 26	19 58
22 Sa	19 57 58	28 58 19	15 11	29 12	19 29	28 35	7 03	12 30	6 17	22 29	27 34	29 08	8 59	5 21	16 38	11 50	19 58
23 Su	20 1 54	29 55 36	27 04	29 07	21 06	28 36R	7 40	12 38	6 14	22 31	27 33	29 06	9 19	5 48	17 11	12 13	19 58R
24 M	20 5 51	0♌52 54	9♎04	29 04	22 42	28 35	8 17	12 45	6 11	22 33	27 33	29 05	9 39	6 16	17 44	12 36	19 58
25 T	20 9 47	1 50 12	21 15	29 03	24 15	28 32	8 54	12 53	6 08	22 34	27 32	29 04	9 59	6 43	18 17	12 59	19 58
26 W	20 13 44	2 47 31	3♏42	29 03	25 46	28 26	9 31	13 00	6 04	22 36	27 31	29 02	10 20	7 11	18 50	13 22	19 58
27 Th	20 17 40	3 44 49	16 32	29 02	27 16	28 18	10 08	13 07	6 01	22 37	27 30	29 01	10 40	7 38	19 23	13 45	19 57
28 F	20 21 37	4 42 09	29 47	29 01	28 43	28 07	10 45	13 14	5 57	22 39	27 30	28 59	11 01	8 06	19 55	14 08	19 57
29 Sa	20 25 33	5 39 28	13♐31	28 57	0♍09	27 54	11 22	13 21	5 54	22 41	27 29	28 58	11 22	8 33	20 28	14 30	19 57
30 Su	20 29 30	6 36 49	27 44	28 51	1 32	27 39	12 00	13 28	5 50	22 42	27 28	28 56	11 43	9 01	21 01	14 53	19 57
31 M	20 33 27	7 34 10	12♑26	28 42	2 54	27 21	12 37	13 35	5 46	22 44	27 27	28 55	12 04	9 28	21 33	15 15	19 56

Tables are calculated for midnight Greenwich Mean Time

August 2023

DATE	SID.TIME	SUN	MOON	NODE	MERCURY	VENUS	MARS	JUPITER	SATURN	URANUS	NEPTUNE	PLUTO	CERES	PALLAS	JUNO	VESTA	CHIRON
1 T	20 37 23	8♌31 31	27♑29	28♈32R	4♍14	27♌01R	13♍14	13♉41	5♓43R	22♉45	27♓26R	28♑54R	12♎25	9♍56R	22♋06	15♊38	19♈56R
2 W	20 41 20	9 28 53	12≈45	28 21	5 31	26 39	13 51	13 47	5 39	22 46	27 25	28 52	12 47	10 23	22 38	16 00	19 55
3 Th	20 45 16	10 26 16	28 02	28 11	6 47	26 15	14 29	13 53	5 35	22 48	27 24	28 51	13 08	10 51	23 11	16 22	19 55
4 F	20 49 13	11 23 40	13♓10	28 04	8 00	25 49	15 06	13 59	5 31	22 49	27 23	28 49	13 30	11 18	23 43	16 45	19 54
5 Sa	20 53 9	12 21 05	27 59	27 59	9 11	25 20	15 44	14 05	5 27	22 50	27 22	28 48	13 51	11 46	24 15	17 07	19 54
6 Su	20 57 6	13 18 31	12♈23	27 56	10 20	24 50	16 21	14 11	5 23	22 51	27 21	28 47	14 13	12 13	24 47	17 29	19 53
7 M	21 1 2	14 15 59	26 21	27 55D	11 26	24 19	16 59	14 16	5 19	22 52	27 20	28 45	14 35	12 41	25 20	17 50	19 52
8 T	21 4 59	15 13 28	9♉52	27 55R	12 30	23 46	17 36	14 21	5 15	22 53	27 19	28 44	14 57	13 08	25 52	18 12	19 52
9 W	21 8 56	16 10 58	23 00	27 55	13 31	23 11	18 14	14 26	5 11	22 54	27 18	28 43	15 19	13 36	26 24	18 34	19 51
10 Th	21 12 52	17 08 29	5♊47	27 54	14 30	22 36	18 52	14 31	5 07	22 55	27 17	28 41	15 41	14 04	26 56	18 55	19 50
11 F	21 16 49	18 06 02	18 17	27 50	15 25	22 00	19 29	14 36	5 03	22 56	27 15	28 40	16 03	14 31	27 28	19 17	19 49
12 Sa	21 20 45	19 03 36	0♋35	27 44	16 18	21 23	20 07	14 41	4 58	22 57	27 14	28 39	16 25	14 59	27 59	19 38	19 48
13 Su	21 24 42	20 01 12	12 42	27 35	17 08	20 46	20 45	14 45	4 54	22 58	27 13	28 37	16 48	15 26	28 31	19 59	19 47
14 M	21 28 38	20 58 49	24 43	27 24	17 54	20 08	21 23	14 49	4 50	22 59	27 12	28 36	17 10	15 54	29 03	20 20	19 46
15 T	21 32 35	21 56 27	6♌39	27 12	18 37	19 31	22 01	14 53	4 45	23 00	27 10	28 35	17 33	16 21	29 34	20 41	19 45
16 W	21 36 31	22 54 06	18 32	27 00	19 16	18 54	22 39	14 57	4 41	23 01	27 09	28 33	17 55	16 49	0♌06	21 02	19 44
17 Th	21 40 28	23 51 47	0♍23	26 49	19 51	18 18	23 17	15 01	4 37	23 01	27 08	28 32	18 18	17 17	0 37	21 22	19 42
18 F	21 44 25	24 49 29	12 13	26 39	20 22	17 43	23 55	15 05	4 32	23 01	27 07	28 31	18 41	17 44	1 09	21 43	19 41
19 Sa	21 48 21	25 47 12	24 06	26 32	20 49	17 08	24 33	15 08	4 28	23 02	27 05	28 30	19 04	18 12	1 40	22 03	19 40
20 Su	21 52 18	26 44 56	6♎02	26 27	21 12	16 35	25 11	15 11	4 23	23 02	27 04	28 28	19 27	18 39	2 11	22 24	19 39
21 M	21 56 14	27 42 42	18 06	26 25D	21 29	16 03	25 49	15 14	4 19	23 03	27 02	28 27	19 50	19 07	2 43	22 44	19 37
22 T	22 0 11	28 40 28	0♏19	26 25	21 42	15 33	26 27	15 17	4 14	23 03	27 01	28 26	20 13	19 35	3 14	23 04	19 36
23 W	22 4 7	29 38 16	12 48	26 26	21 49R	15 04	27 05	15 19	4 10	23 04	27 00	28 25	20 36	20 02	3 45	23 24	19 34
24 Th	22 8 4	0♍36 05	25 35	26 27R	21 51	14 38	27 44	15 22	4 05	23 04	26 58	28 24	20 59	20 30	4 16	23 43	19 33
25 F	22 12 0	1 33 55	8♐46	26 26	21 47	14 13	28 22	15 24	4 01	23 04	26 57	28 23	21 23	20 57	4 46	24 03	19 31
26 Sa	22 15 57	2 31 47	22 23	26 25	21 38	13 50	29 00	15 26	3 56	23 04	26 55	28 21	21 46	21 25	5 17	24 22	19 30
27 Su	22 19 54	3 29 40	6♑28	26 21	21 22	13 30	29 39	15 28	3 52	23 04	26 54	28 20	22 09	21 52	5 48	24 42	19 28
28 M	22 23 50	4 27 34	21 00	26 15	21 00	13 12	0♎17	15 29	3 47	23 04	26 52	28 19	22 33	22 20	6 19	25 01	19 26
29 T	22 27 47	5 25 29	5≈56	26 08	20 33	12 56	0 56	15 31	3 43	23 05R	26 51	28 18	22 57	22 48	6 49	25 20	19 24
30 W	22 31 43	6 23 25	21 07	26 01	20 00	12 43	1 34	15 32	3 38	23 05	26 49	28 17	23 20	23 15	7 20	25 39	19 23
31 Th	22 35 40	7 21 23	6♓24	25 54	19 21	12 32	2 13	15 33	3 34	23 04	26 48	28 16	23 44	23 43	7 50	25 57	19 21

201

September 2023

DATE	SID.TIME	SUN	MOON	NODE	MERCURY	VENUS	MARS	JUPITER	SATURN	URANUS	NEPTUNE	PLUTO	CERES	PALLAS	JUNO	VESTA	CHIRON
1 F	22 39 36	8♍19 23	21♓36	25♈48R	18♍37R	12♌28R	2♎51	15♉34	3♓29R	23♉04R	26♓46R	28♑15R	24♎08	24♍10	8♌20	26♊16	19♈19R
2 Sa	22 43 33	9 17 24	6♈33	25 45	17 48	12 17	3 30	15 34	3 25	23 04	26 45	28 14	24 32	24 38	8 50	26 34	19 17
3 Su	22 47 29	10 15 27	21 07	25 43D	16 55	12 14	4 09	15 35	3 20	23 04	26 43	28 13	24 56	25 05	9 21	26 52	19 15
4 M	22 51 26	11 13 32	5♉15	25 43	16 00	12 12D	4 47	15 35R	3 16	23 04	26 42	28 12	25 20	25 33	9 51	27 10	19 13
5 T	22 55 23	12 11 39	18 54	25 45	15 02	12 13	5 26	15 35	3 11	23 04	26 40	28 11	25 44	26 01	10 21	27 28	19 11
6 W	22 59 19	13 09 48	2♊07	25 46R	14 04	12 17	6 05	15 35	3 07	23 03	26 38	28 10	26 08	26 28	10 50	27 46	19 09
7 Th	23 3 16	14 07 59	14 56	25 46	13 06	12 22	6 44	15 34	3 02	23 03	26 37	28 09	26 32	26 56	11 20	28 03	19 07
8 F	23 7 12	15 06 12	27 26	25 46	12 10	12 30	7 23	15 34	2 58	23 03	26 35	28 08	26 56	27 23	11 50	28 21	19 05
9 Sa	23 11 9	16 04 27	9♋41	25 43	11 16	12 40	8 02	15 33	2 53	23 02	26 34	28 08	27 20	27 51	12 20	28 38	19 03
10 Su	23 15 5	17 02 44	21 44	25 39	10 27	12 52	8 41	15 32	2 49	23 01	26 32	28 07	27 45	28 18	12 49	28 55	19 01
11 M	23 19 2	18 01 03	3♌40	25 33	9 44	13 07	9 20	15 31	2 45	23 00	26 30	28 06	28 09	28 46	13 18	29 11	18 58
12 T	23 22 58	18 59 24	15 32	25 26	9 07	13 23	9 59	15 29	2 40	23 00	26 29	28 05	28 33	29 13	13 48	29 28	18 56
13 W	23 26 55	19 57 47	27 23	25 20	8 37	13 41	10 38	15 28	2 36	22 59	26 27	28 04	28 58	29 41	14 17	29 44	18 54
14 Th	23 30 52	20 56 12	9♍15	25 13	8 16	14 01	11 17	15 26	2 32	22 58	26 25	28 04	29 22	0♎08	14 46	0♋00	18 51
15 F	23 34 48	21 54 39	21 09	25 08	8 04D	14 23	11 56	15 24	2 28	22 57	26 24	28 03	29 47	0 36	15 15	0 16	18 49
16 Sa	23 38 45	22 53 07	3♎08	25 05	8 00	14 47	12 36	15 22	2 24	22 57	26 22	28 02	0♏11	1 03	15 44	0 32	18 47
17 Su	23 42 41	23 51 38	15 13	25 03D	8 06	15 12	13 15	15 19	2 20	22 56	26 20	28 02	0 36	1 31	16 13	0 47	18 44
18 M	23 46 38	24 50 10	27 27	25 02	8 22	15 39	13 54	15 17	2 16	22 55	26 19	28 01	1 01	1 58	16 42	1 03	18 42
19 T	23 50 34	25 48 44	9♏51	25 03	8 47	16 08	14 34	15 14	2 12	22 54	26 17	28 00	1 26	2 26	17 10	1 18	18 39
20 W	23 54 31	26 47 20	22 28	25 05	9 21	16 38	15 13	15 11	2 08	22 53	26 15	28 00	1 50	2 53	17 39	1 33	18 37
21 Th	23 58 27	27 45 57	5♐21	25 06	10 04	17 09	15 53	15 08	2 04	22 52	26 14	27 59	2 15	3 21	18 07	1 47	18 34
22 F	0 2 24	28 44 36	18 33	25 07R	10 55	17 42	16 32	15 05	2 00	22 50	26 12	27 59	2 40	3 48	18 36	2 01	18 32
23 Sa	0 6 21	29 43 17	2♑05	25 08	11 54	18 16	17 12	15 01	1 56	22 49	26 10	27 58	3 05	4 16	19 04	2 16	18 29
24 Su	0 10 17	0♎42 00	16 01	25 07	13 00	18 52	17 52	14 57	1 53	22 48	26 09	27 58	3 30	4 43	19 32	2 29	18 27
25 M	0 14 14	1 40 44	0♒18	25 05	14 12	19 29	18 31	14 53	1 49	22 47	26 07	27 57	3 55	5 11	20 00	2 43	18 24
26 T	0 18 10	2 39 30	14 56	25 03	15 31	20 07	19 11	14 49	1 45	22 45	26 05	27 56	4 20	5 38	20 28	2 56	18 22
27 W	0 22 7	3 38 18	29 49	25 00	16 54	20 46	19 51	14 45	1 42	22 44	26 04	27 56	4 45	6 06	20 56	3 09	18 19
28 Th	0 26 3	4 37 07	14♓49	24 57	18 22	21 27	20 31	14 40	1 38	22 43	26 02	27 56	5 10	6 33	21 23	3 22	18 17
29 F	0 30 0	5 35 58	29 49	24 55	19 54	22 09	21 10	14 36	1 35	22 41	26 01	27 56	5 35	7 00	21 51	3 35	18 14
30 Sa	0 33 56	6 34 51	14♈40	24 54D	21 30	22 50	21 50	14 31	1 32	22 40	25 59	27 55	6 00	7 28	22 18	3 47	18 11

Tables are calculated for midnight Greenwich Mean Time

October 2023

DATE	SID. TIME	SUN	MOON	NODE	MERCURY	VENUS	MARS	JUPITER	SATURN	URANUS	NEPTUNE	PLUTO	CERES	PALLAS	JUNO	VESTA	CHIRON
1 Su	0 37 53	7♎33 47	29♈13	24♈54	23♍08	23♌35	22♎30	14♉26℞	1♓29℞	22♉38℞	25♓57℞	27♑55℞	6♏25	7♎55	22♌46	3♋59	18♈09℞
2 M	0 41 50	8 32 44	13♉24	24 54	24 48	24 20	23 10	14 21	1 25	22 37	25 56	27 55	6 50	8 22	23 13	4 11	18 06
3 T	0 45 46	9 31 44	27 10	24 55	26 15	25 05	23 50	14 16	1 22	22 35	25 54	27 54	7 16	8 50	23 40	4 22	18 03
4 W	0 49 43	10 30 46	10♊29	24 57	28 15	25 52	24 30	14 10	1 19	22 34	25 53	27 54	7 41	9 17	24 07	4 34	18 01
5 Th	0 53 39	11 29 50	23 24	24 58	29 59	26 39	25 11	14 04	1 16	22 32	25 51	27 54	8 06	9 44	24 34	4 45	17 58
6 F	0 57 36	12 28 57	5♋58	24 58℞	1♎45	27 28	25 51	13 59	1 14	22 30	25 49	27 54	8 32	10 12	25 01	4 55	17 55
7 Sa	1 1 32	13 28 06	18 14	24 58	3 31	28 17	26 31	13 53	1 11	22 28	25 48	27 54	8 57	10 39	25 27	5 05	17 52
8 Su	1 5 29	14 27 17	0♌18	24 58	5 17	29 07	27 11	13 47	1 08	22 27	25 46	27 54	9 22	11 06	25 54	5 15	17 50
9 M	1 9 25	15 26 31	12 13	24 57	7 04	29 57	27 52	13 40	1 05	22 25	25 45	27 54	9 48	11 33	26 20	5 25	17 47
10 T	1 13 22	16 25 46	24 04	24 56	8 50	0♍49	28 32	13 34	1 03	22 23	25 43	27 54	10 13	12 01	26 46	5 34	17 44
11 W	1 17 19	17 25 04	5♍55	24 55	10 36	1 41	29 13	13 28	1 01	22 21	25 42	27 54D	10 38	12 28	27 12	5 43	17 41
12 Th	1 21 15	18 24 24	17 49	24 54	12 22	2 34	29 53	13 21	0 58	22 19	25 40	27 54	11 04	12 55	27 38	5 52	17 39
13 F	1 25 12	19 23 47	29 49	24 53	14 08	3 28	0♏34	13 14	0 56	22 17	25 39	27 54	11 29	13 22	28 04	6 00	17 36
14 Sa	1 29 8	20 23 11	11♎57	24 52	15 53	4 22	1 14	13 07	0 54	22 15	25 37	27 54	11 55	13 49	28 30	6 09	17 33
15 Su	1 33 5	21 22 38	24 16	24 52D	17 37	5 17	1 55	13 00	0 52	22 13	25 36	27 54	12 20	14 17	28 55	6 16	17 31
16 M	1 37 1	22 22 06	6♏45	24 52	19 21	6 12	2 36	12 53	0 50	22 11	25 34	27 54	12 46	14 44	29 21	6 24	17 28
17 T	1 40 58	23 21 37	19 28	24 53	21 04	7 08	3 16	12 46	0 48	22 09	25 33	27 54	13 12	15 11	29 46	6 30	17 25
18 W	1 44 54	24 21 10	2♐23	24 53℞	22 47	8 04	3 57	12 39	0 46	22 07	25 31	27 54	13 37	15 38	0♏11	6 37	17 22
19 Th	1 48 51	25 20 44	15 32	24 53	24 29	9 01	4 38	12 31	0 44	22 05	25 30	27 54	14 03	16 05	0 36	6 43	17 20
20 F	1 52 47	26 20 20	28 55	24 53	26 11	9 59	5 19	12 24	0 43	22 03	25 29	27 55	14 28	16 32	1 01	6 49	17 17
21 Sa	1 56 44	27 19 58	12♑33	24 52	27 51	10 57	6 00	12 16	0 41	22 01	25 27	27 55	14 54	16 59	1 25	6 55	17 14
22 Su	2 0 41	28 19 38	26 26	24 52D	29 32	11 56	6 41	12 08	0 40	21 58	25 26	27 55	15 20	17 26	1 50	7 00	17 12
23 M	2 4 37	29 19 20	10≈33	24 52	1♏11	12 55	7 22	12 01	0 39	21 56	25 25	27 56	15 45	17 53	2 14	7 05	17 09
24 T	2 8 34	0♏19 03	24 52	24 53	2 50	13 54	8 03	11 53	0 37	21 54	25 23	27 56	16 11	18 20	2 39	7 09	17 06
25 W	2 12 30	1 18 47	9♓20	24 53	4 29	14 54	8 44	11 45	0 36	21 52	25 22	27 56	16 37	18 47	3 03	7 13	17 04
26 Th	2 16 27	2 18 34	23 54	24 54	6 06	15 55	9 25	11 37	0 35	21 49	25 21	27 57	17 02	19 14	3 26	7 16	17 01
27 F	2 20 23	3 18 22	8♈29	24 54	7 44	16 55	10 07	11 29	0 34	21 47	25 20	27 57	17 28	19 41	3 50	7 20	16 59
28 Sa	2 24 20	4 18 12	22 59	24 55℞	9 20	17 57	10 48	11 21	0 34	21 45	25 18	27 58	17 54	20 07	4 14	7 22	16 56
29 Su	2 28 16	5 18 03	7♉17	24 54	10 57	18 58	11 29	11 13	0 33	21 42	25 17	27 58	18 19	20 34	4 37	7 25	16 53
30 M	2 32 13	6 17 57	21 19	24 54	12 32	20 00	12 11	11 05	0 32	21 40	25 16	27 59	18 45	21 01	5 00	7 27	16 51
31 T	2 36 10	7 17 53	5♊01	24 52	14 08	21 03	12 52	10 57	0 32	21 38	25 15	27 59	19 11	21 28	5 23	7 28	16 48

203

November 2023

DATE	SID.TIME	SUN	MOON	NODE	MERCURY	VENUS	MARS	JUPITER	SATURN	URANUS	NEPTUNE	PLUTO	CERES	PALLAS	JUNO	VESTA	CHIRON
1 W	2 40 6	8♏17 51	18♊22	24♈51R	15♏42	22♍05	13♏34	10♉49R	0♓31R	21♉35R	25♓14R	28♑00	19♏37	21♎55	5♍46	7♋29	16♈46R
2 Th	2 44 3	9 17 51	1♋20	24 49	17 17	23 09	14 15	10 40	0 31	21 33	25 13	28 01	20 02	22 21	6 09	7 30	16 43
3 F	2 47 59	10 17 53	13 57	24 47	18 50	24 12	14 57	10 32	0 31	21 30	25 12	28 01	20 28	22 48	6 31	7 30R	16 41
4 Sa	2 51 56	11 17 58	26 17	24 45	20 24	25 16	15 38	10 24	0 31D	21 28	25 11	28 02	20 54	23 15	6 54	7 30	16 38
5 Su	2 55 52	12 18 04	8♌22	24 45D	21 57	26 20	16 20	10 16	0 31	21 25	25 10	28 03	21 20	23 41	7 16	7 29	16 36
6 M	2 59 49	13 18 12	20 18	24 45	23 29	27 24	17 02	10 08	0 31	21 23	25 09	28 03	21 45	24 08	7 38	7 28	16 34
7 T	3 3 45	14 18 23	2♍09	24 46	25 01	28 29	17 44	10 00	0 31	21 20	25 08	28 04	22 11	24 34	8 00	7 27	16 31
8 W	3 7 42	15 18 35	14 00	24 47	26 33	29 34	18 25	9 52	0 32	21 18	25 07	28 05	22 37	25 01	8 21	7 25	16 29
9 Th	3 11 39	16 18 50	25 56	24 49	28 05	0♎39	19 07	9 43	0 32	21 16	25 06	28 06	23 03	25 27	8 42	7 22	16 27
10 F	3 15 35	17 19 06	8♎00	24 50	29 36	1 45	19 49	9 35	0 33	21 13	25 05	28 07	23 29	25 54	9 04	7 20	16 24
11 Sa	3 19 32	18 19 24	20 17	24 51R	1♐06	2 51	20 31	9 27	0 33	21 11	25 04	28 07	23 54	26 20	9 25	7 16	16 22
12 Su	3 23 28	19 19 44	2♏49	24 51	2 37	3 57	21 13	9 20	0 34	21 08	25 03	28 08	24 20	26 47	9 45	7 13	16 20
13 M	3 27 25	20 20 06	15 37	24 50	4 07	5 03	21 55	9 12	0 35	21 06	25 03	28 09	24 46	27 13	10 06	7 08	16 18
14 T	3 31 21	21 20 30	28 41	24 47	5 36	6 10	22 38	9 04	0 36	21 03	25 02	28 10	25 12	27 39	10 26	7 04	16 16
15 W	3 35 18	22 20 56	12♐02	24 43	7 05	7 17	23 20	8 56	0 37	21 01	25 01	28 11	25 37	28 06	10 46	6 59	16 14
16 Th	3 39 14	23 21 23	25 36	24 38	8 34	8 24	24 02	8 48	0 38	20 58	25 00	28 12	26 03	28 32	11 06	6 53	16 12
17 F	3 43 11	24 21 51	9♑23	24 34	10 02	9 31	24 44	8 41	0 39	20 56	25 00	28 13	26 29	28 58	11 26	6 47	16 10
18 Sa	3 47 8	25 22 21	23 19	24 30	11 30	10 39	25 27	8 33	0 41	20 53	24 59	28 14	26 55	29 24	11 45	6 41	16 08
19 Su	3 51 4	26 22 52	7♒21	24 27	12 58	11 47	26 09	8 26	0 42	20 51	24 58	28 15	27 20	29 50	12 05	6 34	16 06
20 M	3 55 1	27 23 25	21 28	24 25D	14 24	12 55	26 51	8 19	0 44	20 48	24 58	28 16	27 46	0♏16	12 24	6 27	16 04
21 T	3 58 57	28 23 58	5♓37	24 25	15 50	14 03	27 34	8 11	0 45	20 46	24 57	28 18	28 12	0 42	12 42	6 19	16 02
22 W	4 2 54	29 24 33	19 47	24 27	17 16	15 11	28 17	8 04	0 47	20 43	24 57	28 19	28 37	1 08	13 01	6 11	16 00
23 Th	4 6 50	0♐25 08	3♈56	24 28	18 41	16 20	28 59	7 57	0 49	20 41	24 56	28 20	29 03	1 34	13 19	6 02	15 58
24 F	4 10 47	1 25 45	18 02	24 29R	20 05	17 28	29 42	7 51	0 51	20 38	24 56	28 21	29 29	2 00	13 37	5 53	15 57
25 Sa	4 14 44	2 26 23	2♉03	24 29	21 28	18 37	0♐24	7 44	0 53	20 36	24 56	28 22	29 54	2 26	13 55	5 44	15 55
26 Su	4 18 40	3 27 03	15 56	24 27	22 49	19 46	1 07	7 37	0 55	20 33	24 55	28 24	0♐20	2 51	14 12	5 34	15 53
27 M	4 22 37	4 27 43	29 37	24 23	24 10	20 55	1 50	7 31	0 58	20 31	24 55	28 25	0 46	3 17	14 30	5 24	15 52
28 T	4 26 33	5 28 26	13♊05	24 18	25 29	22 05	2 33	7 24	1 00	20 29	24 55	28 26	1 11	3 43	14 47	5 13	15 50
29 W	4 30 30	6 29 09	26 16	24 10	26 47	23 14	3 16	7 18	1 02	20 26	24 54	28 28	1 37	4 08	15 03	5 02	15 49
30 Th	4 34 26	7 29 54	9♋09	24 02	28 03	24 24	3 59	7 12	1 05	20 24	24 54	28 29	2 02	4 34	15 20	4 51	15 47

Tables are calculated for midnight Greenwich Mean Time

December 2023

DATE	SID.TIME	SUN	MOON	NODE	MERCURY	VENUS	MARS	JUPITER	SATURN	URANUS	NEPTUNE	PLUTO	CERES	PALLAS	JUNO	VESTA	CHIRON
1 F	4 38 23	8✗30 40	21♋45	23♈54℞	29✗17	25♎34	4✗42	7♉06℞	1♓08	20♉22℞	24♓54℞	28♑30	2✗28	4♏59	15♍36	4♋39℞	15♈46℞
2 Sa	4 42 19	9 31 28	4♌05	23 48	0♑28	26 44	5 25	7 01	1 11	20 19	24 54	28 32	2 54	5 25	15 52	4 27	15 44
3 Su	4 46 16	10 32 17	16 10	23 42	1 36	27 54	6 08	6 55	1 13	20 17	24 54	28 33	3 19	5 50	16 08	4 15	15 43
4 M	4 50 13	11 33 07	28 06	23 39	2 42	29 05	6 51	6 50	1 16	20 15	24 53	28 34	3 45	6 15	16 23	4 02	15 42
5 T	4 54 9	12 33 59	9♍57	23 38D	3 44	0♏15	7 34	6 44	1 19	20 12	24 53	28 36	4 10	6 41	16 38	3 49	15 41
6 W	4 58 6	13 34 52	21 47	23 39	4 41	1 26	8 17	6 39	1 23	20 10	24 53	28 37	4 36	7 06	16 53	3 36	15 39
7 Th	5 2 2	14 35 46	3♎42	23 39	5 34	2 36	9 01	6 34	1 26	20 08	24 53D	28 39	5 01	7 31	17 07	3 22	15 38
8 F	5 5 59	15 36 41	15 48	23 41℞	6 21	3 47	9 44	6 30	1 29	20 06	24 53	28 40	5 26	7 56	17 22	3 08	15 37
9 Sa	5 9 55	16 37 38	28 08	23 41	7 02	4 58	10 27	6 25	1 33	20 04	24 53	28 42	5 52	8 21	17 36	2 54	15 36
10 Su	5 13 52	17 38 36	10♏47	23 39	7 37	6 09	11 11	6 21	1 36	20 01	24 53	28 43	6 17	8 46	17 49	2 40	15 35
11 M	5 17 48	18 39 35	23 48	23 35	8 03	7 21	11 54	6 17	1 40	19 59	24 54	28 45	6 42	9 11	18 02	2 25	15 34
12 T	5 21 45	19 40 36	7✗12	23 29	8 21	8 32	12 38	6 13	1 43	19 57	24 54	28 47	7 08	9 36	18 15	2 10	15 33
13 W	5 25 42	20 41 37	20 57	23 20	8 29℞	9 43	13 21	6 09	1 47	19 55	24 54	28 48	7 33	10 00	18 28	1 55	15 33
14 Th	5 29 38	21 42 39	4♑59	23 10	8 27	10 55	14 05	6 05	1 51	19 53	24 54	28 50	7 58	10 25	18 40	1 40	15 32
15 F	5 33 35	22 43 42	19 15	23 00	8 14	12 07	14 49	6 02	1 55	19 51	24 55	28 51	8 24	10 50	18 52	1 25	15 31
16 Sa	5 37 31	23 44 45	3♒39	22 51	7 49	13 18	15 33	5 59	1 59	19 49	24 55	28 53	8 49	11 14	19 04	1 09	15 31
17 Su	5 41 28	24 45 49	18 03	22 44	7 13	14 30	16 16	5 56	2 03	19 47	24 55	28 55	9 14	11 39	19 15	0 54	15 30
18 M	5 45 24	25 46 53	2♓24	22 39	6 25	15 42	17 00	5 53	2 07	19 45	24 56	28 56	9 39	12 03	19 26	0 38	15 29
19 T	5 49 21	26 47 57	16 38	22 36D	5 27	16 54	17 44	5 50	2 12	19 44	24 56	28 58	10 04	12 27	19 36	0 22	15 29
20 W	5 53 17	27 49 02	0♈43	22 36	4 19	18 06	18 28	5 48	2 16	19 42	24 56	29 00	10 29	12 51	19 46	0 07	15 29
21 Th	5 57 14	28 50 07	14 38	22 37℞	3 04	19 18	19 12	5 45	2 21	19 40	24 57	29 02	10 54	13 15	19 56	29♊51	15 28
22 F	6 1 11	29 51 12	28 23	22 37	1 44	20 30	19 56	5 43	2 25	19 38	24 57	29 03	11 19	13 39	20 06	29 35	15 28
23 Sa	6 5 7	0♑52 18	11♉59	22 35	0 22	21 43	20 40	5 42	2 30	19 37	24 58	29 05	11 44	14 03	20 15	29 19	15 28
24 Su	6 9 4	1 53 24	25 25	22 31	28✗59	22 55	21 24	5 40	2 34	19 35	24 59	29 07	12 09	14 27	20 23	29 03	15 27
25 M	6 13 0	2 54 30	8♊42	22 24	27 40	24 08	22 08	5 39	2 39	19 33	24 59	29 09	12 34	14 51	20 32	28 47	15 27
26 T	6 16 57	3 55 36	21 47	22 14	26 27	25 20	22 52	5 38	2 44	19 32	25 00	29 10	12 59	15 14	20 40	28 32	15 27
27 W	6 20 53	4 56 43	4♋40	22 01	25 25	26 33	23 37	5 37	2 49	19 30	25 01	29 12	13 23	15 38	20 47	28 16	15 27D
28 Th	6 24 50	5 57 50	17 21	21 48	24 33	27 45	24 21	5 36	2 54	19 29	25 01	29 14	13 48	16 01	20 54	28 00	15 27
29 F	6 28 47	6 58 57	29 48	21 35	23 36	28 58	25 05	5 35	2 59	19 27	25 02	29 16	14 13	16 25	21 01	27 45	15 27
30 Sa	6 32 43	8 00 04	12♌02	21 22	22 59	0✗11	25 50	5 35	3 04	19 26	25 03	29 18	14 37	16 48	21 08	27 30	15 27
31 Su	6 36 40	9 01 12	24 05	21 12	22 33	1 24	26 34	5 35D	3 09	19 24	25 04	29 20	15 02	17 11	21 14	27 15	15 28

The Planetary Hours

The selection of an auspicious time for starting any activity is an important matter. Its existence tends to take on a nature corresponding to the conditions under which it was begun. Each hour is ruled by a planet, and the nature of any hour corresponds to the nature of the planet ruling it. The nature of the planetary hours is the same as the description of each of the planets. Uranus, Neptune, and Pluto are considered here as higher octaves of Mercury, Venus, and Mars.

Sunrise Hour	Sun	Mon	Tue	Wed	Thu	Fri	Sat
1	☉	☽	♂	☿	♃	♀	♄
2	♀	♄	☉	☽	♂	☿	♃
3	☿	♃	♀	♄	☉	☽	♂
4	☽	♂	☿	♃	♀	♄	☉
5	♄	☉	☽	♂	☿	♃	♀
6	♃	♀	♄	☉	☽	♂	☿
7	♂	☿	♃	♀	♄	☉	☽
8	☉	☽	♂	☿	♃	♀	♄
9	♀	♄	☉	☽	♂	☿	♃
10	☿	♃	♀	♄	☉	☽	♂
11	☽	♂	☿	♃	♀	♄	☉
12	♄	☉	☽	♂	☿	♃	♀

Sunset Hour	Sun	Mon	Tue	Wed	Thu	Fri	Sat
1	♃	♀	♄	☉	☽	♂	☿
2	♂	☿	♃	♀	♄	☉	☽
3	☉	☽	♂	☿	♃	♀	♄
4	♀	♄	☉	☽	♂	☿	♃
5	☿	♃	♀	♄	☉	☽	♂
6	☽	♂	☿	♃	♀	♄	☉
7	♄	☉	☽	♂	☿	♃	♀
8	♃	♀	♄	☉	☽	♂	☿
9	♂	☿	♃	♀	♄	☉	☽
10	☉	☽	♂	☿	♃	♀	♄
11	♀	♄	☉	☽	♂	☿	♃
12	☿	♃	♀	♄	☉	☽	♂

Table of Rising and Setting Signs

To find your approximate Ascendant, locate your Sun sign in the left column and determine the approximate time of your birth. Line up your Sun sign with birth time to find Ascendant. Note: This table will give you the approximate Ascendant only. To obtain your exact Ascendant you must consult your natal chart.

Sun Sign	6–8 a.m.	8–10 a.m.	10 a.m.–12 p.m.	12–2 p.m.	2–4 p.m.	4–6 p.m.
Aries	Taurus	Gemini	Cancer	Leo	Virgo	Libra
Taurus	Gemini	Cancer	Leo	Virgo	Libra	Scorpio
Gemini	Cancer	Leo	Virgo	Libra	Scorpio	Sagittarius
Cancer	Leo	Virgo	Libra	Scorpio	Sagittarius	Capricorn
Leo	Virgo	Libra	Scorpio	Sagittarius	Capricorn	Aquarius
Virgo	Libra	Scorpio	Sagittarius	Capricorn	Aquarius	Pisces
Libra	Scorpio	Sagittarius	Capricorn	Aquarius	Pisces	Aries
Scorpio	Sagittarius	Capricorn	Aquarius	Pisces	Aries	Taurus
Sagittarius	Capricorn	Aquarius	Pisces	Aries	Taurus	Gemini
Capricorn	Aquarius	Pisces	Aries	Taurus	Gemini	Cancer
Aquarius	Pisces	Aries	Taurus	Gemini	Cancer	Leo
Pisces	Aries	Taurus	Gemini	Cancer	Leo	Virgo

Sun Sign	6–8 p.m.	8–10 p.m.	10 p.m.–12 a.m.	12–2 a.m.	2–4 a.m.	4–6 a.m.
Aries	Scorpio	Sagittarius	Capricorn	Aquarius	Pisces	Aries
Taurus	Sagittarius	Capricorn	Aquarius	Pisces	Aries	Taurus
Gemini	Capricorn	Aquarius	Pisces	Aries	Taurus	Gemini
Cancer	Aquarius	Pisces	Aries	Taurus	Gemini	Cancer
Leo	Pisces	Aries	Taurus	Gemini	Cancer	Leo
Virgo	Aries	Taurus	Gemini	Cancer	Leo	Virgo
Libra	Taurus	Gemini	Cancer	Leo	Virgo	Libra
Scorpio	Gemini	Cancer	Leo	Virgo	Libra	Scorpio
Sagittarius	Cancer	Leo	Virgo	Libra	Scorpio	Sagittarius
Capricorn	Leo	Virgo	Libra	Scorpio	Sagittarius	Capricorn
Aquarius	Virgo	Libra	Scorpio	Sagittarius	Capricorn	Aquarius
Pisces	Libra	Scorpio	Sagittarius	Capricorn	Aquarius	Pisces

Blank Horoscope Chart

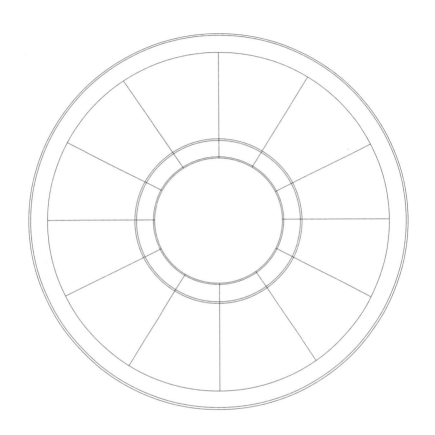